"All too often, our understanding of conflict dynamics in a given region is from 80,000 feet up and we thus miss the local texture of relationships that matter on the ground as well as the non-linear events that can both benefit or plague peacebuilding. This book is the opposite—it is a cliff-hanger, telling the story of the role of international third parties intervening in the Venezuelan conflict (2002–04) from the perspective of two of the third party actors. The narrative is rich in close-up detail, the kind that is almost never seen in public and reveals the "theory-in-use" of the parties, telling the story of the sense they made, and at the second order level, how the sense-making impacted the peacebuilding process itself. For this reason, it is a hearty and substantive contribution to our collective understanding of peacebuilding and an excellent resource for practitioners and researchers working at the international level to untangle the knots of protracted conflicts."
—**Sara Cobb,** School for Conflict Analysis and Resolution, George Mason University

"This is a superb, indispensable, and courageous book about the mediation of international actors in national conflicts. Superb, because it meets the highest standard of scholarship in its analysis of theoretical and practical issues involved in the resolution of conflict and the prevention of violence. Indispensable, because in a world fractured by political strife it offers invaluable instructive experiences and concrete proposals useful for a range of circumstances. And brave, because in the highly polarized context of Venezuelan politics, where political debate has become locked in Manichean extremes, this book dares to confront tough questions by presenting careful arguments. This account provides a fascinating analysis of Venezuelan political processes and analyzes the Carter Center's role, a subject of acrimonious debate in Venezuela. Far from a provincial case study, it is a book of major importance for the study of global politics."
—**Fernando Coronil,** Presidential Professor of Anthropology, The Graduate Center, City University of New York

"*International Mediation in Venezuela* is a fascinating account of the interactions between the evolving government of Hugo Chávez in Venezuela, the changing constellations of the political opposition to Chávez from 2002 through 2004, and the international efforts to mediate between them, especially those of the Carter Center and the Organization of American States. It is written from the perspectives of Jennifer McCoy and Francisco Diez, senior advisers to the

Carter Center, who worked closely with former president Carter in a period of dangerous polarization. Theoretically and practically informed by the growing experience of international efforts at conflict resolution, self-aware and self-critical as participant observers, McCoy and Diez illuminate the personal, institutional, political, and cultural obstacles to defusing Venezuela's internal confrontation. They provide a balanced appraisal of the skills of Hugo Chávez as a political actor, and of the misjudgments of the Venezuelan opposition in seeking to constrain him. A worthwhile study, useful for understanding Venezuela and for building the craft of third-party conflict management."
—**Abraham F. Lowenthal,** professor of international relations, University of Southern California

"Between 2002 and 2004 we Venezuelans lived dangerously. Our society was torn by a frantic political polarization that seemed to drive it toward a bloody confrontation. That, however, did not happen. Why? More than seven years later, this book provides details of unpublished or forgotten events, provided by the Carter Center, which for more than two and a half years played facilitation, mediation, and international electoral observation roles. It is a singular narrative, reconstructed by McCoy and Diez, extracting theoretical and practical lessons to help people who, like them, dedicate their lives to build peace on this planet. For those who lived those days, reading this book means continuing the dialogue with these peacemakers and with ourselves in the struggle for a better country."
— **Margarita López Maya,** historian and political analyst, senior researcher of Universidad Central de Venezuela

"This is an interesting and analytically sharp manuscript that sheds considerable light on the complicated and challenging political situation in Venezuela. The authors provide a highly detailed insiders account of external interventions by the Carter Center and the Organization of American States to promote a path towards reconciliation between sharply polarized political forces."
—**Michael Shifter,** president, Inter-American Dialogue

"In this lucidly documented and deeply reflective case study of the Carter Center's work to help transform conflict and prevent possible civil war in the troubled country of Venezuela, Jennifer McCoy and Francisco Diez offer a valuable set of lessons for theorists and practitioners alike. Usually we have the account of a diplomat or a third-person account by an academic, but in this case the diplomats are academics and so we have the rare privilege of hearing theory and practice seamlessly interwoven. Highly recommended!"
—**William Ury,** Harvard University and co-author of *Getting to Yes* and author of *The Third Side*

"For almost two years between 2002 and 2004, following an abortive coup that almost dislodged Hugo Chavez from the Venezuelan presidency, the Carter Center, based in Atlanta, worked with the Organization of American States and the UNDP to prevent deadly conflict and to promote political dialogue. This thorough and insightful account combines gripping first hand testimony with the thoughtful analysis of the lessons to be learned. The authors display a deep understanding of the complexities of this deeply divisive period in Venezuelan politics. At the same time they remain steadfast in their commitment to democratic reconciliation, and they are also realistic about the limits of external mediation in such disputes."
—**Laurence Whitehead,** Nuffield College, Oxford

INTERNATIONAL MEDIATION
IN VENEZUELA

INTERNATIONAL MEDIATION
IN **VENEZUELA**

JENNIFER McCOY AND FRANCISCO DIEZ

UNITED STATES INSTITUTE OF PEACE
Washington, D.C.

The views expressed in this book are those of the authors alone. They do not necessarily reflect the views of the United States Institute of Peace.

United States Institute of Peace
2301 Constitution Avenue, NW
Washington, DC 20037
www.usip.org

First published 2011

To request permission to photocopy or reprint materials for course use, contact the Copyright Clearance Center at www.copyright.com. For print, electronic media, and all other subsidiary rights, e-mail permissions@usip.org.

Printed in the United States of America

The paper used in this publication meets the minimum requirements of American National Standards for Information Science—Permanence of Paper for Printed Library Materials, ANSI Z39.48-1984.

Library of Congress Cataloging-in-Publication Data

McCoy, Jennifer.
  International mediation in Venezuela / Jennifer McCoy and Francisco Diez.
    p. cm.
  Includes index.
  ISBN 978-1-60127-068-9 (alk. paper)
  eISBN 978-1-60127-107-5
  1. Mediation, International. 2. Conflict management--Venezuela--International cooperation. 3. Venezuela--Politics and government--1999- 4. Venezuela--History--Attempted coup, 2002. 5. Democracy--Venezuela. I. Diez, Francisco, 1958- II. Emory University. Carter Center. III. Organization of American States. IV. United Nations Development Programme. V. Title.
  JZ5584.V46M33 2011
  303.6'9--dc22
                                2011014017

Contents

Foreword

Preventing violence is more important than ending it; it is unusual for international organizations to become deeply involved in a serious political dispute early enough to prevent widespread violence. In Venezuela in 2002, the Carter Center, the Organization of American States, and the United Nations Development Program had the opportunity to do so when President Hugo Chávez and the opposition grouping under the Coordinadora Democrática invited our three organizations to facilitate a dialogue between them. After a short-lived coup and massive protests that turned deadly, we believed that the conditions were ripe for the continuing street demonstrations and for deep divides to erupt into civil war and that we had an obligation to try to protect human life.

We thought the dialogue might last two months and the Carter Center hired an Argentine mediator, Francisco Diez, to be on the ground to help set up that dialogue. In the end, the Carter Center was officially involved as facilitator or election observer for two years instead of two months, and I personally visited Venezuela six times. The director of the Carter Center's Americas Program, Jennifer McCoy, led our efforts from Atlanta and traveled to Caracas regularly. César Gaviria, the OAS secretary general, made an unprecedented personal contribution, spending seven months almost full-time in Venezuela facilitating negotiations between the two sides.

All of these efforts, I am convinced, helped to prevent widespread deadly conflict in Venezuela. Yet sacrifices were made by Venezuelans who lost their lives or were injured in protests, who lost their jobs after the petroleum strike, and whose families became trapped in the ideological divides. I was particularly touched by the young Venezuelans working with Diez in Caracas who responded to conflict expert William Ury's calls to form a "third side" to ameliorate the political conflict. These young people formed networks to offer dispute resolution classes to communities, training to journalists willing to correct their contribution to polarization, and cultural events to unite Venezuelans. They are the hope for the future of Venezuela.

This book is a candid account of the international community's role, and especially the Carter Center's role, in alleviating the Venezuelan crisis. The authors document our analysis as we saw it at each moment of the intervention, and acknowledge our failures as well as successes. Their goal is to contribute to the historical record so that others may assess our work and draw lessons that may be useful for future conflict prevention efforts.

Since our intervention in Venezuela, President Chávez has continued to win elections and remain in office, with the option to run for continuous reelection. At the same time, we have seen opposition parties winning important positions in regional and legislative elections. Since the beginning of our participation in Venezuela, we have encouraged the government and the opposition to find ways to coexist because both represent large segments of the Venezuelan people. The key will be to maintain the social gains of recent years while strengthening independent democratic institutions and protecting the rights enshrined in the 1999 Constitution. The Venezuelan people deserve nothing less.

—Jimmy Carter
February 2011

Acknowledgments

Over the course of more than two years, we collaborated with many people inside and outside Venezuela in carrying out mediation efforts in Venezuela. First and foremost among those with whom we collaborated are former U.S. president Jimmy Carter and former OAS Secretary General César Gaviria, whose personal efforts and sacrifices had an important impact on the course of events in Venezuela. In addition, our collaborations with Fernando Jaramillo, Gaviria's chief of staff, Antonio Molpeceres, the resident representative of the United Nations Development Program (UNDP), Elena Martínez, the director of the UNDP's Bureau for Latin America and Caribbean, and Raul Alconada, a UNDP consultant, were extremely helpful. Within the Carter Center, former peace director Gordon Streeb and two former directors of the Conflict Resolution Program, Ben Hoffman and Matthew Hodes, contributed to the design and conduct of the mediation efforts; Rachel Fowler managed the ten-month election observation mission, and many other staff members contributed to the mediation efforts. William Ury of Harvard University, John Paul Lederach of the University of Notre Dame, and Juan Gutierrez of the Guernica Foundation inspired our approach to mediation and conflict transformation and personally traveled to Venezuela to provide advice on mediation and lead training seminars.

Within Venezuela, Carter Center staff and consultants from several countries played important roles, including Marcel Guzman (Bolivia) and Eduardo Mimíca (Chile), who provided electoral expertise; Ana Cabria Mellace (Argentina), who was the coordinator for the team of Venezuelan consultants leading the Strengthening Peace in Venezuela Program, among whom were Gabrielle Guerón, Victor Hugo Fébres, Nestor Alfonso Santamaría, and Mamilia López; and Pedro Antonuccio and Josefina Blanco (Venezuela), who provided media advice. Mireya Lozada (Venezuela) coordinated the Aquí Cabemos Todos initiative, whose most active members included Ana María San Juan, Arnaldo Esté, José Virtuoso, José María Cadenas, María Isabel Bertoni, Manuel Gándara, and Antonio González. All of them provided valuable advice to Francisco Diez throughout the exercise. Finally, we thank the many political and social Venezuelan leaders we mention in this book, both government and opposition leaders, for their receptivity to and cooperation with our efforts.

We have also incurred debts in writing this book. A grant from the United States Institute of Peace gave us the time and support needed to conduct research and write the initial drafts of the book; the Rockefeller Foundation provided a residency at its villa in Bellagio, Italy, that provided us a place to collaborate on the design of the book. A Senior Scholar Support grant from Georgia State University allowed Jennifer McCoy to complete a draft of the manuscript. Priscilla da Silva and Annette Cabria Mellace collected and organized the many documents, internal memos, correspondence, and press releases that allowed us to verify (and correct) our sometimes fallible memories. We owe special gratitude to our families for providing the moral support and the time for us to work on this book on weekends and on vacations over the last five years.

We hope the events and analysis that we document here may prove useful for scholars and practitioners who wish to assess our work or draw lessons for use in future conflicts. We especially hope the lessons we have learned may somehow be useful to Venezuelans to continue to work toward reconciliation and a reconstructed society.

Introduction

Flying toward Angel Falls in Venezuela, one flies over and among the *tepuyes*—tall rock formations with deep abysses between them, making it impossible to traverse by land. These tepuyes serve as a metaphor for the growing divide among Venezuelans in the late twentieth century. The Bolivarian Revolution under Hugo Chávez Frías exposed these divisions and fueled deeper polarization, affecting families, neighborhoods, and even the capital city such that its eastern half was the zone of the *"sifrinos,"*[1] those who opposed the government, and its western half the zone of the *"chusma,"*[2] those who supported the government. Chávez opponents claimed that he was turning the country into a new Cuba, and his supporters responded that he was finally addressing the severe poverty and inequality ignored for too long in this oil-rich nation of 27 million people. Many believed they were engaged in an "existential struggle" over core values and basic ways of life.[3] Each side wanted to eliminate the other, believing they could no longer coexist.

When the authors began their work with the conflict in June 2002 under the auspices of the Carter Center, the country appeared to be on the brink of domestic violence and possibly civil war. The authors hoped to build bridges across the divides of the tepuyes. On April 11, 2002, a massive demonstration

---

1. This is a favorite term used by Chavistas to refer to their opponents from the upper and middle classes. It is derived from a song in the late 1970s that referred to the sifrina of Caurimare (a Caracas housing development) and described a rich, superficial, brainless woman who cared only about consumption, luxury, and so on.

2. Slang for "gang" often used by anti-Chavistas to refer to Chávez's followers.

3. The term "existential struggle" was used by Maria Pilar Garcia, Ana Mallén, and Maryluz Guillén to describe the Venezuelan conflict in "The Multiples Faces Of Venezuelan Civil Society: Politization and Its Impact on Democratization" (paper presented at the annual meeting of the Latin American Studies Association, Las Vegas, Nevada, October 7–9, 2004). These authors cite Carl Schmitt, *The Concept of the Political* (Chicago: University of Chicago Press, 1996).

Chavista's demonstration with a sign saying, "They will not return!"
Courtesy of SURpress

against the Chávez government ended with nineteen people killed in unclear circumstances, leading the military to remove President Chávez from power. Within forty-eight hours, an outpouring of support for President Chávez in the streets, international condemnation, more deaths, and splits within the armed forces led military officers to reverse course and reinstall the president to his post.

Shocked by the coup and feeling vulnerable, Chávez invited Jimmy Carter, and later the Organization of American States (OAS) and United Nations Development Program (UNDP), to facilitate a dialogue to help reconcile the country. That invitation led to two years of intensive involvement by the three organizations to help resolve the conflict and prevent violence in Venezuela. The international efforts, which included a six-country Group of Friends formed in 2003, spawned a "dialogue table" personally led by the secretary general of the OAS for seven months, a number of peacebuilding activities sponsored by the Carter Center and UNDP for two years, and the monitoring of a ten-month electoral process representing the world's first presidential recall referendum. The international involvement persisted through various manifestations of the conflict in Venezuela, from massive marches and countermarches, at times erupting in violence, to a two-month petroleum strike that paralyzed the country, an open military rebellion in a four-month "sit-in" by active military officers, and social mobilization at different levels across the country seeking both to exacerbate and to defuse the conflict.

The international involvement in Venezuela was unusual in many ways.

- First, it was a conscious attempt by the international community to try to defuse a social and political conflict before it erupted into full-scale violence.
- Second, it represented an unusual alliance between two intergovernmental organizations (OAS and UNDP) and a nongovernmental organization (Carter Center).
- Third, it was a multilevel and multisector conflict within a country lacking clear dominant cleavages based on ethnicity, race, religion, or class (although many of those elements were also present as part of the conflict).
- Fourth, it involved significant personal effort by many world leaders (e.g., Jimmy Carter, "Lula" da Silva, Álvaro Uribe, Fidel Castro, and other Latin American leaders), especially by OAS secretary general

César Gaviria, to mediate the conflict and to navigate complex relationships within the international arena.

Approach of the Book

The book analyzes the two-year effort of the Carter Center and the broader international community to prevent violent conflict, try to reconcile a deeply divided society, and preserve democratic processes in Venezuela between 2002 and 2004. It tells the inside story of negotiations at the national and international level from the perspective of the authors, facilitators who represented the Carter Center during the entire process.[4] As participant-observers who are both scholars and practitioners, the authors describe their participation and the sometimes unexpected events that shaped the Carter Center's efforts. The volume explains their thinking, analysis, and strategies in real time, as they were developed, citing their internal notes and memoranda. The volume also examines missed opportunities and unintended consequences of the many interventions and identifies lessons learned. It is hoped that this case study will serve not only as a source of experience for practitioners in similar situations but also as a source of information to inform scholarly evaluation of conflict prevention efforts in this particular case and theory building in conflict prevention, peacebuilding, and international relations.

In order to analyze what happened in Venezuela from June 2002 to late 2004 and account for the Carter Center's intervention as a third party, this volume presents a narrative that progresses along two basic tracks, a chronological track and a multilevel track. This approach reflects the way in which the authors worked. The chronological track provides a sequential account of the conflict cycles and the Center's interventions and offers "real-time" analysis that reflects the authors' thinking and decisions at the time. The multilevel track, meanwhile, provides analysis of the different political spaces and activities that constituted various levels of the conflict and the Center's interventions, which often developed along parallel paths.

This volume identifies as the central axis in the conflict dynamic the confrontation between the Chávez government and its opponents in an open

---

4. Jennifer McCoy has been the director of the Americas Program at the Carter Center in Atlanta since 1998, and Francisco Diez has worked as a consultant for the Carter Center since 1991. He was the Carter Center's representative based in Venezuela from 2002 to 2004 and its representative in Latin America from 2007 to 2009. Ben Hoffman and Matthew Hodes, as directors of the Conflict Resolution Program in 2002 and 2003–06, respectively, worked closely with the authors in the Venezuelan case. The authors led a team in Atlanta and Caracas that ranged from seven to forty members. The exact size of the team varied depending on the needs of the mission (for example, a larger number of individuals were involved during the various periods of electoral observation).

struggle for power. It describes the conflict cycles emanating from this struggle for power through time and analyzes the Carter Center's interventions at the elite level as facilitators of multiple negotiations; the peacebuilding initiatives that the Center promoted together with many Venezuelans; and the influence of the international context in Venezuela. It thus analyzes the cumulative layers of interventions that the Carter Center and other international actors engaged in—layers that became increasingly complex.

Chapter 1 describes the historical roots of the crisis beginning with the emergence, consolidation, and unraveling of Venezuelan democracy under the Pact of Punto Fijo from 1958 to 1998, followed by the emergence of Hugo Chávez and his Bolivarian Revolution. It describes in greater detail the events leading up to the coup and countercoup of April 2002 and the invitation to the international third parties.

Chapter 2 characterizes the nature of the conflict, describes the nature of the main domestic actors, and gives a schematic overview of the five cycles of the conflict. Analyzing the internal dynamics of the two main protagonists as "archipelagos," it assesses the implications for the dynamics of the conflict interaction itself. It then turns to the theoretical approaches of the authors' analysis and the assumptions that underlay the Carter Center's efforts in Venezuela; finally, the chapter discusses the influence of the international arena on the domestic conflict and in turn the dilemmas faced by international actors.

Chapters 3 through 8 tell the story of the conflict and trace the international participation, beginning with the invitation to the Carter Center and the establishment of the Tripartite Working Group (OAS, UNDP, and Carter Center), moving through the seven-month "dialogue table" facilitated by the OAS secretary general and the launch of the program "Strengthening Peace in Venezuela," and concluding with the observation of the ten-month recall referendum effort. Each chapter analyzes the central conflict for power, discussing the motives and actions of the government and opposition as actors. The chapters describe the continually evolving strategies of the international facilitators and explain the bases of the Carter Center's approach, decisions, actions, and inactions, referring to its memoranda and e-mail communications at the time. They also examine the international context as various other countries and actors became involved at different points. They include discussions aimed at practitioners that analyze specific episodes and methods. Finally, each chapter concludes with an analysis of lessons learned with the benefit of hindsight.

Chapter 9 analyzes the aftermath of the international intervention—the evolution of the internal dynamics in Venezuela from the disengagement of the international actors following the recall referendum of August 2004 to the end of 2010. It describes the consolidation of power of the Chávez government in late 2004 and 2005, Chávez's reelection in 2006 and his unsuccessful attempt to introduce new constitutional reforms in 2007, and the continued development of "twenty-first century socialism" in 2008–10.

Chapter 10 concludes the volume with our theoretical insights and lessons learned for scholars and practitioners of conflict prevention and resolution, peacebuilding, democratization, and international relations.

1

Roots of the Crisis

Venezuela was viewed as a "model democracy" in the hemisphere for four decades prior to the election of Lt. Col. Hugo Chávez in 1998. After a history of strongmen, violence, and a short-lived attempt at democracy in 1945–48, Venezuelans forged a representative democracy under the banner of the Pact of Punto Fijo in 1958.[1] Through a series of economic and political accords, Venezuelan economic and political elites, the military, and the labor unions agreed on a political and economic model based on the distribution of externally derived rents (oil revenues), consensus-seeking mechanisms, and centralized control under a strong presidential system.

The Unraveling of Venezuelan Representative Democracy

Crushing a leftist insurgency and rightist military uprisings in the 1960s, the new democracy faced no serious threats by 1975. Its continued success rested in no small part on the unprecedented income that the Venezuelan state received from the international sale of petroleum after 1973.[2] In late 1982,

---

1. The Pact of Punto Fijo was a power-sharing agreement among the political parties Acción Democrática, Copei, and Unión Revolucionaria Democrática that was signed in December 1958 at the house of Copei leader Rafael Caldera, which was referred to as "Puntofijo." Additional agreements included the Declaration of Principles for Peace and Democracy and the Minimal Program for Government, which set boundaries in the political economy between the public and private sectors; the Labor-Business Accord between unions and the private sector; informal assurances to church leaders that Catholic education would prosper in the new democracy; and eventually the 1961 Constitution. Together, these documents represented six points of elite agreement that underlay the new political regime: power sharing, reconciliation of old antagonisms, respect for individual liberties, reliance on the state as an engine of economic development, postponement of proposals that would redistribute wealth until procedural democracy was secure, and support for the United States in the Cold War.

2. Although the percentages vary by year, the oil sector accounted for roughly 25 percent of Venezuela's GDP; 50 percent of its export earnings; and 75 percent of the government budget in the 1960s and 1970s.

however, the price of crude oil began a decline that lasted, except for a brief period during the Persian Gulf War of 1990–91, until early 1999. During that seventeen-year period, the political regime initially forged at Punto Fijo began to unravel.[3]

Clear signals of the unraveling erupted with the protests known as the caracazo (a large spontaneous protest in Caracas) in February 1989, when the government of Carlos Andrés Pérez attempted to raise gasoline prices as part of an International Monetary Fund (IMF) package in the face of the government's serious international and domestic debt. The consequent rise in bus fares unleashed spontaneous riots across the country, during which a heavy-handed military and National Guard killed hundreds of protestors.[4] The Pérez government's politically inept attempt to open up the economy further alienated the protected business class and contributed to discontent within the military.

On February 4, 1992, a secret club of mid-ranking military officers known as the Movimiento Bolivariano Revolucionario (MBR-2000, or Bolivarian Revolutionary Movement) attempted a coup against Pérez. The coup was put down by generals loyal to Pérez, and the coup leader, Lt. Col. Hugo Chávez, was arrested. Pérez permitted Chávez, though, to make a televised statement calling on his comrades to lay down their arms. His thirty seconds of live television time made him a hero to millions of disgruntled Venezuelans, as he criticized the corrupt democracy and uttered his famous line that he and his followers would put down their arms *"por ahora"* (for the moment).

Before the attempted coup, the apparent consolidation of control over the political system by the two main political parties Acción Democrática (AD, or Democratic Action), a social-democratic party, and the Comité de Organización Política Electoral Independiente (Copei, or Independent Political and Electoral Organization Committee), a social-Christian party, left many Venezuelans extremely dissatisfied with their leadership but unable to visualize an alternative. The overwhelming majority wanted "democracy" but were split between those supporting a democracy with AD and Copei and those supporting one without them.[5] Studies of Venezuelan public opinion

3. For explanations of the unraveling of Punto Fijo democracy and the rise of the Bolivarian Revolution, see Jennifer L. McCoy and David J. Myers, eds., *The Unraveling of Representative Democracy in Venezuela* (Baltimore, MD: Johns Hopkins University Press, 2004) and Steve Ellner and Daniel Hellinger, *Venezuelan Politics in the Chavez Era: Globalization, Social Polarization, and Political Change* (Boulder, CO: Lynne Rienner Press, 2003).

4. The government put the official death toll at three hundred, while human rights groups estimated that a thousand people died in the protests.

5. José Antonio Gil Yepes, "Public Opinion, Political Socialization, and Regime Stabilization," in *The Unraveling of Representative Democracy in Venezuelan,* ed. Jennifer L. McCoy and David J. Myers (Baltimore, MD: John Hopkins University Press, 2004), 231–62.

at the time revealed that most Venezuelans viewed the two dominant political parties as corrupt and incompetent.[6] They also blamed the parties for the country's economic decline. For decades, petroleum had fueled growth and the middle class grew, with per capita income peaking in 1978. Then came a sharp and persistent drop in real per capita oil revenues, a poverty rate that shot up from 25 percent in the 1970s to 65 percent in the 1990s, and the massive disappointment of middle-class aspirations.[7]

Institutionally, the democratic political regime had remained highly centralized, with an ineffective Congress, a weak civil society penetrated by the political parties, and policymaking dominated by a powerful president who occasionally consulted labor and business in devising a state-led development strategy based on external rents, protection of domestic interests, and burdensome social commitments to the lower and middle classes. The early priority given to political stability and democratic survival through consensus-based mechanisms eventually gave way to concerns about the political survival of individual political parties and leaders. The centralized system of political decision making failed to incorporate new groups that had gained influence as economic and political modernization unfolded. These groups, which included the urban poor, intellectuals, emerging middle-class civil-society movements, and junior ranks of the military, became increasingly resentful and eventually found their voice, with many of them deserting the Punto Fijo political regime completely.

Decentralization pushed by the neighborhood associations and new civil society movements in 1989, combined with the political errors of elites, led to a fragmentation of the political party system in 1993, when, for the first time, AD and Copei lost the presidency and achieved less than 50 percent of the congressional vote.[8] This "deinstitutionalization" of the party system also opened space for charismatic leaders who came to personify the new competitive political parties. This was particularly evident in the 1998 elections with the emergence of Irene Saez and her Integración y Renovación Nueva Esperanza (IRENE, or Integration and Renovation New Hope

---

6. David J. Myers, "Institutional Performance, Political Culture, and Political Change," *Studies in Comparative International Development* 30, no. 1 (1995): 84–91.

7. The steepest rise in poverty occurred during the 1990s: the percentage living on less than $1 per day increased from 12 percent in 1989 to 23 percent in 2000, and estimates of those living under the national poverty line doubled from 31 percent in 1989 to 67 percent in the late 1990s. United Nations Development Program (UNDP), *Human Development Report 1999: Globalization with a Human Face* (New York: UNDP, 1999); World Bank, www.worldbank.org; and CIA, "The World Factbook," https://www.cia.gov/library/publications/the-world-factbook/.

8. Ironically, Rafael Caldera, a founder of Copei, left the party, joined the presidential race, and won the election.

Party), Henrique Salas Romer and his Partido Proyecto Venezuela (PPV, or Venezuela Project Party), and Hugo Chávez and his Movimiento Quinta República (MVR, or the Fifth Republic Movement).[9]

By the 1998 elections, real per capita income had eroded to the level it had been in 1963, representing a one-third drop from the peak in 1978. Few Venezuelans recognized that oil revenues per capita had dropped precipitously. Most continued to view Venezuela as a rich country.

The Rise of Hugo Chávez Frías

President Rafael Caldera (1994–99) released the failed coup leader from prison and restored his political rights. During his two years in prison, Chávez had become acquainted with intellectuals and politicians from the old Venezuelan Left, particularly José Vicente Rangel and Luis Miquelena, who saw a chance to emerge from their long marginalization.[10] On his release, Chávez quietly organized his own political party and prepared to run for the presidency.[11] Caldera's victory in 1993 and the perception that AD and Copei could be beaten were important in establishing antiparty candidates as viable challengers.

Chávez's antielite message capitalized on Venezuelan frustrations about the slide in living standards in the 1980s and 1990s—and anger toward the traditional political class. He campaigned on a promise of radical change—to rewrite the constitution (a symbol for a political overhaul) and to eliminate the corruption of the "oligarchs" who had "stolen" the country's riches. He mercilessly attacked the traditional political parties and eventually defeated his primary opponent, Henrique Salas Romer, who also promised radical change but who at the last minute received the endorsement of AD and Copei. Before that, Irene Saez had led in the polls until she accepted the backing of Copei. Thus, Venezuelans' deep desire for change did not necessarily mean

---

9. José Molina and Carmen Pérez, "Radical Change at the Ballot Box: Causes and Consequences of Electoral Behavior in Venezuela's 2000 Elections," *Latin American Politics and Society* 46, no. 1 (2004): 103–34.

10. Several bibliographies of Chávez have been published, most of them sympathetic to the leader. See, for example, Hugo Chávez Frias, *Understanding the Venezuelan Revolution: Hugo Chavez Talks to Marta Harnecker,* trans. Chesa Boudin (New York: Monthly Review Press, 2005); Richard Gott, *Hugo Chavez: The Bolivarian Revolution in Venezuela* (New York: Verso Press, 2005); Aleida Guevara, *Chavez: Un hombre Que Anda Por Ahi [Chavez, Venezuela, and the New Latin America: An Interview with Hugo Chavez]* (New York: Ocean Sur, 2005); Bart Jones, *Hugo!: The Hugo Chavez Story From Mud Hut to Perpetual Revolution* (Hanover: Steerforth Press, 2007); and Cristina Marcano, *Hugo Chavez: The Definitive Biography of Venezuela's Controversial President* (New York: Random House, 2007).

11. Jennifer L. McCoy, "Chávez and the End of 'Partyarchy' in Venezuela," *Journal of Democracy* 10, no. 3 (1999): 64–77.

that Chávez would be the one to carry it out. Chávez won when his competitors' acceptance of support from the traditional parties signaled to the populace that they would not, after all, represent a clean break from the past.[12]

Chávez received 56 percent of the vote in an election endorsed by the Organization of American States (OAS) and the Carter Center. Those votes came not only from the poor: while 55 percent of the poor voted for him, so too did 45 percent of the nonpoor.[13] Chávez was able to mobilize large sectors of the lower classes that had felt excluded by the established parties and that did not possess institutionalized forms of political expression.

Inaugurated on February 2, 1999, Chávez had an approval rating that topped 80 percent and he enjoyed support across all classes and sectors. During his first year in office, he moved decisively to consolidate political power. Fulfilling his campaign promise, he held a referendum on April 1 to approve the election of a Constituent Assembly to write a new constitution. The electoral formula selected to choose the members of the assembly was approved by all of the political parties. This disadvantaged the disorganized opposition and advantaged the governing coalition, which gained control of 94 percent of the seats. This same assembly dissolved the Congress elected in 1998 and removed many justices from the courts. Despite opposition from the private sector and the Church to welfare provisions and abortion rights, respectively, a referendum in December 1999 approved the new "Bolivarian" Constitution. The constitution both reassured and alarmed people, as it was less radical than expected yet brought important changes. The 1999 Constitution extended the presidential term from five to six years and provided the possibility for one immediate reelection; gave the president more direct control over the military while reducing congressional oversight; changed the name of the country from the Republic of Venezuela to the Bolivarian Republic of Venezuela; and strengthened the power of the national executive at the expense of the legislative and judicial branches. It eliminated the Senate, created two new public powers (an electoral power and a citizen's power to control corruption), and provided for more direct democracy through the creation of popular referenda with the power to revoke legislation and recall elected officials. It continued the pro-state approach to economic affairs while protecting private property.

---

12. José Molina and Carmen Pérez, "Radical Change at the Ballot Box: Causes and Consequences of Electoral Behavior in Venezuela's 2000 Elections," *Latin American Politics and Society* 46, no. 1 (2004): 103–34.

13. Damarys Canache, "Urban Poor and Political Order," in *The Unraveling of Representative Democracy in Venezuela*, ed. Jennifer L. McCoy and David J. Myers, 33–49 (Baltimore, MD: John Hopkins University Press, 2004).

Chávez decided that all elected positions should be "relegitimated" under the new constitution, and so he ran again in the "megaelections" of July 2000, securing almost sixty percent of the vote (3.9 million votes)—similar to the number of votes he won in 1998 (3.66 million). His main opponent was a former comrade in arms who had become a popular governor, Francisco Árias Cárdenas. The political coalition supporting Chávez's candidacy overwhelmingly defeated the candidates of AD and Copei for seats in the National Assembly and captured all but 5 of the 22 regional governorships. Similar results in the municipal and neighborhood council elections of December 2000 completed the marginalization of the traditional political parties.[14]

The new National Assembly was charged with appointing the members of the electoral and citizen's branches and the Supreme Court. Previously, a small committee from the Constituent Assembly had been designated to make temporary appointments to these branches, but it did so without following constitutional procedures and designated individuals perceived as Chávez sympathizers. When the newly elected National Assembly simply reconfirmed these previous appointments to the court and the citizen's branch, confidence in the independence of the public institutions and their ability to serve as a check on presidential power was seriously eroded.

Meanwhile, the military mission was expanded. Chávez favored the military as an institution over public bureaucracies and political parties, which he saw as inefficient and corrupt. He therefore enlisted military officers as top-level decision makers in his government, employed the military in massive disaster relief and development programs, and intervened in the promotion process, promoting loyal officers ahead of more senior officers. These practices led to growing tensions within the military—both between older and newer generations and between Chávez loyalists and opponents—that played out in dramatic terms in 2002.

The 2002 Coup and Countercoup

With the new political rules in place, Chávez began a systematic attack on organized interests that he portrayed as representing the old order—labor unions, the Roman Catholic Church, some nongovernmental organizations (NGOs), economic elites, and the private media. To begin, following a devastating oil workers' strike in October 2000, the government presented

---

14   Michael Penfold-Becerra, "Federalism and Institutional Change in Venezuela," *Federalism and Democracy in Latin America*, ed. Edward Gibson, 197–225 (Baltimore, MD: Johns Hopkins University Press, 2004).

to the voters a referendum to suspend trade union leadership and to call new, direct secret votes. When the elections for the Confederación de Trabajadores Venezolanos (CTV, or Venezuelan Confederation of Workers) were finally held in October 2001, the Bolivarian slate of candidates lost to candidates backed by union organizations that during the Punto Fijo era had been allies of AD and Copei. The election was marred by contentions of fraud, leading to an inconclusive result that contributed to the tension in 2002.

In addition, a government program to install Bolivarian primary schools (a comprehensive education approach that included music and dance and meals at school) stirred up a hornets' nest of opposition from the Roman Catholic hierarchy and the teacher unions, which feared government ideological intervention in school curricula. Furthermore, the business community clashed with President Chávez when he attempted to regulate private-sector economic and political activities, and the private media and Chávez engaged in a war of words that at times spilled over into harassment of free speech and led to mob attacks on media outlets. Much of this was spurred by Chávez's oratory on his TV program, *Álo Presidente*.

Intellectual support for Chávez's Bolivarian Revolution came particularly from the old Left, and some of his principle advisers were university professors who followed various tenets of Marxism and favored a tutelary approach that would impose direct democracy. They helped draft the Bolivarian Constitution, with its emphasis on new forms of participatory democracy under the guidance of a strong executive with direct links to the populace. Nevertheless, the commitment to democratic principles among Venezuelan intellectuals meant that some of these same critics of the old Punto Fijo democracy became critics of the Fifth Republic as democratic deficits surfaced. In fact, the divide in intellectual support for Chávez often rested on the interpretation of his contribution to democracy—whether he was deepening it through new forms of participation or weakening it through the concentration of power.[15] Some of his earliest intellectual supporters, such as Alfredo Peña and Jorge Olavarria, became some of his fiercest critics within the first two years of his regime.

After two years of pragmatic economic austerity and courting foreign investment, actions necessitated by low oil prices,[16] Chávez moved to make

15. Richard S. Hillman, "Intellectuals: An Elite Divided," in *The Unraveling of Representative Democracy in Venezuela*, ed. Jennifer L. McCoy and David J. Myers, 115–29 (Baltimore, MD: John Hopkins University Press, 2004).

16. From a low of $11 per barrel in 1998, the average price of oil rose to $16 in 1999 and $27 in 2000, with a subsequent decline in 2001.

economic changes in late 2001. In December 2001, near the end of a year-long enabling law in which the legislature granted legislative-making powers to the president,[17] Chávez announced forty-nine decree laws, without prior consultation with economic sectors or political parties, that reformed such sensitive areas as hydrocarbons, fishing rights, and land ownership. The outcry that followed resulted in an unprecedented joint call by labor and business for a national strike on December 10, 2001.

National divisions deepened in 2002 as more actors spoke out against the president. Splits within the Movimiento al Socialismo (MAS, or Movement to Socialism) party, his coalition partner since the 1998 election campaign, reduced the president's strength in the National Assembly below the 60 percent majority that he needed to approve organic laws. Cracks in his own party threatened to reduce his supporters to minority status in the assembly.

When the president's popularity dipped below 30 percent in early 2002, his political opponents began to explore the feasibility of using new constitutional devices, such as the "revocatory" referendum, to remove him by legal means. Even inside of the military, the very institution whose support President Chávez trumpeted as critical to carrying out his Bolivarian Revolution, opposition crystallized.

In January and February 2002, several active military leaders called for Chávez to resign; plans for a reported coup attempt were apparently postponed; and the president's chief political strategist and close confident, Luis Miquelena, left the government. In March, the CTV and the business federation Fedecámaras issued a joint call for the president to resign. The catalyst for the greatest turmoil, however, was Chávez's replacement of the president and board of directors of the national oil company, Petróleos de Venezuela Sociedad Anónima (PDVSA), in an attempt to gain more political control over the independent board and its spending decisions. This move led to a series of clashes and work stoppages between the new board and PDVSA managers and workers that culminated in a strike by white-collar petroleum workers beginning April 4. Five days later, the CTV and Fedecámaras joined the petroleum strike in solidarity while the government declared the petroleum strike illegal and interrupted private television broadcasting of the strike with mandatory government announcements. The demands of the strikers escalated from reinstating the previous PDVSA board and fired workers to a call for Chávez's immediate resignation.

---

17. Such a delegation had been used previously in Venezuelan democratic history, but the granting of power was more extensive in the economic arenas in 2001.

On April 11, the third day of the nationwide strike, a large group of protest marchers in Caracas diverted their planned route and approached the presidential palace, where pro-government demonstrators were gathered. A confused hail of bullets resulted in 19 deaths and over 100 wounded. That night, military commanders reportedly asked the president to resign in light of his order to implement the Plan Avila, the contingency plan for the security forces to provide order during public protest. In another confused series of events, the commander of the armed forces, General Luis Rincón, announced that the president had resigned by letter and removed his entire cabinet, while hours later the attorney general, Isaías Rodríguez, announced that the resignation letter was fake and the president's daughter announced from Cuba that her father was being held prisoner at Fort Tiuna in Caracas.

With an apparent power vacuum and no available succession (based on the presumed resignation of the president, vice president, and cabinet), the military swore in the president of Fedecámaras, Pedro Carmona, as the new president of the republic. Carmona immediately dismissed the National Assembly, announced that he would not recognize the 1999 Constitution, named a new cabinet, announced that new elections would be held within a year, and began to arrest Chavistas (Chávez followers), including governors, legislators, and ministers. The country and the world were shocked at the clearly undemocratic moves.

International reaction was as confused as the events on the ground. In February and March, the Inter-American Commission on Human Rights had reported that press freedoms were endangered, and the U.S. government had expressed concerns about events in Venezuela. Nevertheless, on April 12, after Chávez's detention, the Rio Group of Latin American presidents meeting in Costa Rica "condemned the interruption of the constitutional order" and called for new elections (they assumed that Chávez's resignation was a fait accompli) and a special session of the OAS. In contrast, the initial U.S. reaction was to recognize a transitional government and blame Chávez for his overthrow, asserting that "though details are still unclear, undemocratic actions committed or encouraged by the Chávez administration provoked yesterday's crisis in Venezuela."[18] A joint U.S.-Spain statement hoped that the "exceptional situation Venezuela is experiencing leads in the shortest possible time to full democratic normalization," but the statement did not recognize an alteration or interruption of democracy.

---

18. Statement by U.S. State Department deputy spokesman Philip Reeker, April 12, 2002.

At midnight on April 13, the OAS extraordinary session invoked the Inter-American Democratic Charter and condemned the "alteration of the constitutional regime," calling on the secretary general to conduct a fact-finding mission in order to restore the democratic institutional framework.[19] Meanwhile, in Venezuela, the tide began to turn as Chávez supporters turned out in the streets demanding his reinstatement, which led to more violence and deaths, and military commanders got cold feet in light of Carmona's draconian decrees and Latin American opprobrium. At dawn on April 14, 2002, Chávez was brought back to Caracas from the island to which he had been flown and sworn back into office later that afternoon.

On April 18, OAS secretary general César Gaviria reported on his visit to Venezuela, concluding there was an urgent need to begin a dialogue, to end political statements by the military, to investigate the violence of April 11–14, and to guarantee the separation of powers and checks and balances.[20] The OAS resolution the same day expressed satisfaction with Chávez's restoration and endorsed the government's initiative to call a national dialogue.[21] The U.S. backpedaled in its support of the Carmona government but continued to assert that Chávez did as much to undermine democracy in Venezuela as his opponents who had tried to overthrow him.[22]

These events weakened the presidency, discredited the opposition leaders most closely linked to Carmona, and horrified foreign investors. Chávez immediately made conciliatory gestures, acknowledging that divisions in the country needed to be addressed, reinstating the PDVSA board of directors, and ending subsidized sales of oil to Cuba. He promised to no longer wear his military uniform and he stopped the television "*cadenas*" (chains) in which private TV stations were obligated to carry his remarks live by pre-empting regular programming, and which had been used to an extreme by Chávez. He made several cabinet changes, including the appointment of a new planning minister respected by the business community, and launched a national dialogue under his new vice president, former defense and foreign minister José Vicente Rangel. The National Assembly, meanwhile, announced it would review many of the forty-nine decree laws and establish

---

19. OAS, "Situation in Venezuela," CP/RES. 811 (1315/02), April 13, 2002.

20. OAS, "Report Pursuant to Resolution CP/RES.811 (1315/02) Situation in Venezuela, AG Doc 9, April 18, 2002.

21. OAS, "Support for Democracy in Venezuela," AG/RES 1 (XXXIX-E-02), April 18, 2002.

22. National Security Adviser Condoleezza Rice, in remarks at the Johns Hopkins University's School of Advanced International Studies, April 29, 2002. Colin Powell's speech at the April 18 OAS meeting also contended that the problems leading to the removal of Chávez had begun long before that day, and he implied that Chávez's own actions were in large part responsible for his ouster.

a truth commission to investigate the violence and nearly sixty deaths of April 11–14 (among whom were both pro- and antigovernment demonstrators). The Supreme Court ordered the release from house arrest of four high-ranking military officials who participated in the April 11 removal of the president.

The conciliatory mood did not last long. Venezuela's gross national product shrank by almost 10 percent in the second quarter of 2002, leading organized labor and business to charge that President Chávez was masterminding an economic coup against them. Chávez claimed, in turn, that the economic sectors were plotting an economic coup against him. Pro- and anti-Chávez marches again appeared on May 1 and May 11, with marchers on both sides demanding an investigation into the deaths of April 11–14. Opposition parties called for a constitutional amendment to reduce the president's term from six to four years.

At the OAS General Assembly on June 3–4, 2002, the United States attempted to gain approval of a resolution calling for OAS facilitation of a national dialogue through the Inter-American Democratic Charter. Annoyed by the clumsy attempt of the United States, whose delegation showed up late for the negotiations, the Latin American countries rebuffed the U.S. effort and instead approved a declaration that reiterated the OAS's offer of assistance for dialogue and reconciliation should the Venezuelan government require it, and that welcomed all international assistance to Venezuela.[23] This resolution did not invoke the Democratic Charter, nor did it send an OAS mission to the country.

The Context of Venezuelan Political Culture

Weaknesses of democracy under both the Punto Fijo political system (the so-called Fourth Republic) and the Bolivarian Revolution (the so-called Fifth Republic) produced citizen dissatisfaction and political instability. Venezuelan democracy under Punto Fijo was based on a centralized, presidentialist political model. It relied on the distribution of externally derived rents rather than on redistribution through domestic taxation to ameliorate social conflict and gain the support of hostile elements and was thus vulnerable to volatile international oil prices. Despite a strong electoral system, vertical accountability was weak as the party system and legislature answered to party elites rather than citizen constituents, creating a crisis of representation. In

23. OAS, "Confidence- and Security-Building in the Americas," AG/DEC 28 (XXXII-O-02), June 4, 2002.

other words, the Venezuelan democracy was deficient in achieving greater democratization in the sense of greater equity and participation. Indeed, in the forty years of Punto Fijo politics, income inequality grew, living standards rose and then declined, and political party leaders became increasingly removed from the country's citizenry. Alienation was reflected in growing voter abstention that rose to 18 percent in the 1988 national elections and skyrocketed to 40 percent in 1993.

Several aspects of Venezuelan political culture, in combination with the obvious structural factors of petroleum wealth, help explain the country's democratic weaknesses and vulnerabilities. The first aspect of Venezuela's political culture that helps explain the country's weaknesses is the myth that Venezuela is a rich country and that its citizens are entitled by birthright to share in its wealth, a myth that has been noted by Anibal Romero, Fernando Coronil, and José Antonio Gil, among others.[24] Coronil analyzes in *The Magical State: Nature, Money and Modernity in Venezuela* the mediating orientations of Venezuelans toward a state that "magically" acts as a caregiver. These orientations predisposed policymakers to choose distributive policies over regulative or redistributive policies, even when the latter may have been more efficient or productive. As the oil boom transformed Venezuelan society into a modern culture with easy access to material goods, those who were left behind, or who lost their benefits as the economy deteriorated, easily fell into the refrain noted by Gil: "The country is rich from oil; I am a Venezuelan and am entitled to a share of its riches; if I am not benefitting, it must be because someone is stealing my share."[25]

A second aspect of the country's political culture that helps explain the country's weaknesses is the tutelary nature of Venezuelan democracy. In *Tutelary Pluralism*,[26] Luis Oropeza argues that prior to 1958 there was no "civic culture" predisposing the country toward democracy and that the political values of the society could have supported either authoritarian or democratic alternatives. After pointing out that cultural pluralism in Venezuela was not historically based on racial, linguistic, religious, or regional antagonisms, he argues that Venezuelan political culture exhibits a dualism of democratic

24. Anibal Romero, "Rearranging the Deck Chairs on the Titanic: The Agony of Democracy in Venezuela," *Latin American Research Review* 32, no. 1 (1997): 7; Fernando Coronil, *The Magical State: Nature, Money, and Modernity in Venezuela* (Chicago: University of Chicago Press, 1997); José Antonio Gil Yepes, "Public Opinion, Political Socialization, and Regime Stabilization," *The Unraveling of Representative Democracy in Venezuela*, in ed. Jennifer L. McCoy and David J. Myers, 231–62 (Baltimore, MD: John Hopkins University Press, 2004).

25. Gil, "Public Opinion, Political Socialization."

26. Luis Oropeza, *Tutelary Pluralism: A Critical Approach to Venezuelan Democracy* (Cambridge: Center for International Affairs, 1983).

pluralism and military autocracy. Oropeza identifies three traits within Venezuelan political culture that shaped the nature of the democracy that evolved after 1958: (1) a corporatism in which groups organized and participated in policymaking in a voluntary manner through formal corporatist mechanisms provided by the state; (2) a centralism emanating from Simon Bolívar's interest in a strong executive to protect the executive against the other powers in a republic; and (3) a predilection toward consensus in which prior agreement among established parties in the form of pacts was seen as crucial for avoiding conflict by removing contentious issues from political debate. However, such consensus diminished the effectiveness of participatory institutions by restricting participation in the name of the higher goal of political stability.[27]

A third aspect of political culture that helps explain the country's weaknesses is related to political learning. While Venezuelan leaders learned important lessons from the failed democratic experiment of the *trienio* (three-year) period (1945–48) and applied those lessons to ensure that the Punto Fijo democracy survived severe challenges from the Right and the Left in its first decade, they failed to adapt to new realities. Specifically, after 1983 they relied on the pact-making strategy and distributive politics that served them well during the 1960s.[28] The fear of a return to autocracy and the lessons learned from the participatory explosion of the *trienio* led to elite-imposed limits on opportunities for conflict and controversy.[29] The failure of the same generation to learn new strategies (and the comfortable position of entrenched interests) inhibited the leaders' ability to adapt to a changed demographic and economic context in the 1970s and 1980s. The resistance and delayed response by political leaders to the demand for decentralization and electoral reform is one example of this. The failure of AD and Copei to learn and adapt to a new electoral climate was further evident in their (mis)handling of the 1998 and 2000 election campaigns.

Representative democracy as developed under Punto Fijo, particularly its party system, thus unraveled in the 1990s. Nevertheless, basic democratic values survived and permeated the Fifth Republic. Latinobarómetro shows

---

27. For a discussion of the implications of limited pluralism in Venezuela, see Michael Coppedge, *Strong Parties and Lame Ducks: Presidential Partyarchy and Factionalism in Venezuela* (Stanford, CA: Stanford University Press, 1994) and José Antonio Gil Yepes, *The Challenge of Venezuelan Democracy* (New Brunswick: Transaction Books, 1981).

28. Francine Jacome, "Venezuela: Old Successes, New Constraints on Learning," *Political Learning and Redemocratization in Latin America: Do Politicians Learn form Political Crises?* ed. Jennifer L. McCoy (Miami, FL: North-South Center Press, 2000).

29. Oropeza, *Tutelary Pluralism.*

that strong levels of support for a democratic system continued into the 1998 election campaign and beyond.[30]

Hugo Chávez's rise with support from the urban masses, and his subsequent emphasis on class differences, raises the question of whether and when Venezuela developed a class-based political rift. Venezuelan political culture, as noted earlier, displays a divide between democratic and authoritarian ideals but manifests little evidence of racial, linguistic, or religious cleavages. Likewise, class-based polarization did not historically manifest itself in Venezuelan politics.

Damarys Canache demonstrates that this lack of an open class rift with regard to preferences on the economy and the role of the state persisted into the 1990s.[31] Nevertheless, the poor, as documented in surveys between 1995 and 1998, expected more from the government in terms of economic intervention, jobs, and health care; and they preferred radical over gradual change. These small but significant differences in policy preferences took on new importance in 1998 when Hugo Chávez's campaign messages gave them great prominence.

The ideological confusion of the Bolivarian Revolution further contributed to the difficulty in discerning where Venezuelan democracy was headed. José Antonio Gil points out that Bolivarian ideology stressed both political equality and political liberty, but favored direct citizen participation over pluralist interest-group mediation.[32] Thus, freedom of speech was protected, while organized groups were attacked. Chávez repeatedly asserted that "civil society organizations" do not in fact represent citizens but constitute a small, self-anointed elite.

Chávez's attempts to create a more efficacious and responsive democracy were largely unfulfilled after three years in office. Dissatisfaction with the performance of the government on key policy problems such as crime, unemployment, and corruption was above 80 percent in mid-2002. The government was unable to deliver a clear message to the people about its goals beyond "revenge," and its promises to address long-neglected needs lacked a

---

30. Latinobarómetro polls support these findings. They show that from 1995 to 2001, a strong majority of Venezuelans (ranging from 60 to 64 percent in any given year, with a slight dip in 2001 to 57 percent) consistently said that democracy is preferable to any other kinds of government; these percentages are in the mid range for Latin America. A relatively small minority (ranging from 17 to 25 percent) contended that in certain circumstances an authoritarian government would be preferable to a democratic one, percentages similarly in the mid range for Latin America. As cited in the *Economist*, July 28, 2001.

31. Damarys Canache, "Urban Poor and Political Order."

32. Gil, "Political Opinion, Political Socialization."

clear strategy to accomplish those objectives or to improve the inefficiency of the national government.

The traditional intermediaries between the government and citizens—political parties and interest groups—were seriously weakened. The military replaced these groups as a primary means of mobilizing and socializing Venezuelans through a new "civic-military" party, through its control of fiscal revenues distributed to the state and local governments, and through its increased role in public administration. Politics was increasingly concentrated in the hands of a single, charismatic individual, President Chávez, making the sustainability of the regime tied to his personal popularity.

Following the coup and countercoup in April 2002, countrywide approval of the president stabilized at roughly 30 percent, with his hard-core support concentrated among the urban poor.[33] Nevertheless, a July 2002 poll showed that even among the urban poor, Chávez had lost his majority support and a plurality was prepared to vote against him,[34] making the urban poor the most polarized sector of the population. As the urban poor grew divided in their sentiments toward Chávez, the upper classes came to unite in their rejection of him.

Nevertheless, wide sectors of all classes coincided, both before and during Chávez's government, in their rejection of the traditional political class and a return to Punto Fijo politics. The discrediting of the traditional parties, along with their persistence in the current political struggle, continued to be a characteristic of the system. Chávez used this fact to neutralize and discredit the emergence of any political alternative by always identifying that alternative with the old regime.

These were the broad contours of Venezuelan politics and culture at the height of the conflict that erupted in the coup and countercoup in April 2002. The conflict ushered in unprecedented international involvement in Venezuela's internal affairs, the focus of the rest of this book.

---

33. A June 2002 poll by Datanalisis showed that Chávez's hard-core support had declined dramatically since 1999, with 74 percent of those polled giving him an evaluation of good or very good in February 1999 and only 20 percent in June 2002, and with his hard-core critics rising from 2 percent to 58.5 percent over the same time period. Datanalisis, "Encuesta Nacional Ómnibus," June 2002.

34. A Keller and Associates poll indicated that among the poorest Venezuelans, 35 percent would vote for Chávez and 44 percent would support another candidate if elections were held in July 2002. In contrast, the highest economic class was unanimous in their rejection of Chávez as a candidate. Keller and Associates, "Encuesta nacional de opinión pública," 2002.

2

The Dynamics of the Conflict
and the International Context

T he Venezuelan conflict itself was multilevel and multifaceted, because it involved social, economic, class, ideological, historical, and cultural dimensions. Nevertheless, the authors identified as the central axis of the conflict the struggle between the government and the opposition for political control over Venezuela's bases of power. They also recognized the conflict as a clash of values and ideologies.

The Power Struggle

Overall, the conflict represented a fundamental struggle for political power to control not only the state apparatus and the oil industry but also other important sectors and institutions, including the military, the media, civil society organizations, business, labor unions, the courts, the National Assembly, the National Electoral Council, and all of the accountability mechanisms of the state. Representing the fast-growing lower classes, which had traditionally been excluded from power by the Punto Fijo elites,[1] and disgruntled middle-class groups, the new Chavista government elected in 1998 approached its search for power in a systematic fashion. Using a very aggressive and ideological discourse, it first wrote a new constitution, later moved to control political institutions, and eventually attempted to control all of the aforementioned sectors of society.

Those sectors accustomed to always participating in the country's decision making, such as the social and business elites, the ecclesiastic hierarchy, and the leaders of the large political parties, reacted to the emergence of the new representatives of the poorest sectors by trying to protect their own

---

1. See discussion in chapter 1.

interests.[2] They brought large middle-class sectors to their point of view by raising fears and discrediting the government. The confrontation was thus established, generating two polarized sectors within the society—Chavistas and anti-Chavistas.

Lewis A. Coser's definition of a conflict over resource appropriation and distribution offers one possible way to look at the dynamics of the interaction between the main parties to the conflict—that is, the conflict represented "a struggle over values and claims to scarce status, power and resources in which the aims of the opponents are to neutralize, injure, or eliminate rivals."[3] According to the resource frame, conflict is the natural outcome of competition among individuals and groups over material goods, economic resources, and political power.[4]

As the confrontation evolved, however, underlying questions related to the identity of the groups and the way they perceived their own social position compared to that of others emerged and became more relevant, making the conflict deeper and much more difficult to address. From the Chavistas, there was a desire for retaliation and a need to end their "invisibility" and to be recognized as equal human beings, while the anti-Chavistas felt fear coupled with an absence of recognition by the "other." These structural components impregnated the whole social fabric and, together with the dynamics of interaction between the parties to the conflict, generated new meanings and more confrontation over time, thus pushing the very nature of the conflict beyond mere competition for resource control and distribution to questions of identity and relational positions.[5]

---

2. During a private interview with the authors in 2003, a former diplomat from the Chávez administration who had moved to the opposition described social change in the following way: "What happens in this country is like a landed estate. It was at first run by the real 'owners,' who quarreled a little with one another until the Pérez Jiménez dictatorship (1948–58) complicated matters. Then, in 1958, the owners decided the country should be run by their 'foremen,' that is, political party members. The owners still chose presidents and ministers, and everybody was happy. With Chávez, it is as if rural workers have gone into the landed estates and displaced the foremen. Imagine how the owners feel! Nobody controls these brutish people!"

3. Lewis A. Coser, *The Functions of Social Conflict* (New York: Free Press, 1956).

4. The resource frame focuses on each side gaining control of the bargaining or negotiation situation in order to "maximize" its desired outcome. Compromise is viewed as an acceptable outcome only when total domination is viewed as unnecessary or impossible to win or to sustain. From the perspective of the resource frame, reaching an agreement in which resources have been redistributed to the satisfaction of all sides means that the conflict has been resolved. See Jay Rothman, Randy Land Rothman, and Mary Hope Schwoebel, "Creative Marginality: Exploring the Links between Conflict Resolution and Social Work," *Peace and Conflict Studies* 8, no. 1 (2001).

5. A criticism of the resource frame is that it leads to interventions that emphasize short-term solutions, leaving unaddressed the underlying causes of the conflict. Ignoring the deeper problems may intensify the conflict to a full-blown crisis. See Rothman et al., "Creative Marginality."

The dynamics of the struggle for power using emotionally charged and divisive narratives created a polarization that masked and subjugated other aspects of reality. As Mireya Lozada eloquently expresses, polarization "makes social conflict invisible; generates a restricted representation of political conflict; privileges certain actors in the management of the conflict and its solution; limits the representation of positions to the hard-core actors (violent groups, coup-mongers), while omitting social movements or diverse groups. The more this dynamic penetrates the social fabric, the more cohesive elements of daily life become broken, with its consequent social damage, as those elements are mediated by what the political elites say is the conflict."[6]

The Clash of Values

At yet another level, the conflict represented different values and visions for the country, with some ideological components. Those who opposed the Chávez administration characterized the regime as threatening to the democratic values of individual liberties and private property. These groups generally represented the displaced traditional decision-making groups. Those supporting the Chávez administration characterized the government as one that would finally address the fundamental problems of poverty, inequality, and corruption in the country. Promoting a new participatory democracy, the Chávez government resonated with the dispossessed, empowering and giving hope to the poor in an unprecedented way, but at the same time fueling fears and prejudices among large sectors of the middle class.

This apparent conflict in values became enshrined in the struggle over the nature of the democracy—"representative" versus "participatory"—and the struggle over petroleum strategy—a commercially run enterprise increasing market share and reinvesting in the industry versus a politically run enterprise increasing price to raise revenues to invest in the "revolution."

The struggle for power and control produced a zero-sum game between the main actors and the clash of values pushed protagonists on both sides to perceive themselves in a fundamental struggle for the very future of the country—and to see the struggle as based on irreconcilable differences. Possibilities for reconciliation and coexistence seemed very remote to these groups. Their own propaganda machines painted two opposing "realities" of the country and fomented division and conflict rather than unity and shared

6. Mireya Lozada, "Polarización social y violencia política: Desafíos y alternativas" (paper presented at the XI Jornadas Venezolanas de Psicología Social: Tolerancia y ciudadanía, Ateneo de Caracas, Venezuela, 2002).

Opposition demonstration accusing Chávez of violating basic human rights.
Courtesy of SURpress.

Chavistas cheer Chávez outside the presidential palace.
Courtesy of the Carter Center archives.

values. Each group felt the mere existence of the other put its own identity at risk, which justified the need to eliminate the other. These characteristics indicated not only a lengthy conflict but also an intractable one. Indeed, the struggle was defined by several of the fundamental characteristics of an intractable conflict: actors who perceive insults; a prolonged dispute; issues of identity, values, and beliefs; hostility, violence, and destruction stemming from polarization; irreconcilable moral differences; high stakes of distribution of interests; and conflicts over power and status.[7] The dynamics of such conflicts also commonly evolve in cycles rather than in a progressive fashion. Open violence is always just another "natural" turn in this kind of conflict, as was the case in Venezuela.

The Actors

Within Venezuela, there were two clearly defined opposing camps: the Bolivarian movement represented by President Chávez and his followers, and the Coordinadora Democrática (Democratic Coordinating Commission), composed of opposition political parties, labor, business, and nongovernmental organizations. Within these two camps, however, there were a range of positions and actors with different interests; most were simply characterized as either radicals or moderates, but they had varying positions depending on the issue, timing, or other factors. The leaders of each camp could not necessarily contain or control the efforts of individual followers, and they each had to be constantly cognizant of their most extreme base. In addition to these two main protagonist camps, which will be discussed further, four additional actors in Venezuelan society affected by the conflict must also be briefly recognized: the military, the media, the Catholic Church, and organized citizens.

The military as an institution was extremely important, complicated, and difficult to read. It has traditionally held an institutional role in Venezuela of upholding the constitution, but within its ranks were political factions whose members owed their promotions and positions to various political parties. This historic politicization of the military continued and was amplified under Chavismo (Chávez's movement in government), as Chávez not only sought to promote loyal officers within the institution but also dramatically expanded the role of the military in politics, government, and developmental efforts.

7. Jacob Bercovitch, ed., *Studies in International Mediation* (New York: Palgrave Macmillan, 2003) and Heidi Burgess and Guy Burgess, "What Are Intractable Conflicts?" in *Beyond Intractability*, ed. Guy Burgess and Heidi Burgess (Boulder, CO: Conflict Research Consortium, University of Colorado, 2003), http://crinfo.beyondintractability.org/m/meaning_intractability.jsp.

Chávez also progressively neutralized the fourth armed force in the country, represented by the Metropolitan Police of the City of Caracas, which was under the control of an opposition mayor.

The media was another important actor. On the private side, the owners of the television stations in particular (along with influential radio and print media) played an important political role as they controlled information to the public and consciously sought to influence politics. Most of them had their own economic interests either as part of family-owned media agglomerations or for associated business reasons. Accustomed to participating in the decisions made by political leaders and clearly aware of their enormous influence on the people (almost 90 percent of Venezuelan homes have a television), the owners of the mass media found themselves suddenly excluded from the Chavista power circle and even threatened regarding their property and rights. They openly began to attack the government, using their communication channels to espouse a political viewpoint and to even distort information. For its part, the state media played a similar role, serving as a pro-government propaganda machine rather than as a provider of reliable news. This confrontation dynamic in the mass media favored the creation of two increasingly divorced realities, with each side understanding and explaining reality based on mutually exclusive histories and with each side reinforcing polarization.

The Catholic Church could have played a mediating role, but it had been in conflict with the Chávez government since 2000 and some of its authorities had taken a position supportive of the coup, thus dramatically reducing its ability to mediate. Historically, the Catholic Church has not played the important role in Venezuela that it has in other Latin countries. On the other hand, Evangelical Protestant churches had expanded in recent years, mainly among lower and middle classes, and were often promoted by the government itself as a means of challenging the Catholic Church hierarchy.

Within the society, individual citizens were affected not only by the stalemate and lack of policy progress but also by the pressure to take sides in the conflict. This had a strong psychological impact on the country. Furthermore, the zero-sum attitude of the main protagonists meant that resolving the conflict over the long term would require significant efforts at the intermediate societal levels not only to heal the trauma but also to help push the leaders into resolving their differences.

Among the citizens at large, there were a large number of people and organized groups who, even when they sympathized with one side or the other, began to tire of the conflict and wanted political and social leaders to refocus

on solving the fundamental problems of unemployment, crime, and poor social services. Many of these groups actively engaged in reconciliation efforts
at various levels of society and attempted to influence the perceptions of the
conflict from outside the main core of protagonists. With a peacebuilding
perspective, the authors—and later public opinion—began to refer to these
groups as the "third side."[8]

The Five Cycles of the Conflict

The authors identify five cycles of the conflict between 2001 and 2004, with
each cycle corresponding to one of the five stages in the struggle for power
between the government and opposition. As in any conflict, each movement
by one side corresponds to a "mirror" movement by the other (whether a previous, simultaneous, or subsequent movement), and different milestones can
be used in relating the history of a conflict's cycles.[9] The authors have chosen
to present a chronological development of events and a discrete set of milestones in order to convey the conditions under which the Carter Center's
intervention as a third party took place.

The Struggle over Presidential Power (2001–02)

At the end of 2001, once the constitutional structure had been ensured
and the government had the majority of seats in the National Assembly,
the president announced forty-nine decree laws aimed at a variety of social, educational, and economic arenas, thus affecting the interests and expectations of various national sectors. The opposition forces, led by labor
and business leaders, took advantage of the rage that these measures generated in broad sectors of the middle class and mobilized their followers to
prevent the "advance" of Chavismo. As described in chapter 1, the struggle for power in this cycle culminated in the coup on April 11, 2002, that
ousted Chávez from power for two days. The opposition felt complete victory, while Chavistas experienced true fear based on the persecution they
suffered during the forty-eight hours of Carmona's government. This brief experience exerted a powerful influence on both parties in the cycles to come,
since the illusion of complete triumph experienced by the opposition and the
fear of total defeat felt by Chavismo became entrenched as a basic reflex from

---

8. William L. Ury, *The Third Side: Why We Fight and How We Can Stop* (New York: Penguin Books, 2000).

9. Paul Watzlawick, Janet Helmick Beavin, and Don D. Jackson, *Pragmatics of Human Communication: A Study of Interactional Patterns, Pathologies, and Paradoxes* (New York: Norton, 1967).

both sides, conditioning many of their future decisions. It is key to under-standing the emotional basis of the Chavistas' goal of keeping power for fear of revenge and persecution if the opposition were allowed to regain the reins of power. The cycle closes with Chávez's return to the presidency on April 14.

The Struggle over the Control of Armed Power (2002)

After the April 2002 events, Chávez became aware of the fact that the legal and institutional control of the state he had gained through the elections was not enough to ensure power. While he recovered strength, he decided to open a national dialogue with his opponents and invited international facilitators. The opposition itself was divided into those who were inclined to accept Chávez's presidency and seek effective limits to the expansion of his power and those who wanted to remove him immediately and definitively. Among the latter were a group of military officers who decided to rebel in October 2002 and conduct a "sit-in" in Caracas's Plaza Altamira. They, and many other opposition leaders (including some media owners), expected this rebellion to be the nucleus of an expansive wave of civic-military disobedi-ence that would spread throughout the country and cause the fall of the government. Chávez's reaction was cautious and passive, and he used this challenge to carry out a "legal purge" of the National Armed Forces, dis-charging every rebel and taking control of key units. He did not resort to force but to legality.

His next move was to take control of the Metropolitan Caracas Police, which was under the command of an opposition mayor, through an interven-tion decree issued by the national government. The opposition challenged the measure and the Supreme Court decided in its favor. Only after Chávez had achieved his fundamental goal of disarming and disarticulating the Metro-politan Caracas Police as a potential armed force of political opposition did he decide to obey the court's decision. The government thus succeeded in ex-tending control to a potentially unsafe arena, from which his April defeat had come, while the opposition was left completely out of the armed-forces arena.

The Struggle over the Power of Oil (2003)

The next conflict cycle came as a result of the confrontation generated by the opposition leaders in December 2002, when they called for a national strike that expanded day by day to finally end in a two-month petroleum strike. A large number of PDVSA workers adhered to the strike, and the company's paralysis froze the entire country. The opposition thought that this extreme measure, which halted the source of foreign exchange and almost all economic and commercial activity in the country, would force Chávez to negotiate his resignation and abandon power. Once again, Chávez took advantage of the opposition's challenge: he organized a grand defensive operation importing food and gas, declared the strike a "sabotage," and fired more than 18,000 workers, managers, and technicians from the company. He thus gained total control of the most significant source of revenue for the state and the center of wealth generation in the country, a goal that had eluded him in 2002.

The opposition's defeat was complete, and with the failure of the strike, the two main business and labor opposition leaders fled the country and judicial prosecution. After that victory, the government consolidated control and increased its power considerably as it began to manage without restrictions the resources generated by the state oil company, as well as the multiple peripheral businesses associated with PDVSA.

The Struggle in the Electoral Arena (2003–04)

After the failed oil strike, the opposition, now led primarily by political parties and with a secondary influence from the owners of mass media, shifted tactics and decided to challenge the government again, this time by collecting signatures to petition for a recall referendum against the president. The government resisted the electoral confrontation by all possible means, resorting to a series of procedural maneuvers on the verge of illegality and to controversial decisions made by the National Electoral Council and the Supreme Court.

The opposition finally succeeded in fulfilling the minimum legal requirements and the recall referendum was convened for August 15, 2004. Once Chávez had publicly accepted the recall referendum, he focused all his energy and resources on a very effective mobilization campaign to win votes. The opposition, for its part, was not able to overcome internal divisions, mistrust, and competition, and its campaign was weak and disorderly. It did not succeed in presenting a sufficiently attractive or clear alternative option, and it lost the vote by 59 percent to 41 percent.

The opposition did not accept the result of the recall referendum, accused the government of fraud and of using various and changing arguments, and blamed the international observers for the defeat. Internal divisions within the opposition grew deeper and its political leaders separated further. By year's end it lost most of its governorships and mayoralties to Chavismo in regional elections.

The Struggle over Institutional Power (2004–05)

After its victory in the recall referendum, the government increased its hege-monic control of the key public institutions—expanding the Supreme Court, reinforcing its control of the National Electoral Council, and gaining control of the National Assembly after an opposition boycott. From this position of strength, the government enacted several laws restricting the rights and pre-rogatives of various social sectors considered to belong to the opposition.[10] The opposition, which had been electorally defeated twice and blamed others for its misfortune, could do nothing to stop the advance of the government.

The Three Characteristics of the Conflict

In each of the five cycles, conflict was brought to life by the interaction be-tween the government and opposition in their struggle for power. There was a different dominant axis in each of the cycles, but across the cycles the dy-namic was very similar and characterized by three elements:

- *Total struggle.* In each conflict cycle, the government demonstrated its desire for complete control of power, while the opposition presented a total and definitive challenge, threatening the center of power and demanding the removal or resignation of the president. Both parties played for "all or nothing."
- *Personalization of the conflict.* While the government moved to occupy and control specific arenas of power, displacing its opponents from them, the opposition concentrated all of its resources and efforts on the position and figure of the president, neglecting other arenas. Thus, the opposition progressively lost power in many arenas, such as within the armed forces, the PDVSA, moderately progressive middle sectors, the legislature, governorships, mayoralties, etc.
- *Strong symbolic and emotional content.* Perhaps as a manifestation of the expressive nature of Venezuelans, each event of the entire conflict was (and still is) infused with symbols and messages of strong emotional content.[11] From the start, Chávez made use of very strong symbolic

---

10. These included the law of social responsibility in radio and television, reforms to the penal code, and the land law.

11. As Mireya Lozada says, "Another factor exacerbating the emotional dimension and diminishing rational searches for solutions to the conflict is the use and exploitation on the part of both sides of the conflict of values, beliefs, symbols and myths with militarist, religious and revolutionary referents. This has affected identities, created opponents, and activated desires, passions and fears among the follow-ers of each side." Mireya Lozada, "El otro es el enemigo: imaginarios sociales y polarizacion," *Revista Venezolana de Economía y Ciencias Sociales* 10, no. 2 (2004): 195–210.

language, identifying his "mission" and himself with the national hero Simón Bolívar, and using specific phrases, images, and appeals characteristic of the country's popular imagination. The opposition mirrored this attitude, claiming that it was the defender of the colors of the flag and using alternative symbols and images, some of them religious, that were also deeply rooted in popular sentiment. A paradigmatic example of this symbolic dimension of the conflict was the change in the name of the country itself![12]

The Internal Dynamics of the Parties: The Two "Archipelagos"

The Opposition

There is no doubt that the metaphor that best represents the diverse and fragmented character of the opposition is that of an archipelago—that is, of a group of islands, both large and small, each with its own characteristics, needs, and visions of reality, that are at the same time a sole entity, a "common territory."[13]

When the opposition created the Coordinadora Democrática as a plural space that would allow it to include all those forces that opposed the government and that would provide all opposition groups with a new orientation, the illusion of unity grew stronger. The failed coup in April 2002 had weakened the most radical sectors, and new leaders were striving to emerge. Different people joined in, from those who had organized themselves to protest against the education decree to the new authorities elected in the CTV and leaders of old and new political parties and the chambers of commerce.[14] Those responsible for the private mass media participated as well, though only in final decision making and not during deliberations. The internal dynamics of the Coordinadora Democrática were dizzying and exhausting, and it was never clear to anyone how the system of decision making worked. There were parallel deliberations and very fluid, ad hoc leaderships that responded to specific themes and to the political context of the moment, which did not guarantee a particular rationality when defining political strategies.

---

12. It was changed by the 1999 Constitution to the Bolivarian Republic of Venezuela. Carmona's extremely brief government during the April coup returned to the original name of the Republic of Venezuela. After Chávez returned to power it was changed again.

13. The authors are grateful to Arnaldo Esté, founding member of the group Aquí Cabemos Todos, for the metaphor of the archipelago.

14. In one of the first meetings of the opposition with César Gaviria, Francisco Diez asked the leader of the Coordinadora Democrática who the lady addressing the OAS secretary general at that moment was and he answered that he had no idea!

The opposition's margin for taking action and making proposals became very limited due to distrust among its political actors. That distrust arose from internal differences whose processing was repeatedly postponed for the sake of unity to fight Chavismo. These internal differences seriously affected the opposition's capacity to develop a sophisticated and efficient political strategy. The opposition did have experienced political leaders in its ranks who understood very well the nature of the conflict and who could speak very clearly in private about the limitations and possibilities of the opposition's strategy. But their analyses and the content of those private conversations could not be easily shared in larger political circles without their running the risk of being accused of weakness, fear, or treason. Open, total confrontation with Chávez was the only politically safe position for each of the opposition leaders, and the more radical positions gained the most support. Many times this made the most realistic and pragmatic leaders conceal their fears or simply reinterpret their analyses so that they would be coherent with those of the majority.[15] In general, when meetings were large, those who expressed the most radical positions against the government were the ones who dominated.

At an early stage in the conflict, the strategy of confrontation in the streets gave rise to the leadership of Carlos Ortega, the secretary general of the CTV, and Carlos Fernández, the president of Fedecámaras, who, encouraged by the attention they received from the mass media, represented "the public voice of the opposition" and displaced "politicians" to the background. In a later stage, when the search for an electoral "solution" through the recall referendum was given priority, politicians and their political parties assumed leadership with the creation of the Group of Five (G-5) and relegated other groups to the background.[16] At both stages, the archipelago character was superimposed on the attempts at unity and coherent action, and the circuit of decision making was always hindered by divisions and distrust.

The diverse and plural nature that characterized the opposition often led opposition leaders to think that this diversity reflected the broad social

---

15. This is similar to what John Paul Lederach describes as the characteristics of high-level leadership: very visible leaders with a lot of media attention adopt positions as a result of pressure not only from their adversaries but also from their own supporters, who presume the leaders have great power and influence. In reality, in the majority of cases, power is more dispersed than this perception. John Paul Lederach, *Building Peace: Sustainable Reconciliation in Divided Societies* (Washington, DC: United States Institute of Peace Press, 1997), 67–69.

16. The Group of Five was composed of the secretary general of the AD, Henry Ramos Allup; the governor of the state of Miranda and leader of Copei, Enrique Mendoza; the leader of Proyecto Venezuela, Henrique Salas Römer; the leader of Primero Justicia, Julio Borges; and the leader of the managers displaced from the oil company PDVSA, Juan Fernández.

sectors that they represented and which they considered naturally majoritarian. In turn, they underestimated Chavismo's representativeness and its own broad social base.

Chavismo

How can one understand Chávez and Chavismo? Like a mirror to the opposition, Chávez was (and largely still is) an archipelago in himself. He was the only common territory for all Chavismo, but at the same time he tried to represent plural interests and ideologies with their own internal contradictions. Chávez, the master tactician, adapted to the context and made decisions corresponding to his own peculiar way of understanding the context. Hence, at different times he gave priority to the internal front over the external one, or to the political over the military, or to the social over the economic, or to the party over the institutional, or vice versa. Not even his closest and most reliable collaborators could unequivocally say which position Chávez would take in delicate political matters. There were neither strict ideological guidelines nor permanent strategic concepts that could make his decisions predictable.

The president himself encouraged the tendency to focus the political struggle on his person. By personalizing the confrontation, Chávez enhanced his own image and personal power, both before his opponents and in his own political territory. His combat tactics always included his personal exposure and he consistently appeared as the main challenger to the whole opposition. His discourse was usually pejorative and provocative, discrediting his opponents and encouraging confrontation and even violence.

The great difference between Chávez and the opposition archipelago, and one of the factors that allowed him to win every battle, was that Chávez maintained this strategy of multiple definitions only when he perceived that his own position of personal power was not threatened. But when he perceived that there was a risk to his power or that he needed to present a fight, he decidedly stood in the front line and exercised his leadership with effectiveness and consistency, something almost impossible for the opposition to do.

Within the government and his political movement, Chávez always exercised absolute and undisputed control. His power was never linked to alliances or to the political groups that supported him, nor to a network of personal relations or to the strength of a political project to which the others adhered. Instead, Chávez's power rose from his ability to communicate with the masses and generate massive, unconditional loyalties through direct communication with them. All of his allies and followers recognized that his power arose from popular support, and that it was personal and nontransferable, a power no one dared defy, ever. Chávez took care to maintain it for himself exclusively, preventing and blocking the appearance of potential figures that might compete with him. As the inverted mirror of the opposition, Chavistas were always united behind their leader, despising the contradictions of the opposition, which they considered a permanent minority in the country.[17]

As a third party facing the confrontation between these two parties, the authors—as part of the Carter Center team—were forced to understand their characteristics and adapt. Over time, the authors learned that making "diagnoses" and "predictions" from a traditionally rational point of view and assuming more or less permanent and somewhat coherent strategies, based on the values, interests, and needs declared by each of the parties, would not necessarily work. The Carter Center team had to face the paradox of being prepared for the unforeseeable, always.[18]

The Carter Center as Third-Party Facilitator

The general lines of the Carter Center's initial approach were stated in a strategy memorandum,[19] which was elaborated after the Carter Center's first evaluation mission to Venezuela in June 2002, and in the exchange of documents and e-mails between the authors. Although that general strategy was discontinued after President Carter's initial unsuccessful attempt to bring the two sides together at the beginning of July 2002 (see chapter 3), some elements of that strategy were kept for the next two years, especially the evaluation of risks and limits, the set of principles guiding the Carter Center's actions, and the idea of working at two different levels.

Evaluation of Risks

From the very beginning, the Carter Center was concerned about whether its decision to become involved as a third party would increase the risks

---

17. Chávez himself told the authors on repeated occasions that he thought the opposition "will always have 3,000,000 to 3,500,000 votes against Chávez, no more than that!"

18. On many occasions the authors could not understand the decisions one or the other party took and would repeat like a mantra, "Remember, this is Venezuela..."

19. Jennifer McCoy and Ben Hoffman, briefing memo, The Carter Center, July 2002. For the full text of the memo, see appendix B.

already present in the Venezuela conflict.[20] Unlike past situations in many other countries in which international third parties intervened as mediators, the situation in Venezuela was not openly violent with armed confrontation between opposing sides. Indeed, armed violence had been minimal and very limited, occurring only during the April 2002 coup and in some street confrontations.

Within this context, the Carter Center's fears were twofold. First, it did not want to generate expectations about a negotiation process whose failure would leave violence as the last resort for the parties. The Carter Center team explicitly discussed the importance of designing possible exit strategies that would allow it to face failure without conveying a message of hopelessness to the people in Venezuela.[21] Second, it was quite skeptical about the principal leaders from both sides being truly willing to negotiate and reach a reasonable agreement for coexistence. Following Marieke Kleiboer,[22] the Carter Center team seriously discussed whether its intervention as a third party was justified at that moment, given the scarce negotiating conviction of the main protagonists. It did not see in the parties what Kleiboer refers to as the total willingness or final decision to seek to deescalate the conflict.

As the Carter Center formed the Tripartite Working Group with the UNDP and the OAS secretariat, all three organizations agreed in July 2002 that the conflict's dynamics pointed to the possibility of an escalation to open violence. It was clear to the group that if Venezuelans did not find a peaceful way to "process" the social and political meaning of the phenomenon that Chavismo embodied, open violence would break out. Many of the symptoms of likely violence were already present,[23] and the example of forty years of internal war in neighboring Colombia served as a sobering reminder of possible outcomes. Faced with this scenario, the three organizations acknowledged that they had specific responsibilities well beyond personal wishes or preferences. As Jeffrey Z. Rubin says, "Most conflicts usually have multiple ripe moments rather than only one, and there is no such thing as a wrong time to attempt de-escalation."[24] The Carter Center, the United

---

20. See the excellent analysis on this issue in Mary Anderson, ed., *Options for Aid in Conflict: Lessons from Field Experiences* (Cambridge, MA: Collaborative for Development Action, 2000).

21. See personal e-mails between Jennifer McCoy and Francisco Diez on July 1–2, 2002.

22. Marieke Kleiboer, "Ripeness of Conflict: A Fruitful Notion?" *Journal of Peace Research* 31, no. 1 (1994): 109–16.

23. As identified in Ruddy Doom and Koen Vlassenroot, *Early-Warning and Conflict-Prevention: Minerva's Wisdom?* (Brussels: ABOS, 1995).

24. Rubin also says that the concept of ripeness can be misused as an excuse to procrastinate, making intervention much more difficult the longer nothing is done. Jeffrey Z. Rubin, "The Timing of

Nations, and OAS all have the institutional mission of promoting peace and defending democratic coexistence, and their own collective evaluation of the conflict urged them to try to intervene.

Guiding Principles for Action

Throughout the course of the Carter Center's intervention, it had to make explicit the set of principles that would guide its behavior and decisions. Its starting point was to consider reality, especially political reality, as a complex social construction whose nature and meaning is in constant evolution and that cannot be understood applying defined and permanent categories outside of the existing context. Politics is a system of meanings based on a set of interrelated perceptions about power, intentions, abilities, rules of the game, and purposes. These perceptions belong not only to the main protagonists of the conflict but also to society in general (the electorate) and of course to international actors.[25]

Was the Chávez regime opening the door for true social change or was an authoritarian, repressive regime being born? Did the opposition wish to defend democracy and social inclusion or was it only trying to preserve its own interests? All of these possibilities existed. The decisions of the various protagonists are responsible for shaping reality, and the patterns of interaction construct the meaning. As a consequence, when evaluating whether it would participate as a third party, the Carter Center assumed it would make an impact, no matter what its decision might be.

The Carter Center team assumed that, as mediator, it was not its mission to discover the "true reality" of the political conflict, nor whether the conflict's principal cause lay in injustice, authoritarianism, ideological differences, or the interests of this or that protagonist. Instead, its mission was to try to understand, always inevitably using in its own judgment, how the protagonists of the conflict perceived that reality, what points supported that perception, and what would be the most efficient mechanisms to contribute to a change that would allow them to find a "constructive solution" to their conflict.

Ripeness and the Ripeness of Timing," *Timing the De-Escalation of International Conflicts*, ed. Louis Kriesberg and Stuart J. Thorson, 237–46 (Syracuse, NY: Syracuse University Press, 1991).

25. Huntington criticizes the traditional realist paradigm for its failure to explain world politics after the end of the Cold War. Basically, he argues that realism does not consider the internal cultural factors that would shape intentions, perceptions, and coalitions among states. Samuel Huntington, *The Clash of Civilizations and the Remaking of World Order* (New York: Simon & Schuster, 1996). See also Paul Waztlawick and Marcelo Ceberio, *La construcción del universo. Conceptos introductorios y reflexiones sobre epistemología, constructivismo y pensamiento sistémico* (Barcelona: Herder, 1998) and Jeffrey Checkel, "Social Construction and Integration," Arena Working Papers 14 (1998), www.arena.uio.no/publications/working-papers1998/papers/wp98_14.htm.

The Carter Center team also assumed that to distinguish between a solution that, in its opinion, is "constructive" and a solution that is "not constructive" implies working with a set of values and principles that need to be made explicit. It followed consistent values to orient its efforts, and the way the team worked was not neutral at all. It was impartial with regard to the actors, in that it did not favor a particular "victor" or a particular "solution" to the conflict. But it was not neutral regarding the values it sought to uphold. It knew that some of the protagonists were ready to sacrifice some human lives for what they perceived would be most beneficial for the whole, and this possibility raised the question of whose values should prevail. In this regard, the Carter Center team viewed the protection of human life as an absolute value, above other values, and thus it stood against violence. It also sought to strengthen the democratic system, including respect for fundamental freedoms, human rights, the rule of law, and electoral integrity, and to enhance sovereignty, social justice, and equity.

The Carter Center did not base its work on political power, which it did not have, but on moral authority. Jimmy Carter enjoyed personal political capital due to his moral integrity and the trust he himself inspired in the leaders from both sides.[26] Thus, the Carter Center used transparency as the basic procedure to build trust, which implied that each side would know the nature of the Center's relationship with the other. It was careful to maintain its independence and to abstain from making value judgments about the people in conflict.

The Carter Center participated in those questions and areas of conflict in which all the parties agreed to have it as a third party. It practiced "multipartiality,"[27] which implies understanding the conflict situation from each and every perspective and being able to establish explicit and open alliances with all parties for the defense and preservation of explicitly agreed-upon values (in this case, peace and democracy).

Finally, the Carter Center worked as an external facilitator and sought to provide ownership of the problem and its resolution to the Venezuelan actors, and to contribute to the development of the capacity of Venezuelans at both elite and intermediate levels to negotiate, resolve disputes, and reconcile.

Multiple Levels of Work

The Carter Center's initial assessment demonstrated that the political conflict reflected the tensions generated by structural social change and that

---

26. P. Terrence Hopmann, *The Negotiation Process and Resolution of International Conflicts* (Columbia, SC: University of South Carolina Press, 1996).

27. Francisco Diez and Gachi Tapia, *Herramientas para trabajar en Mediación* (Buenos Aires: Paidós, 1999).

its roots extended beyond the political phenomenon represented by Chávez and his movement. The Carter Center understood (and later confirmed) that polarization was permeating all levels of society and that to work at the elite level alone would not suffice. When the Carter Center began its intervention, it did not know specifically how a more extended process of peacebuilding that might transform the conflict could be stimulated, but it did perceive that it was necessary to have multiple actors at different levels commit themselves to persistent, coordinated efforts to build bridges between the disputing sides. Consequently, in addition to engaging in activities with the OAS secretary general to facilitate negotiations at the level of the principal political leaders in the country, the Carter Center—over the course of its almost thirty months of work in Venezuela—developed two other complementary initiatives—one with the mass media and the second with intermediate-level social sectors. The UNDP joined the Carter Center in the second of these two initiatives.

Within the mass media, the Carter Center worked at two levels: at the higher level, it began facilitating specific negotiations between the media owners and the government, and later between the media and the authorities of the National Electoral Council. Below the level of media owners, it worked on multiple initiatives with editors and journalists from both private and state media, through a number of workshops and activities aimed at peacebuilding. The Carter Center thought it essential to encourage the construction of other narratives—alternative to those of polarization—that could be diffused to the public on a scale that only mass media can offer.

With intermediate-level social sectors, the Carter Center worked on a joint program with UNDP known as the Fortalecer la Paz en Venezuela (Strengthening Peace in Venezuela), which was built and consolidated over two years. The Carter Center and the UNDP started this initiative with the academic community and social activists and sought to maintain a transparent equilibrium in their relations with groups from the two opposing sides. They organized public events with foreign experts as a means of bringing together groups and individuals interested in peacebuilding and in generating safe spaces for followers of both sides to meet and talk. These efforts aimed to promote personal relationships that would support coexistence between Chavistas and anti-Chavistas.[28] The Carter Center and UNDP sought to create trust and consolidate relationships within and among

---

28. According to Lederach, "A sustainable transformative approach suggests that the key lies in the relationship of the involved parties, with all that term encompasses at the psychological, spiritual, social, economic, political and military levels." Lederach, *Building Peace*.

existing social networks, groups, and individuals willing to work for the construction of bridges between the parties to the conflict. They launched educational and training programs on conflict resolution at different levels and in various sectors.

The International Context

The nature of the conflict within Venezuela was affected by the international context of the early twenty-first century. The role of international norms and ideas had an evident impact on the actors, as each sought to enhance their own legitimacy nationally and internationally in the context of post–Cold War democracy-promotion and human-rights norms.[29] Venezuela, along with the rest of the hemisphere, had approved the OAS Inter-American Democratic Charter in 2001, committing itself to a particular form of democratic practice and to international sanctions if that practice were violated. This posed a constraint on the government and served as a potential source of leverage to the opposition.[30] Even so, the limits of international influence and leverage were apparent due to Venezuela's significant foreign revenues from petroleum and the competing foreign policy interests of foreign governments.[31]

---

29. Constructivists argue that power resources may include ideas and social conventions, themselves defined in terms of identities and interests. See Friedrich Kratochvil, *Rules, Norms and Decisions: On the Condition of Practical and Legal Reasoning in International Relations and Domestic Affairs* (Cambridge: Cambridge University Press, 1989); Alexander Wendt, *Social Theory of International Politics* (Cambridge: Cambridge University Press, 1999); Kathryn Sikkink and Margaret Keck, "Transnational Advocacy Networks in International and Regional Politics," *International Social Science Journal* 159 (March 1999): 89–101. Such ideas and social conventions may include sources of moral authority such as sacral or secular legitimacy, democracy, freedom, and self-determination. See Peter Hall, "The Role of Interests, Ideas and Institutions in the Political Economy of the Industrialized Nations," in *Comparative Politics*, ed. Mark Lichbach and Howard Zuckerman (Oxford: Cambridge University Press, 1997) and Jeffrey Checkel, "The Constructivist Turn in International Relations Theory," *World Politics* 50, no. 2: 324–48.

30. For an analysis of the Inter-American Democratic Charter and its provisions for international intervention, as well as limitations on international intervention, see papers by Shelley McConnell and Jennifer McCoy, Pedro Nikken, and Carlos Ayala in *The Collective Defense of Democracy: Concepts and Procedures* (Comisión Andina de Juristas and the Carter Center, 2005).

31. On the varying influence of linkage (through integration and commercial relations) and leverage (ability to use power resources to influence the behavior of another state), see, for example, Steven Levitsky and Lucan Way, *Competitive Authoritarianism* (Cambridge: Cambridge University Press, 2010). They conclude that linkage without leverage will result in little influence. Venezuela's access to oil revenues, particularly as prices began to rise after 2000, reduced the leverage of the international community at large (international financial institutions, multinational corporations, and foreign aid donors). Even further, Venezuela's role as an energy producer and supplier not only to the United States but also to its neighbors in the Caribbean and South America complicated the interests of hemispheric governments that might have sought to influence the conflict but that needed to consider their own commercial interests with Venezuela and security issues such as Colombia's guerrillas.

As in many conflicts with third-party intervention, each domestic side wanted an international ally against the other. The government wanted legitimation of its position in power; the opposition wanted help in ousting the government. Both sides put continual pressure on the international actors to support their own positions, and both sides were very critical of the OAS and Carter Center at various points. Both sides also became increasingly sophisticated in their search for international allies. The Coordinadora Democrática turned its early attempts to gain OAS involvement in the conflict into an international lobbying effort in the capitals of the hemisphere, even pursuing a publicity war by enlisting influential journalists and media outlets such as the Latin American columnist for *The Wall Street Journal*. The government, meanwhile, first tried to control its image and preserve its autonomy by inviting Carter, then by acquiescing to the participation of the OAS and UNDP. It later sought (and failed) to gain international advantage through the creation of a Group of Friends that would be truly friendly to the government, and ultimately used its commercial advantage to seek friendly votes in the OAS.

The Constraints of International Intervention

The international third-party participants faced three particular constraints in the Venezuelan context. The first constraint involved issues of sovereignty. As a reaction to the history of foreign intervention in the region, Latin American countries have traditionally required a high level of respect to the sovereign rights of nations and to the principle of noninterference. The Chávez administration was especially sensitive to foreign intervention. Indeed, its foreign policy goals included challenging U.S. dominance in the region and creating a multipolar world. Thus, the invitation to international actors was strictly limited—first to "facilitating" a dialogue as opposed to "mediating" a negotiated solution; and second to "observing" the referendum process as opposed to "judging" its outcome.

The fact that the conflict had not erupted into civil war or cross-border conflict meant that the UN Security Council was not involved and the United Nations itself was limited in its engagement. The OAS Inter-American Democratic Charter was invoked for the first time after the April 11, 2002, coup against Chávez, but despite efforts by Chávez's opponents, it was not explicitly invoked to require an intervention to resolve the disputes over democratic deficits after Chávez returned to power. Instead, the OAS tradition of "consensus voting" meant that the Venezuelan government could limit the organization's criticism of and role in the country. The OAS secretary general was well aware of the limits to his invitation.

The Carter Center, as a nongovernmental organization, was less constrained by diplomatic requirements, but it, of course, lacked leverage, relying instead on its moral authority and the trust of the actors.[32] Both organizations searched for a balance to achieve effective intervention without being overly intrusive.[33]

The second constraint involved the shifting mandates given to the international actors by the Venezuelan parties to the conflict and the need to navigate the potential contradictions and conflicts between these mandates. From the beginning of the international involvement, there was dissension among the Venezuelans over whether the Tripartite Working Group's role was one of facilitator (the government's view) or of guarantor of a negotiation process that would lead to binding agreements (the opposition's position). As the international participation evolved and an agreement was eventually reached to respect the constitutional right of citizens to petition for a recall of the president, the role of the same international actors (particularly the OAS and Carter Center) shifted to an electoral focus. This role included both facilitation of the negotiations over the rules for the referendum process, and traditional monitoring (and evaluation and judgment) of the referendum process, which included a ten-month process of collecting and verifying signatures and eventually holding the recall vote.

The government formally charged the international community with participating in two distinct and separate stages—specifically, with facilitating the dialogue table from November 8, 2002, to May 29, 2003, and with observing the referendum process from November 2003 to August 15, 2004. The opposition expressed its desire that the international community play a stronger role and act as a guarantor that the eventual agreement on the recall referendum would be honored in a fair and transparent manner.

---

32. Diana Chigas, "Track II (Citizen) Diplomacy," in *Beyond Intractability,* ed. Guy Burgess and Heidi Burgess (Boulder, CO: Conflict Research Consortium, University of Colorado, 2003), www.beyondintractability.org/m/track2_diplomacy.jsp.

33. As I. William Zartman and Saadia Tooval assert, the leverage of third parties can be increased or decreased by the actors themselves. Leverage comes from several sources: persuasion, the capacity to extract attractive offers from the negotiations, and the threat of abandoning the process and its rewards. The courses of influence and leverage acquire relevance according to the needs of the parties of the conflict. The greater the need to obtain an agreement, the greater the influence of the third-party mediator. See Zartman and Touval, "International Mediation in the Post–Cold War Era," in *Managing Global Chaos: Sources of and Responses to International Conflict,* ed. Chester Crocker, Fen Hampson, and Pamela Aall, 445–61 (Washington, DC: United States Institute of Peace Press, 1996).

The shifting roles for the international actors over time raised an important issue—namely, to what extent could and should the actors who mediated the conflict monitor and "judge" its outcome (that is, serve as international observers at the recall referendum). The recall process represented a continuation of the political conflict and an attempt at its resolution. The OAS and Carter Center viewed as part of their mandate facilitating the implementation of, and monitoring compliance with, the agreement that they had facilitated.

The third constraint involved potential competition and conflict between the international actors' own goals in Venezuela. The Carter Center's overall goal was to provide facilitation that could help resolve the dispute in a peaceful way, to prevent the outbreak of violence, and to enable the country to collectively address its significant social transformation and accompanying tensions within a democratic framework.

An important question for both international and domestic actors is whether the goals of peace and democracy are always mutually reinforcing, and whether they can be potentially conflicting at different stages of the conflict. For example, elections are inherently divisive, particularly under conditions of conflict. The Carter Center consciously strove to promote inclusiveness and preserve political space for dissent. It recognized the possibility that pursuing negotiations could simply be buying time for the Chávez government to consolidate its power in an exclusionary manner, or for the opposition to strengthen its own capacity to resist change and remove Chávez from power. In either case, as long as the two sides resisted the concept of coexistence and the possibility of negotiating issues of democracy, such as preserving the separation of powers or guaranteeing political space for the marginalized poor, the ability to preserve and expand democratic space in the country was restricted.

The very definitions of democracy were of course being debated in the country. The Carter Center recognized democratic deficits, yet it did not believe, during the course of its intervention, that democracy itself had been ruptured or that Venezuela had crossed the line to some form of authoritarianism.[34] However, it did refuse to work with nondemocratic

---

34 A large literature on democratization debates the quality of democracy and possible defects within it, as well as the dividing line between "electoral democracy" and "electoral authoritarianism." For examples of the former, see *Democratization* 11, no. 5 (2004), a special issue edited by Aurel Croissant and Wolfgang Merkel; Guillermo O'Donnell, Jorge Vargas Cullell, and Osvaldo Iazzetta, eds., *The Quality of Democracy: Theory and Applications* (South Bend, IN: University of Notre Dame Press, 2004); and Peter Smith, *Democracy in Latin America: Political Change in Comparative Perspective* (New York: Oxford University Press, 2005). For an example of the latter, see Andreas Schedler, ed., *Electoral Authoritarianism: The Dynamics of Unfree Competition* (Boulder, CO: Lynne Rienner Publishers, 2006).

actors who advocated the use of force or otherwise compromised the Carter Center's values, such as the Bloque Democrático, which advocated civic rebellion, the active military officers who openly rebelled in the Altamira protest, and armed gangs.

3

An Invitation to Third Parties to Facilitate Dialogue, June–October 2002

On June 4, 2002, Jimmy Carter received a letter from Venezuelan vice president José Vicente Rangel asking him to facilitate a dialogue between the government and the opposition. Rangel was already running a national dialogue, but the opposition members had been gradually pulling out of it, complaining that it was too government controlled. Indeed, the government, which initiated the dialogue on April 30, 2002, held the dialogue meetings at the presidential palace rather than in neutral territory, chose the members of the opposition that would participate, excluded the leaders of the labor and business organizations who had supported the coup, and controlled the agenda of the dialogue. Realizing that the dialogue was not functioning and facing international pressure, the government invited Jimmy Carter to help.

The government had several incentives to invite Carter. First, Chávez was shaken by the coup and felt weak. The country was still extremely tense, pro- and antigovernment protests continued while labor leaders talked about another general strike, and the government was unsure of its support within the fragmented armed forces. With junior officers upset about the president's alleged politicization of the annual promotion process in the lead up to Venezuela's Independence Day on July 5, rumors were rife of another coup attempt. Within Chávez's camp, there appeared to be several strategies under consideration by various factions, and it was unclear which one the president favored. Some were willing to pursue negotiations, at the minimum for the sake of international legitimacy; others wanted to eliminate the opposition and consolidate the revolution as soon as possible and resort to the use of force if necessary.

On the international front, the government needed to respond to the OAS's call for national reconciliation and dialogue in order to maintain its legitimacy and show that it was following OAS recommendations. At the same time, the government resisted submitting to OAS oversight given the apparent satisfaction of the United States and a few other OAS members with the coup. The government was more open to the United Nations than the OAS, and asked UN secretary-general Kofi Annan to consider technical assistance for a national dialogue.[1] Foremost, however, seemed to be the government's interest in Jimmy Carter as facilitator. Chávez already had a relationship with Carter and the Carter Center from the Center's election observation missions in 1998 and 2000, and apparently believed that Carter's role would give the national dialogue the needed international legitimacy without sacrificing sovereignty.[2]

The opposition believed itself to be in a strong position, despite the reversal of the coup. Many Chávez opponents had repudiated the unexpected authoritarian moves of interim leader Pedro Carmona, but most retained their goal of removing Chávez from power through either constitutional or unconstitutional means. Those favoring constitutional means considered four possible strategies to shorten the president's mandate: a recall referendum in August 2003 that, if Chávez were defeated, would lead to elections within thirty days in which the president might be able to run again (preferred option by Chávez);[3] a constitutional amendment to shorten the presidential term and add a second round to elections (preferred by some of the political parties that knew they themselves needed more time to be able to compete successfully in elections); massive street mobilizations and strikes to reduce the government's ability to finance and arm the Círculos Bolivarianos (Bolivarian Circles) and govern the country,[4]

---

1. In fact, Annan sent Elena Martinez, regional director of the UNDP for Latin America and the Caribbean, on an exploratory mission to Venezuela in May. Jennifer McCoy subsequently consulted with Martinez.

2. In a meeting on July 9, 2002, Chávez told Carter that he was interested in the UNDP and OAS helping facilitate dialogue, in a technical capacity, but that he had some observations about the OAS. Namely, he was concerned that the secretary general had "practically recognized the de facto government, asking our ambassador not to go to the Permanent Council meeting" after the April 11 coup and that the secretary general was a Colombian—a traditional rival of Venezuela. Chávez also wanted to clarify the statutes of the OAS with regard to sovereign governments and be very clear about the role the OAS would have in Venezuela.

3. The constitution allowed for a recall of elected officials midway through their terms; in the case of the president this would be August 2003.

4. The Círculos Bolivarianos were new groups of Chávez's followers—most of them carrying out social work in the poor neighborhoods—financed directly by the presidency. The opposition alleged that the government was financing and arming the Círculos Bolivarianos as a private militia; the government claimed that these were social movements only.

forcing a presidential resignation and new elections (preferred by the social organizations); and impeachment through the courts (preferred by some NGOs and political parties). The most radical appeared to support even another coup attempt.

The opposition in fact followed multiple strategies simultaneously. With the political parties weak and discredited, civil society groups, including the CTV, Fedecámaras, the media owners, and various NGOs, led the opposition strategy of continued mass mobilizations demanding the president's resignation, while some NGOs and political parties looked for means of impeachment through the court system—for example, they introduced law-suits alleging presidential malfeasance for accepting a campaign loan from a Spanish bank, for illegally diverting funds from the Petroleum Stabilization Fund (FIEM), and for ordering the shooting of innocent civilians on April 11 (a crime against humanity). On May 23, 2002, political parties announced they would seek a constitutional amendment to shorten the president's term from six to four years. By late June, the main opposition actors had ceased participating in the national dialogue for various reasons. The CTV with-drew because its president had not been formally recognized, which then led Fedecámaras to withdraw in an act of solidarity with the CTV. The political parties never joined the dialogue, and the media walked out after a particu-larly heated exchange between one media representative and the president in one of the dialogue sessions. Of the thirty dialogue members, only five were seen as nongovernment supporters.[5]

Many in the opposition were suspicious of the government's invitation to Carter, believing that if the government trusted Carter, he must be somehow beholden to the government. Chávez's trust in him could have been inter-preted differently, however. Specifically, he may have seen Carter's involve-ment as a way to foster "effective communication and facilitate the develop-ment of creative options during the negotiation process,"[6] which is in fact what Carter's involvement helped allow. Those opposition figures interested in negotiations pressed instead for the OAS to facilitate a dialogue, believing not only that the OAS, as an intergovernmental organization, could better pressure the government but also that the OAS could enforce any agreement reached through a dialogue. They particularly believed that the OAS could "force" the Venezuelan government to comply with negotiated solutions un-der the Inter-American Democratic Charter.

---

5. McCoy and Hoffman, briefing memo, July 2002, *see appendix B, this volume.*
6. Zartman and Touval, "International Mediation."

The Main Issues of Contention

After a June 24–29, 2002, assessment trip to Venezuela, which included Carter Center staff, conflict resolution specialists, and former Dominican Republic president Leonel Fernandez,[7] the Carter Center staff analyzed the conflict in the following way:

> This is a multi-party, multi-issue, deep-rooted, volatile and potentially lethal conflict. It is marked by extreme hardliners, personalized and vitriolic hostility between certain key actors, especially the President and media and labor. There is little apparent middle ground and only a tenuous balance of power (hurting stalemate) inclining the parties to negotiate rather than prevail by force (whether by non-violent pressure or violent). While focused on the person of President Chávez, suggesting that accommodation on his part may lead to a workable truce, the deeper problems of institutional erosion, structural economic shortcomings, and heightened expectations of the newly mobilized urban poor call for more.
>
> This is more problematic as there is little evidence that the President is capable of honoring commitments in the absence of pressure, resulting in a deep lack of confidence in the possibility of holding meaningful, durable negotiations. In this atmosphere there would naturally be concerns by each of the parties about the nature of any third party intervention: some will want an authority that can arbitrate and impose commitments and enforce them; others will look to "friendly" third parties who will play into their agenda; some will boycott any effort that might lead to a negotiated settlement as they simply wish the other side removed; others will participate, but do so for the express (hidden) purpose of undermining the negotiations.[8]

In addition to the overriding desire of the opposition to remove Chávez from power, the Carter Center staff identified at least seven issues needing resolution:

Disarmament

Personal insecurity was exacerbated by the dominant perception that the Bolivarian Circles, organized by the governing party ostensibly for social programs in poor urban areas, were armed, as the opposition alleged, to "defend the revolution." In response, a growing hysteria among middle and upper classes, particularly in Caracas, appeared to be leading to a new arms race as families and individuals across the board armed themselves for protection and defense. The issues thus included the difficult proposition of a general disarmament of the population.

---

7. Along with Leonel Fernández, Jennifer McCoy, Francisco Diez, Ben Hoffman (director of the Carter Center's Conflict Resolution Program), and Laura Neuman (senior program associate, Americas Program) participated in the assessment mission.

8. McCoy and Hoffman, briefing memo.

Separation of Powers

There was a general concern about the weakening and politicization of the country's institutions and its checks and balances, including the need to reach an agreement, in line with constitutional provisions, on a timetable for appointing citizens' branch authorities (attorney general, controller general, ombudsman); Supreme Court justices; and electoral authorities.

Forty-nine Decree Laws

The laws decreed by the president in December 2001 created a general concern among the private sector about the government's respect for property rights. After Chávez was restored to power in April, the government agreed that seventeen of these laws should be reviewed by the National Assembly in consultation with the private sector.

Labor Sector

The government had still not recognized the legitimacy of the CTV elections from October 2001 and the matter remained unresolved by the electoral authorities and the courts, leading the government to initially exclude the CTV from the national dialogue and to delay negotiation of collective contracts. The CTV demanded official recognition of its leadership.

Freedom of Expression

The private media perceived a tightening of their freedoms and complained of harassment and assaults of their journalists. Television and radio owners were concerned about a new telecommunications law that could allow the government to suspend access to the airwaves for those who opposed the government, and all private media were concerned about a draft law on the social responsibility of the media.

Despite this, the press continued to freely criticize the government (Human Rights Watch noted at the time that the private media were vocal and clearly biased against the government), antigovernment talk shows abounded, and the government perceived the media as its primary political opponent. Indeed, television station owners seemed to play a major behind-the-scenes role in the opposition's political strategizing.

Establishment of a Truth Commission

Following the events of April 11–14, the National Assembly promised to establish an independent and investigative truth commission to determine responsibility for the deaths and arrests on both sides during those chaotic days. The commission had not been established by July, constituting another critical agenda item.

Security for Opposition Marches

The opposition followed the April 11 march with repeat efforts in May and June and planned a large one for July 11. It was especially concerned about security for the July 11 march and its ability to enter the security cordon around the presidential palace to deliver its ultimatum for the president's resignation.

The Carter Center's Strategy

In this environment, which was defined by deep polarization, high levels of anxiety and insecurity, and directly competing interests of the players, the Carter Center devised a strategy to deal with the political crisis. It sought to reduce tensions in the short term and open up political space for concrete negotiations on a dialogue process and agenda. Specifically, its goal was "to develop a process to negotiate a political accord leading to a legitimate, inclusive, multi-sector dialogue seeking reconciliation and the restoration of functioning, trusted political institutions."[9]

Its strategy consisted of a two-step negotiation process among elites in July–August to immediately help reduce tensions and to put in place a longer-term multisector dialogue process. President Carter would visit in early July to try to reach an accord among the actors on a dialogue process and agenda, and then bring them together one month later in a neutral location outside of Venezuela to negotiate substantive accords on the agreed-upon agenda, including on the design of a long-term multisector dialogue process and international and national verification mechanisms. The Carter Center team thought it essential to begin to lower tensions immediately by achieving a truce in the war between the media and Chávez and to help defuse tensions before the scheduled July 11 march. It also planned to build an international coalition, which would include the UNDP and OAS, to facilitate the elite-level negotiations and to provide technical and financial assistance to the longer-term national dialogue, as well as to create incentives and disincentives that would encourage compliance to any agreements reached.[10] Prior to his trip in July, President Carter consulted with UN secretary-

---

9. Ibid.

10. For an analysis of the use of incentives and disincentives, see I. William Zartman and Saadia Touval, eds., *International Mediation in Theory and Practice* (Washington DC: Westview Press for SAIS, 1985).

general Kofi Annan, OAS secretary general César Gaviria, and the U.S. State Department, and received their total support to provide international assistance for a dialogue in Venezuela. The Carter Center assumed the process would take one year.

Following the June assessment mission, the Carter Center was aware that it needed to build confidence in its presence, primarily among the opposition, and in its approach, among both sides.[11] It wanted to ensure that Venezuelans themselves would "own" the process and the outcomes, as that would be the only way to achieve a sustainable resolution.

Carter's First Trip, July 2002

Responding to the vice president's letter of invitation, President Carter and the authors traveled to Caracas on July 6, 2002, to explore a dialogue process and agenda. What actually happened during the four-day trip had little to do with the original strategy first set out by the Carter Center. The Center's first goal was to facilitate a meeting between President Chávez and the private television and major radio and newspaper owners.[12] After listening to Carter's proposal, the media representatives agreed to meet with Chávez on the condition that the full range of opposition groups (the fledgling Coordinadora Democrática) also agreed to meet with the president. Even though the Carter Center had not planned to move ahead during this initial trip with a proposal for a face-to-face meeting between Chávez and a full range of his opponents, President Carter decided on the spot to attempt to arrange such a collective meeting. He met with the many opposition groups individually. Some of them expressed interest but most expressed skepticism about meeting with Chávez so soon. Carter formed a twelve-point agenda based on their more relevant and substantive grievances. The opposition groups asked for time to discuss the proposal with their own members and among themselves.

Meanwhile, Carter went to Chávez with the proposal to meet a full range of opposition groups on neutral ground—Carter's hotel suite—and, per the opposition's request, asked him to invite the Episcopal Conference (Catholic Church), the OAS, and UNDP. Chávez agreed. The opposition groups consulted with their individual group memberships and then met together in marathon sessions to discuss the proposal. At one point, they called Jennifer McCoy to ask that President Carter come to meet them to discuss the

---

11. Diez and Tapia, *Herramientas para trabajar.*

12. Carter Center staff had been assured ahead of time by Gustavo Cisneros and Chávez that such a meeting would be welcome.

President Carter meets with President Chávez in the presidential palace.
Courtesy of the Carter Center archives.

agenda. After McCoy was assured by CTV president Carlos Ortega that the possibility of their acceptance was still on the table, President Carter went to the MAS party headquarters to face more than sixty opposition leaders in a very tense meeting. MAS president Felipe Mújica and Carlos Ortega opened the session by declaring that the group was rejecting the proposal and that they viewed a meeting with Chávez at that time as an attempt to undermine their strength right before the planned opposition march on July 11. Mújica stated that the obstacle to dialogue was President Chávez himself and that the Coordinadora Democrática remained interested in dialogue. He proposed the creation of a government-opposition negotiating team to establish the agenda, beginning *after* the July 11 march.

President Carter replied that, in his view, they were missing an opportunity to meet Chávez on neutral ground, to discuss their agenda, in the presence of the international organizations requested by the opposition. He explained again that the government had not in fact called the meeting—that it was his own proposal and that Chávez had only learned of it the night before. Carter told them that he had the full support of the OAS and United Nations, and that they would be present at the meeting. He closed by stating that he would hold the meeting the following day as planned, and that if any individual changed their mind and decided to come, they would be welcome.

The following morning, Chávez and the international witnesses appeared on schedule, and three pro-opposition civil society representatives and a representative of the Episcopal Conference showed up. Carter stated that the purpose of the meeting, given the lack of opposition figures, would be for him to present Chávez with the list of opposition grievances and to receive Chávez's response to them (whether an explanation of his position or a statement of his plans to act to remedy the grievances). He stated that he would then report to the public the substance of the meeting.[13] That same day the opposition sent a letter thanking President Carter for his efforts and asking him to continue participating in the conflict as a third party.

An Assessment of Carter's First Trip

The June assessment mission had clearly identified the need to design a two-stage negotiation strategy.[14] First, the Carter Center would take the necessary time to build trust and design a process *together with* the key actors, using a single-text strategy to agree on the agenda, place, representation, and procedures to be used.[15] Second, following the agreed-upon procedure, the Carter Center would start a joint negotiation at the elite level in July and August, to be followed by a longer-term multisectoral dialogue.

However, the Carter Center made two mistakes. First, it mixed process objectives with substantive objectives when it added to the principal goal of designing a process with both sides the goals of reaching specific agreements between the government and the mass media and of advancing substantive issues. Second, it lost control of the process both when mass media owners unexpectedly rejected a bilateral meeting with Chávez, asking instead for a joint meeting with all of the opponents to the government, and when Carter agreed to continue to work toward that objective that very same week.[16]

All of a sudden, the strategy that had been designed to evolve in stages over two months turned into an attempt facilitated by Carter to negotiate the "hottest" subjects between the government and all of its opponents the very next day. From an "objective" standpoint, it was a most attractive offer for the

13. Carter's trip report outlining the twelve points and Chávez's response is available at http://carter-center.org/news/documents/doc1042.html.

14. See details in McCoy and Hoffman, briefing memo, and in the e-mails exchanged by McCoy and Diez on July 1–2, 2002, author's private collection..

15. Diez and Tapia, *Herramientas para trabajar.*

16. For a description of this principle, see Bercovitch, *Studies in International Mediation.*

opposition. It had complained that the dialogue called by the government was a farce, and now Carter was offering a real scenario, a neutral place, with the president seated at the table, with international witnesses (OAS and UNDP), and with Carter himself as a facilitator. Undoubtedly, such a meeting would have changed the course of events. The problem was that it was for "the very next day." The opposition was not ready for that. They had called a large protest march for later that week, and sitting down to negotiate three days before such an event would have implied weakening their strategy of confrontation, the only strategy upon which all opposition groups agreed.

I. William Zartman and Saadia Touval explain that the more parties feel they must reach an agreement, the more influence and power the mediator will have to reach an agreement.[17] At that moment in Venezuela, however, one of the parties felt that it had a more valuable alternative to face-to-face negotiations: pressure in the streets. As a result, the mediator's power and influence did not suffice to bring the parties to the table. In the opinion of the authors, President Carter is the kind of mediator who prefers to work with powerful individuals (rather than with groups) and who goes straight to the substantive core of the problem.[18] He is less interested in procedural aspects. However, at this stage of the Carter Center's intervention, a process first needed to be "built." In addition, for its participation as a third party to be feasible and effective, it was first necessary to create trust among opposition members.

Carter made public his analysis of the twelve points on the opposition grievance list and Chávez's responses to the list, and also sought and received a commitment from Chávez to accept the participation of the OAS, the UNDP, and the Carter Center to facilitate a dialogue.[19] Carter also proposed a compromise for the upcoming July 11 march in which security would be guaranteed by the government and a small group of marchers would be permitted to proceed to the presidential palace to present their demands.

In the end, the massive July 11 march was carried out peacefully, and the diplomatic community and even many in the opposition credited the Carter-Chávez talks with achieving the government provision of security to the marchers and with prompting the president's call to his own supporters to avoid confrontation.

---

17. Zartman and Touval, "International Mediation."

18. For an examination of different mediator styles, see Isak Svensson, "Democracies, Disengagement and Deals: Exploring the Effect of Different Types of Mediators" in *Resources, Governance and Civil Conflict*, ed. Kaare Strøm and Magnus Öberg (London: Routledge Press, 2007).

19. The private media declined to publish his report in full, but it did regularly chastise the government for failing to comply with the "promises" made to Carter, even though Carter's report did not constitute a negotiated agreement given the lack of participation of the other side to the conflict. Jimmy Carter, "Trip Report on Venezuela." July 12, 2002, http://cartercenter.org/news/documents/doc1042.html.

The Tripartite Working Group

Immediately after Carter's trip, the Carter Center invited representatives from the OAS and UNDP to meet in Atlanta on July 18 to explore a joint effort to offer Venezuelans assistance in a revamped national dialogue effort. From this meeting, the Tripartite Working Group on Venezuela was born—an unprecedented joint effort of an NGO (Carter Center) and two intergovernmental organizations (OAS and UNDP) setting up the foundations for a multitrack diplomatic effort coordinated in a new and unique way.[20] The three organizations agreed to name an international facilitator, in consultation with the Venezuelan actors, who would represent all three organizations, and to propose a verification mechanism that included the participation of distinguished individuals from Venezuela and from elsewhere in the hemisphere. The UNDP would provide financing and expertise for the technical secretariat in support of the dialogue process and the OAS and the Carter Center would provide political and technical support to the international facilitator. The Carter Center expected at that time that it might take a month to conclude the prenegotiations for the agenda and dialogue format, and another two to five months to conclude the dialogue itself.

In fact, the Tripartite Working Group spent the next three months designing the prenegotiations and attempting to set up a dialogue table. The group's first internal agreement was to ask the opposing parties for a written request asking the tripartite members to serve as third-party facilitators; this would serve as explicit proof of their commitment to enter in a dialogue process.[21] Representatives of each of the international organizations (privately calling themselves the "three musketeers") traveled together to Caracas in late July to offer their services to the government and to the opposition Coordinadora Democrática,[22] conditioned on a written request by both sides, and to clarify some misperceptions (particularly the opposition's misperception that an OAS mediating role would provide for binding and enforceable agreements). The group then waited for responses.

The government accepted the group's participation first, sending a letter of invitation to the three organizations on August 2 asking them to serve

---

20. For a discussion of multitrack diplomacy, see Louise Diamond and John W. McDonald, *Multi-Track Diplomacy: A Systems Approach to Peace* (West Hartford: Kumarian Press, 1996).

21. For theory of commitment, see Bercovitch, *Studies in International Mediation.*

22. The "three musketeers" were Fernando Jaramillo, chief of staff to OAS secretary general Cesar Gaviria; Elena Martinez, assistant UNDP administrator and director of the Latin American and Caribbean Bureau; and Jennifer McCoy, director of the Carter Center's Americas Program.

as facilitators for a national dialogue. The opposition took more time as it debated at multiple levels within the unwieldy Coordinadora Democrática, but on August 14 it too invited the three organizations. On the same day, the Supreme Court dismissed charges against four generals accused of rebellion for the removal of the president on April 11, leading to violent clashes between government and opposition protestors outside the court and devastating criticism by President Chávez against the Supreme Court. Also on the same day, the OAS approved a resolution supporting the tripartite facilitation and recognizing the Venezuelan opposition by the name of Coordinadora Democrática (an important point to the opposition to give it international standing).[23] With the government on the defensive and the opposition emboldened, the political climate began to deteriorate and the confrontation once again became radicalized.[24]

The tripartite group met with OAS secretary general César Gaviria in Washington, DC, on August 20, where he proposed another mission to take the political temperature of the country and to encourage the opposition to get on board before moving forward with plans to propose an international facilitator to the Venezuelans.[25] The secretary general wanted to get involved as a third party at a ripe moment, or at least when the conditions were present for such a moment to arrive.[26] Consequently, the group met again in Atlanta in late August to prepare its next mission to Caracas on September 9–13, 2002. The group identified as its first goal changing the political climate in Venezuela from one of conflict to one of dialogue by convincing both sides of the benefits of dialogue, by urging both sides to give gestures of goodwill, by focusing on issues that required immediate attention and that both agreed upon, like the reform of the National Electoral Council and an emergency social package, and by proposing a document that they could both sign as a first joint action. The group also wanted to get clear statements of commitment from the actors to a process of resolving conflict through consensus mechanisms and to get agreement on the next steps for developing those mechanisms. It ultimately hoped to give Venezuelans the hope that violence was not inevitable.

---

23. OAS, "Support for the Process of Dialogue in Venezuela," CP RES 821 (1329/02), August 14, 2002.

24. See, for example, comments by Movimiento al Socialismo secretary general Leopoldo Pucchi, reported in *El Nacional*, August 27, 2002, that the opposition had four scenarios for removing the president: impeachment, constitutional amendment to shorten his term, extraconstitutional military action, and extraconstitutional civic-military action.

25. Gaviria was quite aware of the political significance the conflict had in the hemisphere and wanted to make sure that what happened to Carter would not happen to him and that he would be able to commit the opposition to the process.

26. See the discussion of ripe moments in Zartman and Touval, "International Mediation."

During the mission to Caracus, the group faced the same confrontational scenario experienced by the Carter Center during its July visit. The two sides continued to emphasize mutually exclusive starting points for negotiation: the opposition insisted that the first item for discussion be the early departure of President Chávez from power, while the government rejected this agenda item. Both sides also persisted in characterizing each other as illegitimate and unworthy of sitting at the table: AD and Copei leaders in particular called President Chávez an "assassin" and a "thief," while President Chávez refused to sit with those he called "*golpistas*" (coup-mongers). Nevertheless, the tripartite mission gained consensus on three issues that could be addressed in terms of international-assistance proposals—the truth commission, implementation of the new disarmament law, and electoral reform.

The tripartite group concluded after its September visit that both sides of the conflict were acceding half-heartedly to dialogue efforts in order to protect their international image and buy time to pursue their more ambitious agendas.[27] For the opposition, that agenda was to oust the government through a street mobilization strategy; for the government, it was to survive in power with the legitimacy gained from having attempted a dialogue with its opponents. The group surmised that the opposition would continue to participate as long as it could simultaneously pursue the street strategy, and the government as long as its authority was not questioned through intrusive international monitoring and judgment.[28]

In the letters that both sides had sent in August to the Tripartite Working Group inviting its members to act as facilitators, it was evident that neither recognized that they had common conceptual grounds with the other. On the contrary, each chance they got, each side tried to distance itself from the other by criticizing its opponent. However, in those very same letters, each side proclaimed itself as the champion of peace and democracy and its opponent as the opposite. Based on the concept of "narrative theory," the tripartite group took idiomatic expressions from the invitation letters it had received and wrote the draft of a Declaration of Principles for Peace and Democracy.[29] It decided to present the draft to the parties and ask them to

---

27. For an analysis of the multiple reasons parties may enter negotiation processes, see Ronald Fisher, "Methods of Third-Party Intervention," in *Berghof Handbook for Conflict Resolution* (Germany: Berghof Research Center for Constructive Conflict Management, 2001), 11.

28. Jennifer McCoy, confidential internal Carter Center report on the international Tripartite Working Group mission to Venezuela, September 9–14, 2002.

29. For a discussion of narrative theory, see Michael White and David Epson, *Narrative Means to Therapeutic Ends* (Adelaide: Dulwich Centre, 1990).

reconfirm their decision to start a process of consensus building that would be facilitated by the group.

The Carter Center staff hoped that the act of signing a joint Declaration of Principles for Peace and Democracy in Venezuela would be a big step forward in identifying interlocutors for each side and in acknowledging consensus on a set of principles as a basis for coexistence. The Carter Center proposed that it would act as facilitator in a "go-between" process of dialogue between Vice President Rangel, who would represent the government, and Timoteo Zambrano, who would represent the opposition. To that end, Francisco Diez remained in the country to pursue the signatures using a "shuttle-diplomacy" strategy.[30]

The "Go-between" Exercise

To begin the exercise, Francisco Diez visited Vice President Rangel. Rangel reviewed the text, made minor changes, and expressed his agreement "in general terms." Diez asked him whether he represented the government's opinion on the text, and Rangel assured him that he did.[31] Then, Diez did the same with Timoteo Zambrano, who made comments and proposed changes that Diez knew (as did Zambrano) would upset the government. Zambrano strongly emphasized the word "negotiation."

Diez talked with the vice president again; Rangel bitterly complained of some public statements criticizing the government that had been made by opposition members. He angrily told Diez that the declaration would have to be reviewed by the political parties allied with the government. He was changing the rules of the game that had previously been agreed on, so Diez rejected his idea,[32] telling him that it would be impossible to agree on a text if dozens of people intervened, and that the initiative would be dropped if he could not represent the government to finalize the text.[33] Rangel asked for time to think about the matter, and he and Diez agreed to meet again in a couple of days.

---

30. For a discussion of shuttle diplomacy, see Eric Brahm and Heidi Burgess, "Shuttle Diplomacy," in *Beyond Intractability*, ed. Guy Burgess and Heidi Burgess (Boulder, CO: Conflict Research Consortium, University of Colorado, 2003), www.beyondintractability.org/essay/shuttle_diplomacy.

31. This is a principle noted in Lawrence E. Susskind and Robert H. Mnookin, "Major Themes and Prescriptive Implications," in *Negotiating on Behalf of Others*, ed. Lawrence E. Susskind and Robert H. Mnookin (Thousand Oaks, CA: Sage, 1999).

32. This reaction as a mediator was very important in terms of process control, since in the same interaction the Carter Center established the rule with the government that the Center could present and withdraw options to the table, not merely witness or facilitate talks. This is also another example of the difference in approaches the Carter Center had with the OAS.

33. A common move in the exercise of mediating negotiations is that of offering to withdraw an initiative or an option created by the mediator from the table, thus showing that the mediator has neither

During the next ten days, Zambrano kept calling Diez to learn about the reaction of the government, but Rangel would not answer Diez's calls.

Diez began to consider how he could get the vice president's attention so that he might speak with him again and decided to get in touch with Carlos Chávez, the individual responsible for the organization of the Bolivarian Circles.[34] After meeting with Carlos Chávez, Diez sent the vice president a fax saying he wished to inform Rangel about that meeting and to review the declaration's text with him. It worked, and Rangel called. The following day a headline appeared in the major newspaper *El Nacional* that read, "The Carter Center Meets with the Bolivarian Circles."[35]

Rangel accepted almost all of the modifications to the text but emphatically rejected the word "negotiation." Zambrano, meanwhile, had to travel abroad and left another member of the Coordinadora Democrática, Jesús Torrealba, in charge of continuing the exercise. When Diez met with Torrealba and presented the vice president's proposal of using the expression "a process of assisted agreements" instead of "a process of assisted negotiation," Torrealba found it suitable and thus the text was completed.[36]

Diez agreed with the opposition that the government should make a public statement expressing its decision to sign the declaration, something which Vice President Rangel did on October 11, 2003, and that the Coordinadora Democrática would sign it first, on the left side of the ensuing page, and that the government would then sign the right side.[37] In the end, to the government's and the Carter Center's surprise, the opposition gave more than thirty signatures and attached a one-page "addendum" to the declaration full of criticism toward the government. The tripartite

---

a personal interest in nor commitment to that initiative or option. This way, the parties will have full responsibility for the decision and, if they go ahead, the commitment will then be reinforced.

34. At the request of the government, the mission of the Tripartite Working Group had scheduled a meeting with the Círculos Bolivarianos for September, which was later called off after the opposition learned about it. The opposition was of the belief that the Círculos Bolivarianos were violent groups (almost paramilitary) and that they should not be internationally legitimized.

35. The meeting was relevant for the government, which knew that the opposition leaders had asked the OAS and the Carter Center not to meet officially with the Círculos Bolivarianos because they said it would "legitimate" these groups. The news did not bring any major consequences and was not commented on by the opposition.

36. The declaration is reproduced in Carter Center, *The Carter Center and the Peacebuilding Process in Venezuela: 2002–2005* (Atlanta, GA: The Carter Center, February 2005), http://cartercenter.org/documents/2138.pdf.

37. The book with the text of the declaration that had been agreed upon was ready some minutes after Gaviria left for the airport. The Carter Center realized his signature was missing, so his press chief rode a Caracas police motorcycle after the retinue to the very runway to get his signature in the only original copy of the agreed-upon text that the Carter Center had. When his press chief came back with the signature on the book, he told us, "I hope the effort was worthwhile and this paper shall go down in history!"

group thus made an allowance for the government to do the same in a separate copy of the book—that is, to add its own "addendum" in which it could criticize the opposition.[38] The "incident" never became public, and the media talked about the declaration as a text that had been agreed upon without problem.

The entire exercise took over a month of hard efforts, including a visit by OAS secretary general Gaviria and an explicit request by him that the two sides accept the document. The chaotic development of this exercise clearly showed that both sides were not completely willing to start a negotiation in good faith, and that their main incentive to work with the international actors was to gain allies in order to ensure victory over their opponent.[39]

A New Escalation of the Conflict

In October 2002, the government took a series of defensive decisions. It tried to ensure control of security forces and disarticulate any chance of a new armed coup. The government made changes in the top ranks of the armed forces and issued a decree to ban helicopters belonging to the metropolitan police (under the control of an opposition mayor) from flying over Caracas without the consent of the air force. It also decided to ban, on national security grounds, opposition marches in some city areas.

The Coordinadora Democrática, for its part, organized several street marches in protest against the government, incorporating more followers each time, with nearly one million people marching in the October 10 protest. Emboldened by this mobilization capacity, it called a general strike for October 21. The climate of confrontation was becoming tenser each day. All the international community became alarmed, and the European Union, the United Nations, and the United States, among others, made statements in favor of the need for dialogue and moderation.

The one-day opposition strike was carried out without major problems, but the following day, a group of fifteen dissident military officers made a proclamation against the government and a call to "occupy" Plaza Altamira, in eastern Caracas.[40] That same day Gaviria issued a statement condemning

---

38. Raúl Alconada Sempé of the UNDP had the idea of photocopying the text signed by Gaviria, duplicating the book, and thus solving the situation.

39. This illustrates the principle described by Fisher in which the conflicting parties always look for an ally, not for a neutral third party. See Fisher, "Methods of Third-Party Interventions."

40. Altamira is the main square of a "zone" of the city, which forms part of the Chacao municipality, and is controlled by an opposition mayor. As the heart of anti-Chavismo, the challenge was not too threatening in the eyes of the government.

the military "sit-in," and Diez, for the Carter Center, started to prepare for what it believed would be a repressive answer from the government.

To Diez's surprise, the president decided to ignore the event. The dissident military officers—together with hundreds of supporters—set up camp in the plaza, which became the center for around-the-clock private television newscasts. As days went by, more rebellious military officers joined the protest in the plaza and were filmed by the television cameras.

In order to understand the position of the government in the face of these events, Diez contacted the president of the Defense Committee of the National Assembly, a former military man very close to Chávez. After spending several hours of conversation, he told Diez in a confidential tone that the Plaza Altamira rebellion was the best thing that could happen to the government. As soon as active officers joined the "rebels" (as he called them), they were discharged, automatically losing their military rank. Thus, the opposition was offering the government the chance to "purge" the National Armed Forces and deactivate the danger posed by opponents who had military rank and fire power. Even so, rebel military officers maintained the "sit-in" in the plaza, thus further escalating the conflict dynamic.

Terms of Reference for the Dialogue Table

By the end of October, Gaviria returned to Venezuela with representatives from the Carter Center and started negotiations with opposition leaders and the government on the conditions that would enable a facilitated process to generate agreements. He focused only on negotiating the structure of such a process, adopting for the agenda of the negotiations the three main subjects for which the international community offered technical assistance—that is, the electoral process, citizen disarmament, and the establishment of a truth commission.[41] He proposed to create a dialogue table with representatives from both sides, with himself as facilitator, that would focus exclusively on a procedural strategy.[42]

As it had done with the declaration of principles, the Tripartite Working Group elaborated a draft of the terms of reference (*sintesis operativo*) for the

---

41. For a discussion of the negotiation process structure, see Jacob J. Bercovitch, Theodore Agnoson, and Donnette L. Willie, "Some Contextual Issues and Empirical Trends in the Study of Successful Mediation in International Relations," *Journal of Peace Research* 28, no. 1 (1991): 7–17.

42. Although the tripartite group had planned to find an independent facilitator to represent all three organizations, Gaviria decided at the last moment, without consulting the Carter Center, UNDP, or the government, to propose himself, in part to gain the acquiescence of recalcitrant opposition members.

dialogue procedures and submitted it to representatives from both parties, in a new "go-between" exercise with the same main representatives from both sides—Zambrano and Rangel—and with César Gaviria as facilitator. More than three "rounds" of text modification were needed to get agreement on each of the document's paragraphs, though not on the title of the exercise. As with the Declaration of Principles, the opposition insisted on referring to a "negotiation table," while the government would only accept the name "dialogue table."[43] The facilitators proposed the name "table for construction of agreements" as a viable option. Gaviria argued to Zambrano that it was impossible to reach agreements without negotiating and this proposed name would imply negotiations; in turn, the opposition stated that it would accept the name "table of negotiation and agreements" but that it would not participate otherwise.

At that point, Gaviria decided to leave the problem in the hands of the government and wait. Two days later, he announced to the parties that he would leave the country.[44] Finally, the day Gaviria was leaving Caracas, the vice president announced that the government would accept the contents of the terms of reference, including the title "table of negotiation and agreements," and that they would appoint a representative to the table.[45]

The Introduction of the "Third-Side" Idea

A fundamental aspect of the Carter Center's initial appraisal was that the country was experiencing divisions of differing nature growing out of a variety of origins and that all of them were concentrated on the chasm opened by Chávez. The dynamics of political polarization were beginning to take root in each of the social spaces, deepening divisions and dragging everyone toward one side or another of the confrontation. Given this situation, the Carter Center decided to request the help of William Ury, a conflict resolution expert at Harvard University and creator of the "third-side" concept, which is conceived of as a social space from which a community can work actively for peaceful coexistence, with no need to renounce its beliefs, pref-

43. Timoteo Zambrano, among others, was again representing the opposition; this time he made the word "negotiation" a condition that could not be waived.

44. It was a very clever and well-aimed move on the part of Gaviria as a facilitator, because it was not a threat but just the recognition that he would not personally make any additional effort. The opposition knew that the highest cost of not "setting up" a dialogue table facilitated by the OAS secretary general would at that moment be borne by the government, and the opposition enthusiastically celebrated that the title had been accepted "at the very last minute." Gaviria was thus able to have the two parties at the dialogue table.

45. See the text of the terms of reference agreed to on November 7, 2002, in The Carter Center, *The Carter Center and the Peacebuilding Process in Venezuela*, 12.

erences, and sympathies.[46] With the sponsorship of the UNDP, the Center organized a "closed" seminar to be held in late October.

It was necessary to generate a balanced and safe space from which to call on participants sympathetic to both the government and the opposition, so that they might work together, at least for a day. The Carter Center decided to present this as an academic event and set up a high-level panel to include two important university presidents (close to the opposition) and two distinguished government representatives, all of whom would be asked to comment on Ury's presentation.[47] The panelists were asked to provide their own list of participants to be invited by the Center, for the event would be closed to the press and attended only by those that the panelists themselves saw fit to invite. The Center recruited the first set of volunteers who helped as facilitators from among the least-polarized human rights organizations, for the purpose of generating working groups after listening to Ury's presentation and the comments from the panelists.

Almost two hundred special guests were in attendance, and for the first time, in the same setting, Chavistas and anti-Chavistas formed ten mixed groups by sector of activity, each with a facilitator, for the purpose of making a list of activities to make concrete the peacebuilding concepts being explored. Ury captivated the audience and many participants were enthusiastic about having the opportunity to talk with people "from the other side" and working together to imagine coexistence.

An important outcome of the activity was to create, through a number of persons and organizations, a symbolic opening of a new and different space, an alternative to the Chavismo–anti-Chavismo polarization. But the most significant achievement for the mediation effort was the set of relations the Carter Center established with mid-level social and academic actors as a result of this initiative.

International Context

Throughout this process, the OAS Permanent Council and the United States government played important roles. The OAS General Assembly declaration of June 4, 2002, encouraging international assistance to Venezuelan national reconciliation, reflected both the international community's concern about

---

46. William L. Ury, *Getting to Peace: Transforming Conflict: At Home, at Work, and in the World* (Boston: Viking Press, 1999).

47. On the opposition side were the presidents of the Venezuela Central University and the Catholic University, and on the government side were the president of the National Assembly and the minister of higher education.

the ongoing conflict and Venezuela's success in defeating a direct invocation of the Inter-American Democratic Charter. The August 14, 2002, OAS resolution made explicit the international support to the Tripartite Working Group but also gave greater standing to the Coordinadora Democrática by referring to it as the body "representing" the opponents to Chávez. The Coordinadora Democrática's desire for such standing reflected its view that, rather than representing a mere political opposition to the government, it represented a civil resistance (similar to a belligerent in a civil war) to the government and should thus have equal status to the government.[48]

Tensions between the U.S. and Venezuelan governments resurfaced as the United States precipitously opened an Office of Transition Initiatives in July. This was an office of the U.S. Agency for International Development (USAID) that could provide rapid deployment of funds, particularly in a country with no USAID mission, but that was typically opened in countries truly in political transition from an authoritarian government, such as Serbia after Slobodan Milosevic or Peru after Alberto Fujimori. The Venezuelan government, which was not consulted ahead of time, took this as an affront and an implication that Venezuela should be in a regime transition. The U.S. ambassador to Venezuela had recommended that USAID not use such a provocative name for the office in Venezuela and was blindsided by an interview with the director of the Office of Transition Initiatives that appeared in a Venezuelan newspaper before the foreign minister had been briefed about the office.[49]

The economic conditions in the country also worried international observers in August and September 2002. With predictions of a fiscal deficit of 5–8 percent, inflation at least 40 percent, and GDP growth at negative 4–5 percent for the year, the Carter Center was worried that tensions would escalate when the Venezuelan school year started on September 15 over expected teacher-contract disputes. Further, domestic debt payments were due in November and December, and the country's oil surplus fund risked being exhausted by December.

Analysis and Lessons

Through this early period of the preparations for international intervention, several procedural lessons for international facilitation in political conflicts became clear.

---

48. The Coordinadora Democrática's periodic attempts to include labor and business in addition to political parties and NGOs also confused the role of the opposition. The Carter Center recognized the dilemma of incorporating nonpolitical actors—church, media, labor, business, NGOs—into political negotiations because, while they certainly held political power, in the long run they could weaken further the political parties if they assumed a recognized political role.

49. U.S. ambassador to Venezuela Charles Shapiro, in conversation with the authors, March 2003.

The first lesson involves the need to sequence process first and substance second. A prenegotiation period in which the sides could agree to what the negotiation would be like—that is, to determine the participants, the location, the rules, the conditions, and the agenda—was imperative in this context. With such high levels of distrust and ambivalence over the merits of negotiating at all, the international facilitators needed to first negotiate an agreement on the mechanisms of consensus building before entering into the substance itself. As Harold Saunders relates, the parties must be able to start generating commitments using a kind of process that provides them with a safe common space and show that they are able to assume and fulfill some procedural commitments, which usually have low cost but are still very significant.[50] This prenegotiation stage includes defining the role third parties will play and usually also the purpose of the negotiation. Such a strategy of "setting" the table first not only postpones the arguments about the contentious issues but also offers an opportunity for the parties to signal or take some confidence-building steps. Without a growing confidence-building process, the possibilities of reaching a sustainable agreement are always more reduced.

Working with the same actors and with only a few months' difference in time, Carter and Gaviria faced very similar objective circumstances. The level of "hurting stalemate" between both sides was the same, the costs and fears were essentially the same, and the external conditions of the conflict did not seem to present extraordinary opportunities. Why was Carter's offer of facilitation not accepted and Gaviria's was? The difference has to do with two aspects related to the same facilitation. The first is that the Tripartite Working Group did detailed and precise preparation work and focused on the prenegotiation, which was not possible to do in Carter's case. The second is the perception of the decision makers from both sides. For the opposition to have the OAS secretary general as facilitator was especially meaningful, both because the government had been reluctant to accept him (what is bad for my opponent must be good for me, and vice versa) and because the opposition attributed to him supranational authority and ability to exert pressure. The government, on the other hand, attributed a different meaning to the same thing (as usually happens in all conflicts): it viewed the OAS secretary general's involvement as a guarantee that the "coupmonger" sectors of the opposition (especially the military sectors condemned by Gaviria) would be controlled, and a reassurance of the government's international legitimacy.

---

50. Harold Saunders, "We Need a Larger Theory of Negotiation: The Importance of Pre-Negotiation Phases," in *Negotiation Theory and Practice,* ed. William Breslin and Jeffery Z. Rubin, 57–70. Cambridge, MA: Program on Negotiation at Harvard Law School, 1991).

The second lesson is the urgent need for a communication strategy of the third-party facilitators. Without such a strategy, misinformation easily turns into misunderstandings that engender distrust. In the case of the Carter Center, the opposition mistakenly believed that the Carter Center had accepted the 2000 election results carte blanche and ignored its complaints about potential fraud and irregularities at the legislative and local levels. In reality, the Carter Center report on its observation of the 2000 Venezuelan elections characterized that election process as flawed and explicitly noted that the results of some of the legislative races could not be known with certainty due to extensive irregularities and politicization of the process. However, the Center had not sufficiently publicized the report in Venezuela.

Likewise, the opposition's lack of information about Carter's trip to Cuba in May 2002 fueled its suspicions that he was too close to Chávez, as it failed to realize (or ignored) Carter's open call for human rights and democracy in Cuba, which was heartily endorsed by the conservative Cuban-American National Foundation in Miami. Finally, in its state of extreme distrust (on the verge of paranoia), the opposition assumed that Carter's trip shortly before its July 11 march was a stratagem of Chávez to undermine its show of strength. In reality, Chávez had not suggested any dates at all for Carter's trip and the dates were chosen because they were the only days that Carter had free the entire summer.

The Tripartite Working Group also learned the communication lesson the hard way when, during the first post-invitation mission in September, it realized it had raised expectations too high, as press reports referred to the formal beginning of the dialogue process, even though it had just begun to explore mechanisms. Consequently, press comments at the end of the trip expressed disappointment that the mission had failed to make progress on reaching substantive agreements.

The inability of third parties to control the information flow also became shockingly clear to the Carter Center as it proved unable to squelch a rumor that it had received up to $2 million in payments from the government.[51] Even though President Carter wrote a personal open letter to the Venezuelan people denying the rumor, the media declined to print the letter.

The third lesson during this period involves the clear need to seek ways to nourish the "third sector"—those groups and individuals who, regardless of their political positions, are willing to work toward a peaceful resolution of

---

51. The rumor started with $150,000 in July and escalated to $3 million by September. As the Carter Center denied that it had received any funds from the government, the rumor then shifted to assert that the funds had gone through a "third party"—namely Citgo.

the conflict and to help open political space and lengthen the time horizon. In the case of Venezuela, such nourishment would allow for a new approach to solving the country's urgent problems.

After the Ury seminar, it was clear these intermediate level social groups, adherents of Chavismo and anti-Chavismo, really wanted to look for ways to try to coexist or at least diminish the cost of the political conflict in their daily lives. As a result, the Carter Center saw the opportunity both to engage itself in a track 1½ peacebuilding initiative and to build a parallel working line that would complement and reinforce its work with the OAS at the negotiation and agreements table.[52] Indeed, as will be shown, the Carter Center began to act on this lesson in the following months.

---

52. For a full explanation of the track 1½ approach, see chapter 10.

4

From the Negotiating Table to the Oil Strike, November 2002–March 2003

The period from November 2002 to March 2003 was perhaps the most intense period of the conflict, with the risk of an open and violent confrontation ever present and the parties competing for control of weapons and money. This power struggle had moments of maximum tension and took place in several arenas—the barracks, the PDVSA state-owned oil company, the international stage, and, needless to say, the rallies and protest marches in the streets.

As a result, the initiatives undertaken by the third parties also increased. The Carter Center continued to accompany the OAS at the negotiation and agreements table, including through active participation by Jimmy Carter. In addition, the Carter Center generated two additional spaces, one for peace-building with social sectors, networks, and intermediate groups, and another for negotiation with mass media owners. It was also during this period that the Group of Friends of the Secretary General of the OAS was created. These initiatives were brought together as a combination of efforts to help contain the escalation of violence and channel the conflict.

The Negotiation and Agreements Table

Throughout this period the negotiation and agreements table functioned as an escape valve that allowed the process to remain relatively contained through the formal parameters of the table and a tepid respect by the parties for peace and democracy, the two main pillars on which the OAS and Carter Center's role as mediators rested.

With the government's approval of the terms of reference text and acceptance of the table's title, the prenegotiation phase drew to a close.[1] A negotiation and agreements table would be installed, with six representatives and one adviser on each side. Nothing had been said regarding the mechanism for choosing these representatives, and given the level of confrontation, the Carter Center and the OAS were concerned that one of the delegations might prove unacceptable to its adversaries, or might not be sufficiently representative, but that did not turn out to be the case.[2]

The Delegations

The government was the first to designate its representatives. It chose a very high-level group, composed of Vice President José Vicente Rangel, Minister of Foreign Affairs Roy Chaderton, Minister of Education Aristóbulo Isturiz, Minister of Labor María Cristina Iglesias, National Assembly deputy Nicolás Maduro, and the governor of the state of Táchira, Ronald Blanco La Cruz. The group's adviser was Venezuela's ambassador to the OAS, Jorge Valero, a man known to enjoy fluid relations with Gaviria and his team.[3]

On the opposition side, things were somewhat more complicated, as the Coordinadora Democrática represented a very wide spectrum of political and social forces, sectors, and interest groups. Ultimately, the opposition chose as its representatives a deputy to the Latin American Parliament, Timoteo Zambrano; National Assembly deputy Alejandro Armas (a former Chávez ally); the governor of the state of Yaracuy, Eduardo Lapi; a representative of Fedecámaras, Rafael Alfonzo; and the undersecretary general of the CTV, Manual Cova. After a very vigorous internal discussion, the NGOs working with the opposition alliance chose the experienced left-wing politician Américo Martín to represent them. The group's adviser was a constitutional expert, lawyer Juan Manuel Raffalli, from the Primero Justicia Party. This delegation encompassed all sectors with representation at the highest level possible without affecting the delegation's coexistence. This meant that none of the "political chiefs" of the Coordinadora Democrática was on the delega-

---

1.   In practice, the government almost never publicly used the agreed-upon title and always referred to the "dialogue table" when dealing with the press. This was done quite deliberately to create confusion about the proper title and to provoke the opposition.

2.   At the time, the Carter Center explored the issue with the vice president and proposed to work on how the two delegations could be made up in such a way as to be mutually acceptable. The vice president cut the initiative short by replying: "No way! Let each side designate its own representatives as it sees fit! It's unthinkable that we would allow them an opinion as to who should represent the government! That is something each group must decide for itself."

3.   Ambassador Valero was later replaced by National Assembly deputy Omar Mezza Ramírez.

tion. At the time, these chiefs included union leader Carlos Ortega, business-man Carlos Fernández, and party politicians such as Eduardo Fernández of Copei, Rafael Marín of AD, Enrique Salas Römer of Proyecto Venezuela, Julio Borges of Primero Justicia, and the governor of the state of Miranda, Enrique Mendoza.

International Facilitation

The terms of reference indicated that the facilitator would be OAS secretary general César Gaviria,[4] and that the Carter Center representative in Caracas, Francisco Diez, would provide technical support. Gaviria could count on the permanent presence of his chief of staff, Fernando Jaramillo, who had been his representative at the inauguration of the Tripartite Working Group. The UNDP, for its part, chose to remain behind the scenes and not join the table. However, the UNDP did not formally pull out from the initiative, and the Carter Center was charged with keeping it informed with whatever was tak-ing place. Regardless, the limelight was always on Gaviria, whose presence lent the facilitation process a very high degree of political visibility.

Meanwhile, the political climate was rapidly heating up as the main leaders of both sides, Chávez for the government and the Ortega-Fernández duo for the opposition, harangued each other in ever-more incendiary speeches. There were already explicit threats of a general strike, and the opposition declared that the table would be allowed one month to reach an agreement, and no more.

The First Meeting of the Table

The OAS and Carter Center had asked the Church to provide a neutral venue, and it was decided that the meetings would be at a seminary in the suburbs of Caracas.[5] On Friday, November 8, 2002, at four o'clock in the afternoon, the table held its first meeting, with the members of both delegations present. The place was packed to overflowing. The national

---

4. At a meeting in Washington, DC, in August 2002, the Tripartite Working Group had agreed to designate an external facilitator to represent the three institutions. However, having conducted negotiations on the terms of reference, Gaviria nominated himself as lead facilitator, with no explicit conversation on the issue with either the UNDP or the Carter Center. The Carter Center later learned that two reasons justified his decision: first, the opposition had told Gaviria that it would not accept a facilitator other than himself (according to what one of its members later told McCoy); and second, the opposition had announced that the table could only last for a month, which made it more feasible for Gaviria to devote his personal time to the effort.

5. This first meeting shall be described in detail to highlight the importance for a negotiation process to establish minimum conditions for its functioning, including those small preparatory and procedural details that often make the difference between an ambience that creates an attitude of collaboration among the parties and one that leads to a pattern of confrontation.

press had practically taken over the seminary with cables, cameras, trucks, and literally hundreds of reporters, photographers, and journalists, while security agents assigned to government officials and Secretary General Gaviria swarmed about. A press room had been set up, but it was too close to where the meetings were to be held, so no journalists could remain there because they would hear everything. The priests that ran the seminary were utterly overwhelmed. There was no space in which the members of the delegations who had arrived early could await the arrival of their colleagues. Taken together, the situation gave the impression of chaos barely contained, and the air was thick with tension.

Upon entering the meeting room, the delegations barely looked at each other. One of Gaviria's assistants, who had vast experience as a mediator in political conflicts, had prepared a set of draft procedural suggestions as the first point to be addressed.[6] Gaviria began to speak about the essence of his colleague's draft, but as there were not enough copies for everyone present, only the heads of delegation and Gaviria himself had been given one.[7] The tension mounted as Gaviria began to make references to what "the paper" he had in his hand said, and confusion increased further because everyone thought he was referring to the terms of reference.[8] Finally, Gaviria decided to ignore the draft paper about questions of procedure and established the rule that only one person would speak at a time and that only he could give someone the floor. Thereafter, the members of the two delegations proceeded to give a round of speeches, and a semblance of order was achieved. But still, no one knew how to proceed.

At one point, when one of the opposition members had the floor, the minister of education began to interrupt him in order to refute what he was saying. Gaviria twice asked the minister not to interrupt the speaker. The first request was pronounced softly, and the second a little more strongly. Finally, Gaviria took the microphone and vehemently insisted on the need for an organized dialogue, saying that he would not allow such interruptions,

---

6. The terms of reference for the table indicated that the procedures were to be agreed upon at the table's first meeting.

7. These were Vice President Rangel, on the government's side, who completely ignored the text, and Timoteo Zambrano, on the opposition side, who read it carefully but failed to share it with any members of his delegation.

8. Gaviria read a point that stated that in addition to the main facilitator there would be secondary facilitators who were to be in charge of the complementary tables foreseen in the terms of reference. The vice president, however, interrupted him forcefully, declaring, "We won't accept any facilitator other than yourself." While Zambrano tried to explain to Rangel that a different text was being discussed, Rangel observed him with extreme mistrust, paying no heed. Other members of both delegations finally asked about or gave their own interpretations of what was happening, only increasing the tension.

nor stand for any lack of mutual respect. By using his authority, Gaviria was able to impose order.

A little later in the proceedings, someone asked who was taking notes of what was being said and what type of minutes would emerge from the meeting. Someone proposed that the television cameras be let in so that the entire meeting could be broadcast live; others suggested that the OAS bring in stenographers. It was finally agreed that the sessions would be recorded.

In mid-afternoon, Gaviria called for a fifteen-minute break, and all participants proceeded to the room next door, where the nuns served tea and pastries. Several members of the delegations sat down together and even had brief informal chats, with far less tension than in the meeting room. Once the meeting resumed, however, the speech making resumed.

When the meeting drew to a close, someone asked how the press should be dealt with. No one dared propose a strategy, and so it was understood that each side could say to the media what it saw fit. That night, Venezuelans saw on their televisions representatives of both delegations giving long speeches in which they railed against their adversaries.

Gaviria had proposed that the table meet each workday at 3 p.m., so the next meeting occurred on Monday, November 11, at the same venue. The second meeting of the table was virtually identical to the first, except that this time the speeches were recorded. This made them less spontaneous. At the end of the session, Gaviria announced his decision to change the meeting venue to the Hotel Meliá in the geographic center of Caracas, where the OAS and Carter Center delegations were staying. Everyone agreed to this change.

The Table's First Steps

Once installed at the Hotel Meliá, the process slowly began to change. The table's plenary meeting took place in a large meeting hall, and two additional rooms were used by each of the delegations. The press was kept in an area sufficiently distant from the meeting rooms, and a comfortable press room was set up for public declarations by participants.

The only regular intervention by Gaviria continued to be alternately giving the floor to members of the two groups. Unlike in the first two meetings, he began to use the breaks as a tool for relationship building. Whenever there appeared to be an opening, however narrow, in the speeches of the participants, Gaviria would call a recess and the parties would leave their seats for the coffee and cookies table, where, cups in hand, informal contacts got under way. Little by little, there was a thawing in the personal relations between the members of each delegation.

During the second week of meetings, Gaviria proposed to cease the recordings, so that the delegations could talk calmly and less self-consciously. This was accepted. Although the delegates stopped talking for the benefit of the tape recorder, they continued to speak past each other. As each side was eager to go before the television cameras after the meeting and report what had happened at the table, when given the floor, delegates generally spoke to gain tacit authorization by their own colleagues and to repeat outside what they had said at the table rather than to communicate with their political adversaries. Although both sides kept to the agreement to take turns in reporting on events at the table, so that whoever reported first one day reported second the next, the reports continued to highlight only the confrontational aspects of the table.[9] As a result, Gaviria appealed to the only common interest the two sides shared—the table's public image. He told them that the public statements made at the end of each session were beginning to undermine the image of the table.[10] The delegations agreed that from then on, only Gaviria would report on the progress achieved at the end of each day's session. At about the same time, Gaviria undertook another procedural innovation: he began to occasionally hold private meetings with each side during breaks.

The positive effect of these moves on the quality of the process was immediate. Finally, two weeks after getting under way, the table began to discuss new and substantive issues, including important "sideline" issues.[11] For example, a true political negotiation took place between the parties regarding the conflict with the metropolitan police. Meetings were held between the main protagonists in this conflict, including mayors and the minister of interior, with members of the government and opposition delegations

---

9. Delegation members seemed to think that whoever made the first declaration would have a stronger impact upon the audience, even though whoever spoke second had the opportunity to defend his or her case and to discredit the opponent's earlier statement. Both delegations were of the opinion that politically the most important session of the day took place not at the table but in front of the cameras.

10. The negotiation table had already begun to appear in polls as a political space that created expectations and, of course, allowed its members an unusual political projection. The very fact that the meetings took place on a daily basis, and that the entire country was anxious to hear results, led to the emergence, once verbalized by Gaviria, of a lukewarm common interest to preserve the space.

11. With this move, Gaviria affirmed himself in his role. Both delegations found themselves in a situation in which they had either to agree on what type of "product" the table was to present to the country each night by means of Gaviria's words, or to depend entirely upon how he chose to describe the day's proceedings. This created a different dynamic and got everyone on the same track. Conversations during recesses became more frequent, and from these informal talks, reinforced at private meetings, proposals for action began to emerge for the table on new and substantive issues, thus strengthening a spirit of collaboration.

serving as facilitators and promoters of dialogue. Indeed, a number of solutions and formulas for conciliation were proposed at the table. Although it proved impossible to reach an agreement on this issue, the table took on an unquestionable political existence, and its members strengthened their commitment to the space for dialogue that had been created. In this context, another issue was raised—the need to resolve the situation of paralysis at the National Electoral Council (CNE). Some exploratory negotiations got under way in an effort to appoint a new board that might enjoy the trust of both sides, but these talks also failed.[12]

With the collapse of these "sideline" efforts, the discussion at the table returned to the core of the political conflict. In essence, the talks boiled down to the single-minded demand by the opposition that the president tender his "immediate resignation," to which government representatives unrelentingly replied that the opposition should stick to the constitution and try to rally enough support to force a recall referendum on Chávez's mandate. Meanwhile, as the month of November came to a close, the government secured its control of all of the country's firepower and rumors were rife that the opposition was preparing to call a general strike.

The Control over Weapons

As described in chapter 3, the "sit-in" by dissident military officers in Plaza Altamira, which began in October, was initially received with enthusiasm by the opposition,[13] but ultimately the "sit-in" only served the government's purpose of "purging" the armed forces. The authorities discharged dozens of officers and staff in the hierarchy and reorganized the command posts, placing them under the orders of Chávez's "centaurs."[14] As a result of the uprising, the government ensured its control over the entire structure of the National Armed Forces.

---

12. At this point in time, the "provisional" CNE was made up of four magistrates who favored the opposition and one who was close to the government. The government was proposing to replace all the provisional magistrates with a permanent body to emerge from an agreement, while the opposition ignored the notion. The "provisional" CNE had been taking decisions by a vote of four to one in favor of the opposition, until the Supreme Court of Justice ruled on an appeal presented to it and disqualified one of the opposition members. This reduced the opposition majority to three to one (four votes were required to take a decision) and left the council totally paralyzed. The entire story would have been different had an agreement been reached at the table to replace the CNE.

13. Private media owners and some of the social leaders were the most enthusiastic, while traditional politicians viewed the military rebels with mistrust.

14. The term "centaurs" was used by a high-level government official in an interview with the authors. He was himself a former Chávez student at the military academy and later the head of the Parliament.

Tanks in Caracas City.
Courtesy of SURpress.

Feeling more secure, the president decided in late November to issue a decree allowing the military to confiscate the assault weapons of the Caracas Metropolitan Police, which was under the authority of the opposition mayor of metropolitan Caracas and represented the fourth strongest armed force in the country in terms of firepower, and allowing him to declare certain areas of the city as "national security" zones in which street protests were not allowed.[15] The mayor's office organized protest rallies and appealed the measure to the Supreme Court of Justice. Shortly thereafter, tanks rolled into Caracas, and soldiers were everywhere to be seen, many performing joint patrols with the now disarmed municipal police force.

The opposition, which had celebrated the Altamira uprising and now kept itself "quartered" in the plaza, protested the move vociferously via television, and its street protests challenged the security zones, but the government did not back down. The Supreme Court of Justice accepted a legal appeal and ordered the immediate "return" of the command of the metropolitan police to the mayor and a demilitarization of the city. The government participated in the negotiations over the metropolitan police which was facilitated by

15. Among the areas declared "off-limits" were the presidential palace, which was completely isolated by barbed wire palisades, and the facilities of the state-owned oil company, PDVSA.

the table, assured everyone that in good time it would comply with the ruling issued by the court, and then continued the intervention beyond the legal deadlines. The military pulled back from the police stations in mid-December only after it had confiscated all of the weapons that it considered "dangerous" and Chávez felt that the force had been neutralized. The opposition and the metropolitan police claimed that it would be impossible to fight common crime without adequate weapons, but by then the government was not about to do an about-face. Eight months after the April military coup, Chávez was in control of all national institutions with firepower.

The Control over Oil and the National Strike

The opposition archipelago's strategy for confronting Chávez as expressed by the Coordinadora Democrática during these months was based on the premise that pressure needed to be exerted on the government from all possible sides. In turn, the table was meant to serve as a space in which to negotiate the terms of his "surrender"—specifically, to obtain Chávez's resignation or a constitutional amendment that would shorten his term in office. In the context of this logic, the daily statements made on television by the two main opposition leaders, Ortega and Fernández, were geared toward keeping up the opposition's fighting spirit and confrontational attitude. There were marches, demonstrations, and all sorts of street activities in the vicinity of the Meliá Hotel and several other emblematic points in town. Plans for a general strike gained momentum toward the end of November.

With a general strike imminent, Gaviria held marathon sessions at the table, proposing discussion of a formal declaration condemning violence and affirming the preeminence of the constitution (of interest to the government), while simultaneously proposing discussion of an "electoral solution" (of interest to the opposition), with the expectation that an agreement would prevent a strike. Although on a couple of occasions the meetings ran until five o'clock in the morning, it was not possible to make progress on a text, nor were efforts made to negotiate those issues that justified the launching of the strike. Gaviria did not introduce any issue for discussion unless the parties explicitly brought it up first, and he moved exclusively within the boundaries of the table. These sessions were characterized by conversations in which everyone knew there were issues that were not being mentioned and that until these issues were dealt with, there was no prospect for a solution to be found. Although never quite made explicit, the opposition demanded, among other things, the approval of the consultative referendum on the recall of the president, an end to the military's intervention with the metropolitan police, and the demilitarization of Caracas.

Finally, the opposition called a general strike for Monday, December 2, 2002. In principle, it was intended to last for a day or two. The union and business leaders said they would be assessing the situation on a day-to-day basis to decide how much longer the strike would go on. Almost immediately following these statements, the government announced it was leaving the negotiation table for the duration of the strike.

Under these circumstances, Gaviria exerted himself to the utmost. He spoke to both sides in private, went to the government's headquarters, called opposition leaders, and spoke to media owners. His goal was to get both the government back to the table and the opposition to negotiate an end to the strike.

On the first day of the strike few people ventured to work and almost no businesses were open. Encouraged, the opposition decided to continue with the measure, but on the second day the strike was not quite as effective. In the afternoon there were incidents in the "off-limits" zones, and the national guard repressed protesters, using tear gas and physical violence. Television stations never tired of repeating the "brutality" of the guardsmen. That night the street protests increased.

Gaviria was able to convene the opposition leadership in the Meliá Hotel and extract from them a commitment to call off the strike if the government announced that it would cease the intervention with the metropolitan police (which the government knew it would have to do sooner or later because it needed to comply with the Supreme Court ruling). The government representatives arrived at the hotel at about 8 p.m., complained of the disturbances, heard out the proposal, and went off to consult. At 10 p.m., Minister of Labor Cristina Iglesias called Gaviria to tell him that the government would only negotiate if the opposition immediately put a halt to the disturbances in the streets of Caracas. Gaviria replied that this was beyond the control of the opposition leaders, who were still at the hotel awaiting an answer. Annoyed, Gaviria added that when the government was ready to negotiate seriously, it could call him again.

At midnight, the opposition representatives, tired of waiting for a response from the government, left the premises. But at 2 a.m. a government delegation made its appearance, ready to accept the proposal. Calls went out to the opposition leaders, but none of them answered their phones. By morning the government was no longer willing to agree to anything, nor was the opposition.

Four days into the general strike, given that the strike was finding an echo only in the urban commercial areas "controlled" by the opposition and given Gaviria's insistence, the government agreed to return to the table. That same day, the full management of the state-owned petroleum company, PD-VSA, joined the strike, and the government denounced that the move was intended to sabotage the table. The decision that the PDVSA would participate in the strike was taken in a rather confused manner by the leaders of the organizations representing the company's top staff during an emotionally driven workers' assembly. Some leading opposition politicians were cautious about the move, but most enthusiastically applauded the decision.[16]

Faced with the oil strike, Chávez installed something akin to a general headquarters in his offices and personally led the operations to take control of the PDVSA, sparing no expenses and ignoring procedural niceties. He himself called officers to take charge of striking oil tankers, purchased gasoline abroad, activated neighborhood markets to ensure food supplies, mobilized the military on all fronts regarding issues of security and logistics, and contracted scores of oil technicians from Brazil, India, Pakistan, and other countries. He described the strike as a sabotage of the nation, requested solidarity from his followers, his grass roots, and other countries, and laid off all employees who had joined the strike, replacing them little by little.[17] By February 2003, after two months of a struggle with no quarters given, the government managed to normalize the company's vital operations, and Chávez had his own men at the helm. He had won the main battle. The strike lasted sixty-two days, cost the country billions in losses, and completely altered the political landscape for years to come. It could all have been avoided had the negotiations succeeded that night in the Melía Hotel.

When the PDVSA's management decided to participate in the strike, daily life in Venezuela's cities and towns underwent a transformation. Gasoline rationing and the disappearance of certain staple foods from the market dealt most everyone a serious blow. There were no movies, no soap operas, no Christmas preparations—only the political conflict in the streets and on the television screens. Many foreign diplomats left Caracas for security reasons. The government fought tooth and nail on all fronts. Every two or three days

16. Almost a year later, a top opposition leader told the authors in private that he had been against extending the strike to the PDVSA because he feared the situation could get out of hand. However, as the PDVSA management had held an assembly and decided on its own to join the Coordinadora Democrática's "quest," it could not then be abandoned to its fate. This meant that the Coordinadora Democrática now found itself obliged to include among its demands the reinstatement by the government of the PDVSA management and workers who were fired because of the strike.

17. According to information from opposition unions, approximately twenty thousand persons lost their jobs.

some member of the opposition assured the Carter Center that the strike would be over in another two days, while foreign oil experts told it over and over that the country would collapse in another forty-eight hours.[18]

The actors perceived completely orthogonal scenarios. One opposition member excitedly stated:

> With the strike we'll kill them! They never imagined we could take control of the spigot that lets the money flow into this country. There won't be a coup because not even the military at Altamira can do a thing without us. It is we who manage the oil business, and in this country whoever controls oil controls everything. They haven't got a clue how to run a monster like PDVSA. In their death throes, they'll come running to the table to negotiate!

On the other side, a member of the government delegation, equally as certain of triumph as his adversary, categorically stated:

> We are extremely pleased with this strike. Now we really have a revolution under way at last! So far everything was just chatter, but if we can control the PDVSA and place it at the service of the people—now, that's really revolutionary! And this has made people support us strongly again. We are driving some pickup trucks out to the neighborhoods with a video showing how the money made at PDVSA never reached the people, and how now this is going to change. This opposition doesn't understand a thing. The oil sabotage has aroused nationalist feelings among the military and in many other people who were a bit lukewarm toward us, and they are now coming over to our side!

The Table during the Strike

Meanwhile, the meetings at the table took place with ever-increasing intervals. Gaviria had drawn up a twenty-two-point proposal covering several pages and including a number of concepts derived from political theory on democracy, institutions, and the need to avoid violence. Points 21 and 22 of the document described the most explicit disagreements: one on guarantees for PDVSA workers and the other on reaching an agreed-upon electoral solution to the crisis. During the first weeks of the strike, the delegations worked on the proposal point by point, and general agreement was achieved on twenty of them.

At this moment in the sessions, the members at the table listened to each other and even enthusiastically discussed a number of issues, expressing their differences in a setting that included mutual acknowledgments. That said, all were operating on the understanding that the actual decision to move toward fundamental agreements could not be reached at the table and would have to be taken by the leaders on both sides.

---

18. The United States embassy organized a private luncheon with the OAS and the Carter Center, specifically so that two American technicians could provide this assessment of the situation.

The Carter Center attempted to convince Gaviria to adopt more proactive interventions in his role as facilitator. In a telephone conversation between Carter and Chávez on November 26, 2002, when the opposition was calling for the strike, Carter offered to host an intensive round of negotiations at the Carter Center or elsewhere outside Venezuela. Chávez replied that he would like Carter to join Gaviria as a facilitator, and that he would personally participate in an intensive round of negotiations hosted by Carter but that he preferred it be held somewhere in Venezuela. Carter had recently been named the recipient of the 2002 Nobel Peace Prize, and he told Chávez he was willing to travel to Caracas right after the December 10 awards ceremony in Norway, as long as there were some concrete proposals to negotiate.

Throughout December, however, Gaviria felt that the timing was not right, and the Carter Center decided to respect his position as the conductor of the process. Gaviria believed that the perceptions of the two sides were mismatched—the Coordinadora Democrática felt stronger with each passing day of the strike and with every massive opposition rally, while the government was slow to react to these changing dynamics and did not yet seem ready to negotiate.[19] By mid-December, the Carter Center's own reading was that time was running out, because it felt that the opposition's expectations and demands would continue to escalate from its original demand for a consultative referendum on Chávez's mandate to a demand for immediate resignation.[20]

In the Carter Center's judgment, Gaviria conceived of the table at that time as a space to which the parties would come to negotiate when their political confrontation in the other arenas led to a capitulation, and not as a place that might generate agreements that would convince their leaders to put an end to the conflict. This difference in approach between Carter and Gaviria was to define the spirit of the facilitation process and circumscribed what the table could be expected to produce.

Christmas came and went in a climate of growing confrontation,[21] and January 2003 found the delegations still reviewing Gaviria's twenty-two-point document and awaiting the outcome of the strike. The Carter Center felt it was time to come up with a proposal that would focus on the core aspects of the negotiation and that had thus far been so carefully avoided by the government delegation: an electoral way out of the crisis.

19. Matthew Hodes and Francisco Diez, internal Carter Center memo titled "Venezuela Summary Status Report," December 16, 2002.

20. Ibid.

21. The opposition decided to hold off on all celebrations "until the tyrant falls" as a result of the ongoing general strike and instead went into the streets and squares of eastern Caracas to protest against Chávez.

The Carter Proposal

In January 2003, Jimmy Carter wished to present the Venezuelans with an electoral exit strategy. He offered Gaviria the option of introducing the strategy as a joint proposal. Gaviria declined to do so jointly, saying he thought it would be a very good idea if President Carter put forth the proposal himself. By now the Carter Center had earned a good level of respect from the two delegations, but it was about to enter into a territory in which the parties, quite explicitly, had thus far chosen not to venture. However, it had good reasons to do so: (1) the table had stagnated and was not producing results, which meant it was losing credibility; (2) the opposition's street initiatives to force the government's hand seemed bound to fail; (3) Gaviria was sticking to his policy of not intervening on substantive matters and was waiting for something to happen in the streets that would bring the two sides to an agreement at the table, an approach the Carter Center disagreed with; and finally, (4) Carter had a previously planned fishing trip to Venezuela for January 2003!

One of the lessons of mediation that was vividly expressed during this experience is that the mediator must be flexible and adaptable at all times to take advantage of unexpected opportunities and pure luck, as well as of circumstances outside his or her control. In this case, Jimmy Carter had prior personal relationships with two of the conflict's main protagonists: President Hugo Chávez and business leader and media owner Gustavo Cisneros. The latter owned a multinational empire, was one of the wealthiest men in Venezuela, and lived most of the time in New York and the Dominican Republic. He had long-standing friendships with many world leaders, including not only Jimmy Carter but also former U.S. president George H. W. Bush, and occasionally invited them to his various properties for fishing vacations.

Knowing of Carter's passion for fly fishing, in early 2002, prior to Carter's involvement in the Venezuelan conflict, Cisneros had invited President Carter and four of his fishing buddies to plan their next annual fishing trip to his "jungle camp" in southern Venezuela, where there was excellent fishing. The date was set for January 2003, one year in advance, as is normal for Carter's busy travel schedule. When the authors realized in early January that this trip was on Carter's schedule—in the middle of a devastating national strike and while the Carter Center was supporting Gaviria's facilitation—their first reaction was, "This will be a disaster for Carter's image in the country." They asked him to cancel the trip, but he declined, saying this was a long-planned personal trip completely unrelated to the conflict. They then decided to try to turn this into an opportunity to try to break the logjam in the negotiations.

The authors advised Carter that he call Chávez to tell him about his planned visit and ask if they might meet. Chávez proposed meeting discreetly at the river camp, not knowing that Carter was being hosted by his principal enemy, Cisneros! They then suggested to Carter that he add a couple of days to his itinerary to visit Chávez in Caracas and present some proposals to the negotiating table. He agreed, and they went into overdrive to prepare the proposals.

In preparation for his visit, Carter showed UN secretary-general Kofi Annan and U.S. secretary of state Colin Powell the Carter Center's proposals for an electoral solution to the crisis. In addition, the Carter Center made some exploratory contacts with both the opposition camp and allies of the government and decided there might be some space in which to negotiate a constitutional amendment mechanism. However, the basic problem continued to be of opposing perceptions: the government felt that it was winning the oil strike, while the opposition believed that precisely because of the oil strike it had the government on the ropes and that this was the time for it to impose high demands.

The Carter Center generated two proposals for negotiation, one for a constitutional amendment to shorten the presidential term and call for new elections, and another to activate a recall referendum. Both proposals also highlighted the need to address the other points underlying the conflict, including those related to the separation of powers (checks and balances), the protection of human rights, the promotion of social justice, and international monitoring of the entire agreement. On Monday, January 20, 2003, Carter met Chávez, who told him that both mechanisms (constitutional amendment and recall referendum) were provided for by the constitution and that if one of them were activated he would abide by the decision.

Carter told Chávez that it was important to guarantee reinstatement to the thousands of petroleum workers on strike and not punish them. Although Chávez did not want to include this point in the proposals, he told Carter that the workers would not be punished (although later they were all fired without any recompense.) Carter then attended a meeting of the table and put forth the two proposals. The delegations expressed their approval of the initiative and promised to consider the proposals and reply in writing.

The move helped to untangle the conversations at the table, as well as to include the electoral issue as part of the formal discussions between the delegations, but it did not lead to an agreement, nor did it alter the dynamics of the meetings. It was agreed that there would be an exchange of documents from each side in response to Carter's proposals. On January 29,

Carter and the authors meeting Chávez on January 20, 2003.
Courtesy of the Carter Center archives.

Carter with opposition leaders, from left to right, Alberto Quirós Corradi, Timoteo
Zambrano, Juan Manuel Raffalli, Asdrúbal Aguiar, Felipe Mujica, and Julio Borges.
Courtesy of the Carter Center archives.

the opposition replied that the most suitable mechanism was the constitutional amendment, referencing an initiative already circulating among opposition deputies that it knew the government would never accept. On February 3, the government replied that the recall referendum was the appropriate constitutional mechanism by which to pursue the opposition's objective, but that this was a task entirely up to the opposition to carry through.

By deciding that Carter's proposals would be a "contribution" to the table facilitated by Gaviria, the initiative became part of the dynamics in that space and thus its potential as a trigger for negotiations that would lead to actual decisions was diluted. It was clear that the table was not the space for decision making and that the most it could do was formalize decisions coming from the outside. The Carter Center could not provide follow-up to the proposals outside the context of the table or set up parallel negotiations without affecting Gaviria's authority.

The End of the Strike

The opposition had for months been insisting on holding a consultative referendum that had been set for February 2, 2003, and that had then been blocked by a Supreme Court decision. This date was highly symbolic, and as the strike was losing strength, the opposition decided to convoke a massive "*firmazo*" (sign-up) day for Sunday, February 2, and simultaneously end the strike. The indefatigable NGO Súmate proposed to collect signatures for thirteen different initiatives, including a recall referendum on Chávez and a constitutional amendment to shorten the presidential mandate. The "*firmazo*" was the object of massive media coverage, gave back to the opposition some of its enthusiasm, and allowed the opposition in some measure to save face in view of the failure of the strike.

By mid-February, the country had not exploded—although it was not clear how well and efficiently Chávez would be able to manage PDVSA—and it was becoming evident that Chávez no longer needed the striking employees, as little by little the situation was returning to normal. Further, the table was losing its raison d'être and significance as a space for negotiation. Carter's proposals had been diluted by the many disagreements at the table, and the government was feeling stronger than ever. However, the Chavistas were concerned about the possibility of violence erupting, and, as usual, fearful that the opposition might once again find a way to orchestrate a coup. In this setting, the members of both delegations revived the idea of making a joint declaration against violence, and they resurrected the text that the

Carter Center had worked on in December. At that time, the opposition had been reluctant to sign it, but it was now eager to produce movement that might neutralize, even partially, its defeat regarding the strike. Indeed, in an unofficial demarche, it requested that the Group of Friends of the Secretary General of the OAS formally ask both sides to sign the agreement against violence, making it appear that the opposition was "agreeing" to a petition put forth by the international community.

On February 18, 2003, at a solemn ceremony, the "Declaration against Violence, for Peace and Democracy" became the first agreement signed at the table. All parties felt encouraged that it might be possible to come to an agreement on the issue of elections. However, only two days after the signing ceremony, Fedecámaras leader Carlos Fernández was arrested by judicial order, and an arrest warrant went out for CTV union leader Carlos Ortega. Both were accused of civil rebellion, treason, and conspiracy for having called the general strike. Ortega fled the country. The government averred that this did not mean that a witch hunt was under way or that it would embark upon a wave of repression, but that rather the measure was simply the outcome of a court case opened in November 2002. The truth is that the government thus consolidated its triumph over the strikers, and the opposition had to begin to forge a new leadership for the next cycle of confrontation that loomed ahead.

The International Context

Nearly concurrent with Carter's visit, another move on the international scene was under way that would exert influence upon Venezuela. Brazilian president Lula da Silva and Chávez had spoken, and the latter had asked the Brazilian president to use his good offices to help set up a group of countries that would be known as the Friends of Venezuela. Lula agreed. Gaviria immediately perceived the initiative as an effort to diminish his influence and moved rapidly and intelligently to counter it. He began to contact the governments of the region and eventually generated a climate of opinion favorable to the idea of establishing a "balanced" group that would include the United States and other countries that the Venezuelan government did not consider to be "allies." Chávez expected to form a group of countries whose leaders were friends of his, while the group that emerged was made up of friends of Gaviria, so much so that the official title became the aforementioned Group of Friends of the Secretary General of the OAS.

At a previously scheduled regional meeting in Ecuador in January 2003, it was decided that the group would be made up of Brazil, the United States,

Mexico, Chile, Spain, and Portugal. Lula was charged with calling Chávez and telling him of the decision. The final confirmation of the group was received with great excitement by the opposition, and from that moment onward the Coordinadora Democrática decided to incorporate an "international front" in its battle against the government. For his part, Chávez took the blow and became more aware of his limitations in the international arena. If his relationship with Gaviria had never been warm, this episode cooled it off once and for all.

The foreign ministers of the six countries in the group met for the first time on January 24, 2003, in Washington, DC, and elected Brazil as the group's coordinator. The group decided to focus its efforts on the nonviolence pact and urge the parties to the conflict to lower their rhetoric. Although Gaviria asked it to act as a mediator, and the United States was quite interested in this option, the group refrained and wanted only to serve as support to Gaviria and the table. The group also declined to endorse Carter's proposals, although the Brazilian foreign minister expressed support for them in a press conference held after the group's first meeting. Representatives were sent to Caracas the following week to meet with the parties and urge a peaceful resolution to the conflict, but clearly they were not prepared to take on a more active role. The main contribution of the group over the next months was the periodic press statements it released supporting the work of the table, and the sense it gave to all Venezuelans that the international community was closely following their internal conflict.

Individual governments also had particular interests in Venezuela that influenced their attitudes toward the strike. The United States, in particular, was planning to invade Iraq in March 2003 and very much wanted the Venezuela oil strike to end. The U.S. State Department pressured Gaviria to present substantive proposals, but he resisted. Brazil, meanwhile, had substantial commercial investments in Venezuela and supplied oil and food during the strike.

The "Third-Side" Redux

Throughout November and December 2002, the Carter Center had focused on events around the negotiation and agreements table, but in January 2003 it decided to continue with the "third-side" initiative it had started in October with UNDP. While the tensions caused by the strike and street confrontations dominated the public scene, the Carter Center planned William Ury's second visit to the country for February 2003 and, with support from

USAID, organized a small team that included some foreign colleagues in order to magnify the initiative's impact.[22]

The Carter Center designed workshops in which William Ury provided conflict management training to broadcast and print journalists and editors from both state-owned and "alternative" (Chavista) media and traditional private (anti-Chavista) media, allowing them to come together for the first time in a space of learning and reflection. It also worked with community networks and NGOs to find concrete examples of social spaces in which Chavistas and anti-Chavistas coexisted peacefully and constructively and began to establish connections between them, asking for their support in organizing Ury's public conference. At the Carter Center's invitation, Gaviria made the opening speech at that event. Four mid-level social leaders whom the Carter Center had identified as activists for peace and reconciliation between Chavistas and anti-Chavistas composed the panel. The working groups that met after hearing the presentations were given the goal of agreeing to some concrete, feasible activities that participants could undertake immediately, with a view toward building a "third side" in Venezuela.[23]

With the event having significant repercussions,[24] the Carter Center decided to hold a third conference with Ury in March to accelerate the process of building a space for the articulation of social and community groups willing to work in favor of a peaceful solution to the conflict. The third visit was cosponsored once again by the UNDP and also by the Center for Peace of the Universidad Central de Venezuela. This time the center invited two members of the negotiation and agreements table to serve as panelists: civil-society representative Américo Martín, for the opposition, and Minister of Education Aristóbulo Isturiz, for the government.

Starting with those initiatives, the Carter Center was able to establish a solid basis of support for the many Venezuelans who wished to become involved in the different peace-building processes, known as the Strengthening Peace in Venezuela Program (SPV). This Carter Center and UNDP initiative became a permanent parallel line in their work as mediators. From this platform, indispensable relationships and links were forged with many

---

22. Mediators Ana Cabria Mellace, Carmen McCormack, and Gachi Tapia traveled from Argentina to Caracas and took over the preparation and design task, including activities prior to William Ury's visit and his follow-up. The basic aim was to provide the "third-side" concept with a scale and footing and to start a process intended to create a "critical mass" of citizens willing to work for peace and reconciliation among Chavista and anti-Chavista forces.

23. The founding of the nongovernmental organization Constructores de Paz (Peacebuilders) was one outcome of these later meetings. As this book goes to press, it continues working on peace and reconciliation initiatives at the community level.

24. A video of this conference was made and is available at the Carter Center Americas Program.

mid-level social actors and a number of national organizations that began to connect with each other and join the peacemaking efforts. These relationships with civilians closer to either side of Venezuela's polarized society allowed the Carter Center to learn about the hopes of people who had felt ignored by the traditional leaders for decades and who had become loyal to Chávez, as well as the fears and resentment of many others who had been attacked and harassed by government supporters. The Carter Center heard hundreds of personal stories of fear and human suffering caused by the political conflict on both sides, gaining a broader perspective and a deeper understanding of the conflictive situation.

Negotiations between the Media and the Government

The confrontation between the private media—both print and television— and the government was always an issue to which the Carter Center paid full attention. Chávez identified the private media as his main internal enemies, accused them of being putschist, and exposed them to all sorts of attacks and insults with his own public comments, whether about individual owners or specific media outlets. For their part, the media exerted an enormous influence upon leaders of the social and political opposition, and habitually took the most radical positions against the government. All public communication that circulated through the mass media, whether owned privately or by the state, was based on this confrontation and fed into the polarization.[25]

Ury's visit to Venezuela in February of 2003 was not motivated solely by the need to hold events that would promote the "third-side" idea. During his first visit in October 2002, Ury had met with representatives of Chavismo and the opposition, and there had been a few interviews in the media. Now, in his second visit, Ury met with César Gaviria, U.S. ambassador Charles Shapiro, and President Chávez. The chemistry between Chávez and Ury was excellent.[26] The Carter Center therefore decided to organize a breakfast

---

25. The penetration of television in Venezuela is very important, as almost all homes have a television set. The largest share of the market belonged to channels 2 (RCTV) and 4 (Venevisión), both opposed to the government. The lone news-only channel, Globovisión, was also private and radically opposed to the government, while the other private channel, Televen, although in opposition to the government, was considered by the government to be the least radical. Chávez called the owners of these four private televison channels "the Four Horsemen of the Apocalypse" and attacked them constantly in his speeches and extensive national radio and television addresses, which all stations were obliged to broadcast. He also almost always took the offensive on his Sunday television program, *Aló Presidente*, broadcast live by state-owned channel 8 (VTV), which had a considerably smaller audience.

26. Chávez declared himself "the greatest promoter of the third side in Venezuela" and was delighted to hear of the personal relation between Ury and John Kenneth Galbraith, the Harvard economist who was critical of neoliberalism and much admired by the president. Ury was given an English-language book on

with the owners of the private media outlets and explore the possibility of opening channels for negotiation between them and the government (taking up again the initiative that had begun, and failed, during Carter's first visit in July 2002). The Carter Center and Ury were aware that a meeting with the entire group would be very difficult, but by the end of the breakfast, which lasted for almost three hours, the owners expressly stated their willingness to try to embark upon negotiations with the government and to accept the Carter Center's help.

The Carter Center team carefully prepared for the working breakfast with the media owners, for although some good individual meetings had been held with some of them, all group meetings had been very difficult and unproductive. Usually the most radical individuals took the initiative and established the "mood" for the meeting, effectively blocking the development of a real conversation. This had happened in the meetings with Carter, and no one wanted to repeat that experience. Diez and Ury therefore decided to put in practice all of the recommendations set forth in Ury's "third-side" framework.

First, the Carter Center team listened very patiently and carefully to all of the owners' complaints and demands, and demonstrated that it understood very well what was happening to the owners (thus giving their views legitimation). Once the owners had gotten everything off their chests and were ready to listen, Ury told them how important they were to the country, and how what might happen in Venezuela depended in great measure on them (thus giving them recognition). This recognition and affirmation of their public role was described both in laudatory terms and as an affirmation of their social responsibility. Finally, waiting for the appropriate moment, Ury described what he saw as the worst-case scenario in the absence of negotiations:

> As a foreigner, I can only tell you what I see. A year ago I was here in Caracas and at that point, March of 2002, the president was attempting to take control of PDVSA, but failed. One year later, due to the failure of the ongoing oil strike, in which the managers responded to the government's provocations in an irresponsible manner, the president is taking control of PDVSA. The same thing happened with the military who responded to his provocations by rebelling, also irresponsibly. Today they have been discharged for having gone to Plaza Altamira, and the president is in full control of the armed forces. I see that the same thing could happen to the television stations. If you respond irresponsibly to the provocations, you will provide reasons so that when I come back next time, they are under government control.

Bolívar titled *The Liberator* and, upon reading it, came to understand a good part of the "model" Chávez had devised and the way in which he understood his "mission" in Venezuela and Latin America.

At this point, there was a long silence, and one of them asked the magic question: "And what do you think we can do?" To this, Ury replied: "Not fall prey to provocations, and negotiate a reasonable coexistence."

With the objective of the meeting having been achieved, Ury expressed willingness to come back in March, while Diez was left in charge of preparing a methodological proposal that would allow for opening up the dialogue between the government and the owners of private mass media. Jimmy Carter proposed to Chávez that he open a line of communication with media owners to be facilitated by Ury. Chávez accepted the proposal.

The Carter Center team was well aware that Chávez would not participate personally and that a real negotiation between the two sectors required involving decision makers directly. The commitment of the minister of infrastructure, Diosdado Cabello, who was in charge of negotiations and the government's strongman, and the owners of the private television stations was needed.[27] Diez and Ury designed a methodological negotiation scheme based on a single text, using the go-between technique,[28] with a view toward identifying "baby steps" to build confidence between the media and the government. The objective of the exercise was that each side would identify "goodwill signals" that might unilaterally lead to measures not linked to a reciprocal act from the opponent and that might demonstrate each side's willingness to deescalate the confrontation. Diez checked the design with the media owners and sent it by fax to Cabello, but the minister did not reply to it or answer his repeated calls. It was necessary to wait until Ury came back in March and another meeting with Chávez was held before Cabello was explicitly authorized by the president to participate in the talks as government representative.[29]

With the idea of linking the exercise to the negotiation and agreements table, the Carter Center invited the OAS to participate in the talks. Gaviria declined the invitation and wished the team luck, saying that in his opinion such a negotiation was bound to fail. However, as the initiative gained steam, Gaviria, who had been kept well informed of the proceedings, agreed to create a media commission at the table. It was set up with Alejandro Ar-

27. Cabello was one of the few who could represent the president and speak for him. The Carter Center also needed someone whom the media owners would respect and perceive as a legitimate counterpart. Diez spoke to Cabello regarding the initiative, and he responded favorably.

28. The go-between technique implies that the two parties are in separate rooms, without direct contact between them. The facilitators move between rooms, helping the two sides to prepare a single text that reflects the remarks and contributions of both.

29. The authors ran into Cabello in the lobby of the presidential office and asked him why he had not returned their calls, to which he replied: "Well, now we'll see what the boss says." It was only when Chávez personally instructed his minister to intervene that Cabello became involved.

mas representing the opposition and José Vicente Rangel representing the government.[30]

The "Baby-Steps" Exercise

One of the most serious difficulties regarding relations between the television station owners and the government had been that whenever one of the two contenders—or both—had goodwill and wished to send positive "messages" to the other side, these messages were not being "read" correctly because they got lost in the "din" of the television screens, the unstoppable dynamic of confrontation and the constant appearance of "pundits" who furiously attacked the opposing side in order to call attention to themselves. With both sides primed to see and hear attacks, they were not prepared to recognize positive signals or gestures of goodwill. The Carter Center therefore decided to propose a negotiating exercise that Ury calls "baby steps."

At Ury's meeting with the president in March, Chávez stated that he was not willing to negotiate privileges that would exonerate the media from the enforcement of legal norms, but that he was open to taking a few steps and establishing some measures that might facilitate coexistence. The Carter Center team proposed to start these steps immediately, the very next day, and both sides agreed. Work was conducted at a small hotel east of the city that was not very well known and that had a large number of small, pleasant places in which to meet in a setting of trees, plants, and gardens. This allowed the team to have Cabello in one space and all the media leaders in another, without their meeting face to face. The team began by presenting the "methodological proposal" in writing, making clear that the exercise would take place based on what had been discussed earlier, thus providing the parties with the greatest level of security possible. This document was very important because it allowed everyone to relax and provided the team a "road map" to go by.

The advantage of the proposed exercise was that no one was risking anything by participating, but that both sides stood to win if they complied with the agreement. After three full days of work, the minister and the media owners agreed upon a very detailed text of unilateral actions for each side, with a timetable for carrying out the "baby steps" and a mechanism for weekly meetings between the minister and individual private media representatives.[31] The Carter Center team also included in the text a clause linking

---

30. The two had been close friends in the past, but now were bitter adversaries. In private talks with the authors before his death caused by cancer one year later, Alejandro Armas recognized the end of his long friendship with Rangel as one of the most hurtful consequences of the political conflict for him.

31. See a copy of the text in The Carter Center, *The Carter Center and the Peacebuilding Process in Venezuela*, 18.

the exercise to the table's media commission in order to affirm the deference due to Gaviria.

Both sides complied with the first steps of the agreement during the first week of implementation at the end of April, but none of the weekly meetings ever took place. The Carter Center team made the mistake of "linking" the small unilateral gestures established in the agreement to the scheduled weekly bilateral meetings, which never occurred because Cabello did not attend.[32] Because these meetings did not take place, both sides disavowed their commitments and went back to their earlier behavior, based on open confrontation. Although the agreement was not complied with, the exercise helped open the possibility of direct negotiations between the government and the media, which the Carter Center team ended up facilitating later down the road.

Analysis and Lessons

This period of international intervention was characterized by overpowering intensity. The levels of confrontation had risen to unforeseen heights, and the Carter Center as facilitator multiplied its interventions in an effort to keep pace.

The first lesson gleaned from this period is the need to carefully consider whether the facilitator should continue to perform its role in the way it was established at the beginning of a process no matter the circumstances or adapt to changing conflict dynamics by altering its role. In the Venezuelan case both sides wanted Gaviria to be the facilitator. Indeed, his standing as OAS secretary general was always seen by the parties to the conflict as reassurance that the international community was playing a role by witnessing and helping to contain the conflict. This objective was undoubtedly achieved. There were any number of occasions in which full-scale violence could have broken out, and this did not occur. Gaviria's presence in the country and his decisive interventions at unilateral meetings with both the government and the opposition "saved" the table on several occasions.

---

32. Failing to attend the first scheduled bilateral meeting with one of the television stations, Cabello excused himself due to the illness of his mother, who lived in the interior of the country, which the Carter Center later verified was true. But he did not attend the next two meetings either, giving neither notice nor explanation. Months later, Diez met with Cabello again and asked why he had never attended the planned meetings, nor returned the Carter Center's calls. His reply: "The truth is that for me personally the idea of having to sit down and talk to Marcel Granier was unbearable—I can't stand that man!" Cabello apologized, saying that he was aware of his commitment to the Carter Center, but that when he was on his way to the meeting, he had received a phone call from his office reporting a minor problem, and that he decided to attend to it instead, feeling much relieved at the fortuitous excuse to skip the meeting! (Granier was the RCTV representative and the first person with whom he was scheduled to meet.)

When the Carter Center team proposed a more active role as facilitator, Gaviria told it that in his experience, when people spend a lot of time together, even if only making speeches, little by little the desire to kill each other passes and at some point in time opportunities arise for reaching agreements. Their own political needs compel them to do so. "And when that occurs, we'll be here," was how he put it. Thus, Gaviria's approach was to handle himself within the boundaries of the table and wait for the initiative to spring from the participants. He was acting more as a witness than as an intervener, which was clearly what the parties required at the beginning of the process.[33]

But it was also clear that decision makers on both sides (Chávez for the government and—at that time—Ortega and Fernández for the opposition) would not be sitting down at the table. In the Carter Center's view, when the conflict escalated, the facilitator might have taken a number of initiatives to expand the boundaries of the table in order to involve the real decision makers more, as well as to help the decision makers' delegates on both sides to more effectively influence the building of momentum that could lead to the reaching of agreements. On several occasions, the Carter Center became very aware that it was possible to reach agreement between the delegates, but that these steps forward could not be taken because the decision makers, who were not at the table, would not validate them. The facilitator never took action to help the delegates solve the basic dilemmas of negotiating on behalf of others.[34]

In the Carter Center's view, it was possible to consider the table as a "generating" space that could decisively contribute to political decision making by both parties. But if the facilitation procedure does not include a methodology encouraging open-minded listening, a true dialogue, and the constant exploration of options that may have an impact on the decision-making process, the efficacy of the space diminishes considerably. In particular, when the conflict escalates and the prospect of a violent outcome is more evident, the facilitator should move from being a witness to being more active in changing perceptions that might emerge from the talks, as well as in constructing alternative narratives for the participants, something which could provide new room for decision making at difficult moments.

---

33. It is also true that these "hard and inflexible" boundaries that the facilitator generated around the table, basically by refusing to "operationalize decisions" beyond that space, served to maintain and preserve it as a valuable arena. It is possible that a more active approach that failed to produce results would ultimately have weakened the table.

34. For a discussion of the dilemmas of negotiating on behalf of others and possible solutions, see Susskind and Mnookin, "Major Themes and Prescriptive Implications."

The second lesson gleaned from this period is the need to recognize that in such high-level political conflicts, third parties always play a political role. Here, there are at least three relevant issues to consider. First, it is very important to be able to "read" signals in politics and to position oneself in a sphere of influence that promotes clear values and objectives, while simultaneously avoiding competition with political actors on their own turf. A very unstable and delicate balance must be struck. This demands extraordinary flexibility and openness. Still, minor friction and disagreements with political actors are bound to occur, and the facilitator must be able to address them to maintain its ability to perform the role.

Second, mediators have specific interests and principles that are always healthy to make manifest, as transparency is a golden rule in the exercise of this role. Mediators explicitly work to maintain peace, democracy, and the rule of law. In the case of Venezuela, this made it impossible for the OAS or the Carter Center team to include the rebellious military officers in the negotiations, or to provide space for groups that promoted violent solutions or condoned illegal acts.

Third, it was the Carter Center's intention to be "multipartial" rather than impartial, because the only way to "operate" in a highly polarized context is to build relations and generate trust with a large number of persons on both sides of the spectrum and to show an in-depth understanding of each side to the conflict.

Accepting the political aspect of the facilitation role, acting transparently, promoting values, and forging personal relations based on trust with key actors of both sides characterizes Jimmy Carter's mediation style. Indeed, this was his rationale and his modus operandi with the two main political enemies in this conflict. For example, on his first visit to Chávez, when the Carter Center team told Carter he was being too complacent with the president, he replied: "I need this man to trust me." Likewise, when the team remarked it seemed to be a mistake that amid the political conflict Carter planned to stick to his plan to go fishing as a guest of Gustavo Cisneros, he said: "He is a magnificent host and my friend."

In the authors' view, it is not the fact that Carter is a former president of the United States or Nobel Peace Prize winner that allows him to behave in this manner and employ a "multipartial" mediating style, but rather it is his honest and transparent behavior that invests him with the moral standing and international stature that he enjoys.

The third lesson learned during this period is the need to be conscious of one's own cultural differences in performing the role of mediator. The idiosyncrasies of the Chavistas and the opposition were always very different. The opposition leaders were (and continue to be) persons of upper-middle-class background with a comfortable and open view of the outside world, while Chavista leaders tended to be from the middle or lower middle class and more suspicious of anyone who came from abroad. Facilitators must work conscientiously to build trust and personal relations with all, and to that end must develop the necessary sensitivity. Gaviria did not conscientiously cultivate trusted personal relationships with both parties. Although his facilitation style was always very respectful of the decisions taken by either side, he made a concerted effort to keep a personal distance from all of the actors. Even so, the owners of media outlets and some opposition politicians managed to seek him out in his eastern Caracas hotel to speak to him and attempt to establish personal relations with him. Government supporters, on the other hand, never went to his hotel or made efforts to contact him. As a result, his conversations with the opposition had no counterbalance. In addition, Gaviria's dialogue with Chávez was always uneasy, and this inhibited government supporters from fully trusting him even further. Little by little, he came to be perceived by the government as being biased in favor of the opposition, thereby limiting the table's possibilities.

For the Carter Center's part, it made a "cultural" mistake by not paying adequate attention to the personal characteristics of Minister Diosdado Cabello, a former military officer and an engineer, when weekly bilateral meetings were agreed to between him and individual media owners in the "baby-steps" exercise. The Carter Center team knew beforehand that he always felt intimidated by the television owners. This was the main reason the Carter Center's team proposed a go-between exercise for the initial negotiations, so that he would not need to be in the same room with them. But the team then included the face-to-face meetings in the agreement and took his acceptance of the text as a personal commitment, which proved not to be the case. As he explained to the Carter Center much later, he was on his way to the first meeting as planned but stopped a few blocks before reaching the meeting place and returned to his office when he realized he would not be capable of talking with a person he perceived as a "hypocritical coupster."

5

From the May Agreement to the Recall Petition, March–October 2003

The failure of the petroleum strike and the departure of its leaders signaled a dramatic change in the balance of power and ushered in a period of transition in the dynamics of confrontation between the parties. The government had already consolidated its control over the armed forces and now with its control over PDVSA proceeded to control the main economic resources of the country. The opposition made every effort to adapt to the new situation and reinvigorate itself in order to keep up the pressure in the streets and take the first steps down the road of confrontation in the electoral arena.

The cycle of the negotiation and agreements table thus came to an end, and after several efforts, a basic agreement was signed in May 2003. The opposition changed leaders, and the government changed priorities. The role of the mediators was limited to working with the "follow-up liaison committee" for the May agreement, while Carter Center initiatives with the media and social sectors expanded around the Strengthening Peace in Venezuela Program.

The Supreme Court of Justice became a temporary referee in the conflict and appointed the persons who were to make up the National Electoral Council (CNE) amid a cross-fire of pressures and maneuvers by the mass media. Meanwhile, international actors positioned themselves to begin the electoral observation tasks derived from the activation of the first popular referendum to recall an elected president in history.

The Negotiation and Agreements Table

The failure of the strike dealt the leadership of "the two Carloses" (Fernández and Ortega) within the business and labor sectors a political death blow, and the government moved in to mop up by arresting Fernández and forcing Ortega to flee. Political party leaders and the media owners also felt the impact caused by the strike's failure. In this context, the Coordinadora Democrática's delegates to the table took on more significant roles as opposition figures, and in March 2003 they began to seek options for reaching an agreement. Once again mention was made of Carter's proposals. The choice of a recall referendum would legally come into play in August of that year, at the midpoint of the presidential term, and what had once seemed far-off in time now appeared more feasible to the opposition—mainly because it saw no other viable alternative, and the government had stated that this was the appropriate electoral option.

The Beginning of the End of the Table

By March 2003, government delegates were arriving late or simply failing to attend the meetings of the table called by Gaviria and over time showed less and less interest in the process. Following the Group of Friends' fruitless visit to Caracas in February, Chávez put his relationship with Gaviria on ice and on several occasions made public his dissatisfaction with him. Gaviria thereupon decided to leave Caracas for a couple of weeks. When Gaviria announced this intention at a meeting of the table, Vice President Rangel explicitly recognized his efforts and patience, thanked him for having kept the table alive, and reiterated the government's willingness to continue participating. He asked that the meetings be facilitated by Gaviria's chief of staff Fernando Jaramillo and the Carter Center's Francisco Diez in Gaviria's absence.

At the few meetings that were possible to be held during what remained of March, the delegations spoke very openly about what the necessary conditions would be for holding a recall referendum. At smaller meetings, several points on which agreement could be reached were identified, such as the designation of a CNE considered reliable by both parties; the role of the mass media during the campaign; the provision of economic resources by the government; the role of the armed forces in the implementation of the "Plan República" (the deployment of the armed forces on election day); the system for gathering and validating the signatures necessary to activate the referendum; the possibility that a government official who had been recalled might participate in a later election for the same post; the acceptance of international technical assistance; and the strengthening of the electoral system and the electoral verification mechanisms.[1]

---

1. Points mentioned in the memo of March 20, 2003, sent by Francisco Diez to the Carter Center, author's private collection.

After several working sessions, the two delegations tasked the facilitators with writing a draft text on the mechanism for a recall referendum that would then be considered by both parties. In private, the two delegations had on several occasions made clear to the Carter Center that they were tired and wished to put an end to the table exercise. They both wanted to replace it with a better "product." This further heightened the Carter Center's expectations.

Fernando Jaramillo, with the support of Francisco Diez, worked on a proposal for the recall referendum. Soon thereafter, the OAS produced a comprehensive document that harkened back to the twenty-two points put forth by Gaviria, including the last two points that referred to an election exercise that had never gained consensus. There were several working meetings on these documents and finally, at the table's session on April 10, 2003, led by Jaramillo, the members of the two delegations present that day agreed on a full text. A follow-up meeting was scheduled for the next day to seal the commitment by all of the other members (among them the vice president and the leader of Fedecámaras). On April 11, Jaramillo and Diez met first with the opposition. The feeling of discontent among its members was evident. Businessman Rafael Alfonzo said that accepting an agreement for a recall referendum was equivalent to obtaining nothing. As his presence was not helpful to reaching an agreement, Timoteo Zambrano asked Alfonzo to leave. After Alfonzo's departure, Jaramillo and Diez brought together the two delegations (which included only three of the six government members) and read them the agreed-upon text. They made a few finishing touches to the text and declared work on the text "closed." On April 11, 2003, a year to the day after the coup that had fleetingly removed Chávez from office, three government representatives (not including the vice president) and five members of the opposition confirmed their agreement on a text. The date set for its signature was April 22.

Upon request from Deputy Omar Meza Ramírez, Francisco Diez sent the complete text by fax to Vice President Rangel and by e-mail to President Chávez's secretary, who called to confirm receipt. As those present were getting up from the table, Jaramillo loudly said that it was clear that this was the final text, that it would no longer be worked on, and that while it still had to be "officially" approved by the two sides, it would be a good idea if he read it publicly, asking if anyone was opposed. No one stated a clear opinion. Timoteo Zambrano said, "Go ahead, go ahead, of course," though others muttered, "I don't know." On the government side, Meza Ramírez declared, "Well, perhaps that's not all that prudent as yet, it depends." The remainder hurriedly left without replying. Upon leaving the table's meeting, Jaramillo proceeded to read the text to the press. Publicly at least, there was now an agreement.

That entire week was spent by the government in the "megacelebrations" to celebrate the two-year anniversary of Chávez's return to power after the coup of April 11–13, 2002. A large number of foreigners from Socialist, Communist, and a variety of leftist parties had been invited and one could sense in the air the sensation of triumph that had taken hold among the Chavistas. The strike had fizzled, as had the military "sit-in" at Altamira, and at the negotiation table the opposition had been forced to accept that the next step would be a recall referendum, the constitutional right it had always possessed.

Within the Coordinadora Democrática, the text of the agreement caused heated debate, as a significant part of the opposition was of the opinion that it made no sense to sign an agreement that only recognized constitutional rights and legal obligations already in force. Others countered that even if this were the case, the very fact that the government was about to sign an agreement would stop it from "maneuvering" to block the recall referendum and would, in addition, keep the international community committed to the process. On the Chavista side, some spokespersons said that no agreement had been reached and that they would need to meticulously examine the text. It was obvious the signing was not very important to the government and the facilitators heard no more from them for more than two weeks. Finally, through an adviser, the government sent the facilitators an almost entirely new text that, while keeping the overall structure of the previous document, included a significant number of changes, both in terms of language and content.

Initially, the opposition was irate. Jaramillo had to work very hard with it, and eventually managed to get an agreement from it according to which the original text would be used and the new version would be delivered by the government as the foundation for a consensus text that would gather the most pertinent aspects of both. Jaramillo then produced a text that reflected a balance between the substance that mattered to the opposition and the new language introduced by the government. This was sent to both sides, and Jaramillo and Diez sat back to await their reactions. Two or three days later, the opposition told the facilitators it would only reply after hearing the government's reaction, and that for it the valid text continued to be the one agreed upon at the table on April 11.

The government sank into silence and nobody returned the facilitators' calls. In May, Gaviria returned to Venezuela. He installed himself at his usual hotel and asked to see the vice president, but there was no response to his request for an audience. Gaviria instead met the ministers of foreign relations and education, both members of the table, but got no answer on the text of the agreement. With this stalemate, Jimmy Carter called President Chávez and got a commitment from Chávez to receive Jennifer McCoy on the evening of May 19.

Direct Negotiations with Chávez

The government's silence regarding the text proposed in late April by Jaramillo was ominous. The Carter Center truly did not know what to expect. When Jennifer McCoy arrived in Caracas on May 18, she and Diez spoke to some opposition representatives, as well as to Gaviria. It was clear the government wanted to do away with the table and Gaviria's presence as soon as possible. On the morning of May 19, McCoy and Diez went to see the vice president and other members of the government's delegation to the table. Talking about the situation in general terms, the government representatives expressed their opinion that the table had served its purpose and that nothing more could be expected of it. But when asked to state whether they accepted the text as proposed, their reply was elusive. They said only that "the various political forces that support the government have a right to express an opinion and this is a process that takes time because it is very complex." As McCoy and Diez were leaving, already standing and on the way out, the vice president said: "You have a meeting with the President tonight, don't you? Well . . . ask him!" It was abundantly clear that the opinion regarding the complexity of the political forces boiled down to none other than the president himself. That afternoon McCoy and Diez told Gaviria that they would be seeing the president and would seek a clear answer. He asked for them to call him upon leaving the meeting, no matter what the hour.

That night McCoy and Diez arrived at Miraflores Palace at 9 p.m. and were received by the president, who was alone in his office. They sat in armchairs and a brief, formal conversation ensued. McCoy went directly to the point and stated that they were perplexed by the government's silence, that they thought the text of the proposed agreement to be very positive, and that they wanted to know his personal opinion of it. Chávez said that yes, he had been taking a look at it, and that it had a few "little things" that he did not like. McCoy insisted that they look at the text together, so Chávez called in his assistant and asked for "those papers I have been working on."

Moving over to a table, the three sat down to compare the texts. The president began to read changes he had made on the margins of the document in his own handwriting, and together they proceeded to read the proposed agreement point by point. There were a number of grammatical corrections that Chávez made and general expressions that worried Chávez because they could be interpreted in different ways. McCoy and Diez knew the grammatical corrections would be of no interest to the opposition. But with respect to Chávez's last three points, which made reference to the suffrage law, the closing down of the table, and the continuation of international facilitation, McCoy and Diez made clear to Chávez what the opposition's fears and interests were. In turn, they suggested reformulations to the text and analyzed with Chávez each of the words employed in the document. In doing so, McCoy and Diez wrote down the president's corrections on their copy of the text and carefully drafted new sentences. Chávez, for his part, took notes and read each point in great detail. When analyzing the text together, it became quite clear that Chávez's main interests were in putting an end to the negotiation and agreements table and preserving his image vis-à-vis the international community. The annual Rio Group meeting of Latin American presidents was to be held in Cuzco, Peru, on May 23–24, and there was great interest in the Venezuelan negotiations. This was the chance to "close the deal" with Chávez, and the Carter Center took it.

The Deal with Chávez

Several key moments from the conversation between McCoy and Diez and President Chávez are worth relating in detail here because they are very illustrative of both the issues of substance that were at stake and the negotiation methodology used. The most important substantive issue was the commitment not to modify paragraph 17, which related to not changing the suffrage law while the effort was under way to activate the recall referendum. The opposition was afraid that the government, using its majority in the National Assembly, would change the electoral rules of the game. The government had already eliminated this reference in its version that modified the text agreed upon on April 11, which the opposition read as a sign that its worst fears were coming true. In McCoy's and Diez's discussion with Chávez, the president again eliminated the reference, but he was told: "Mr. President, if we take that out, the opposition won't sign." To this, he replied:

"But we can't take on rights or commitments that are not incumbent upon us! This is a competence of the National Assembly, as they'll assert!" McCoy and Diez understood that the opposition's fear and the president's concern reflected different motives, not opposed interests, and thus asked: "But would you promote any change in the electoral law at this point?" "No, no, I wouldn't," Chávez replied. "Then," McCoy and Diez countered, "how do you think we can put what you're saying down in the text as a commitment on your part? What commitment are you willing to take on, as executive branch?" And so a sentence was written that would allay the opposition's fears, a reformulation that saved the point in question.

With regard to Chávez's main interests, McCoy and Diez knew full well how much President Chávez valued his international image. Thus, they asked: "Can you imagine, Mr. President, arriving at the Rio Group meeting with an agreement under your arm and Gaviria by your side?" His eyes shone as he answered: "Hey, that would be a miracle!" McCoy and Diez also spoke frankly about his interest in finishing off the table, to which he replied: "Look, I respect the work that Gaviria has done here. He stood his ground and the truth is that he helped a great deal! Without the table who knows what might have happened in this country. But enough already! Enough!" From his expression it was obvious that there was no more space for the table. But the sentence he had suggested to signify the closing of the table was frankly aggressive and ultimately unacceptable. So McCoy and Diez proposed the turn of phrase, "with the signing of this Agreement, the table constructively concludes its functions." Thus, this point was resolved as well.

Upon concluding the review of the text, Jennifer McCoy said: "Mr. President, I need your word that no one else needs to approve this text from your side." At first Chávez did not understand what she meant. But she insisted, placing her hand on his arm, and looking him straight in the eye: "I need your commitment that if the opposition accepts this text, the government will sign the agreement. That we are not going to be told afterward that the parties and social movements that support you need to give their opinion on the text." Chávez broke out laughing: "No, Jennifer, don't worry, I give you my assurance."

The authors left the presidential palace at one o'clock in the morning on May 21, 2003, with a text that the president had committed himself to. On the way back to their hotel, they called Gaviria, who was sleeping, and told him of the agreement. The authors agreed to meet him at his hotel later that morning at 7 a.m.

The Deal with the Opposition

Hours later, at his hotel, Gaviria was a happy man. As he heard the changes and the nature of the conversation, he could not stop congratulating the authors and saying, "This is good, very good, very good." The authors made a clean copy of a final version of the text and sent it to the president's secretary. Upon receiving the green light from Miraflores, a copy was also faxed to Vice President Rangel, head of the government delegation. Gaviria had already scheduled a meeting with him for that day at 10 a.m., and it was agreed that Diez would participate in it. As they left for the meeting, Gaviria made some cryptic remarks to the press, saying only that there was a "response" from the government and that he would review it with the opposition.

The next forty-eight hours were a marathon. Gaviria and Diez installed themselves in the hotel suite used by the OAS in order to receive, first of all, the opposition delegation. Gaviria challenged them to consider the text very seriously and was able to control the angry discussions among them. In the following hours, the different political actors of the broad opposition spectrum came filing through—heads of political parties, businesspeople, union leaders, media owners, and so on. Gaviria was patient, though firm, with all of them. Meanwhile, McCoy was meeting with the leaders of the various political parties to present them the text that Chávez had accepted and to encourage them to sign an agreement based on it. The owners of two of the television stations (Alberto Ravel for Globovisión and Víctor Ferreres for Venevisión) became Gaviria's "political operators" in favor of the agreement. They spoke with everyone, brought in the more recalcitrant leaders to meet Gaviria personally, pressured others, and held long talks with stragglers in an effort to see the agreement accepted. At one critical juncture of this confusing process, Gaviria demanded to know from the opposition representatives to the table whether they were going to work on the text, because if they were not willing to work on it, to improve on one specific point or another, with a view toward reaching consensus, he would retire from the negotiations and abandon Caracas. This proved very effective.

The next day, May 22, McCoy and Diez and Gaviria began very early on to introduce some changes to the text upon the request of opposition representatives. Once each of these changes had been defined, Gaviria spoke by telephone with the vice president, and McCoy and Diez sent him each proposed paragraph by fax. In turn, Rangel consulted with the president, who was traveling about the country, and came back with counterproposals that McCoy and Diez then discussed with the opposition. It was exhausting. Amid the exchange of messages, the secretariat of the presidency confirmed to Gaviria that Chávez was extending an invitation to him to travel together to the Rio Group meeting in the presidential airplane, which was leaving at midnight. This presented a very clear deadline. If consensus on a text could not be reached before the trip, there would be no deal after that.

At 11:45 p.m., the last point up for discussion was finally approved. This was a very important point for the opposition, which insisted that the table continue to function in some form. McCoy and Diez knew full well the government would not accept this. The solution was to once again float the idea of the *mecanismo de enlace* (liaison mechanism) described in the "Declaration against Violence" that both sides had signed in February.[2] Gaviria and Diez drafted a text, made the proposal to both sides, and it worked. After the entire agreement had been reviewed once more, Gaviria told the opposition representatives that were still in his suite: "The text cannot be changed any more. When I get back from my trip, and if you're ready, we sign. But I'm not accepting a single further change, neither from the opposition nor from the government. This was the first time we had Chávez himself negotiating from the other side of the line, and that will not happen again." They agreed. Gaviria left immediately for the presidential jet that would fly him to the meeting in Cuzco. As for Chávez, he would be arriving, as first suggested by Diez and McCoy, with the agreement under his arm and Gaviria by his side.

The Signing Ceremony

Once the complete and finished text began to circulate among all sectors of the opposition, the few voices expressing praise were virtually drowned out by the din of harsh criticism. Columnists, pundits, leaders of the most miniscule political factions—all were extremely critical of the text. With Gaviria and McCoy out of the country, Jaramillo and Diez had to move through a barrage of meetings in which they explained why the text said what it did, and why they thought it worth signing. From May 23 to May 29, the day agreed upon for the public signing ceremony, multiple efforts were made to change or add paragraphs to the agreement, but Jaramillo and Diez steadfastly supported Gaviria's last statement and refused to tamper with it any further.

Finally, on the morning of May 29, the stage was set for the solemn ratification ceremony to take place in a Caracas hotel, with the two delegations

---

2. The idea of using this mechanism, which was envisioned in the already-signed declaration, came from a brilliant opposition "operator" who called Diez to suggest the solution. Among opposition ranks, every paragraph of the agreement was hotly debated at several levels in parallel fashion, and this individual had not been able to make herself heard among the other party members.

signing the text of the agreement in the presence of representatives from the OAS, the Carter Center, and the UNDP.[3] Businessman Rafael Alfonso and Governor Eduardo Lappi, the two most recalcitrant members of the opposition delegation, ultimately decided to attend the ceremony,[4] and close to midday, the agreement was signed before the television cameras.[5] Minutes later, Chávez called each of the facilitators to express his congratulations.

The Content of the Agreement

The agreement itself fell short of what Carter had proposed in January. In his proposals, the strike would end and striking workers would face no retribution; the president would agree to a recall referendum no later than August 19, 2003, if the opposition gathered sufficient signatures; a joint national-international commission would be established to supervise all electoral processes; deadlines were proposed for the naming of the new CNE; the table agreement would ensure that provisions would be agreed on to renew the public powers of the Supreme Court and the attorney general, comptroller general, and ombudsman; international human rights commitments would be respected; and the government and opposition would agree in advance of any electoral process to a process of reconciliation and promotion of social justice.[6]

In contrast, the final agreement recognized the constitutional right of Venezuelans to petition for a recall referendum to contribute to solving the Venezuelan crisis, recognized freedom of expression as well as the need for equitable media access and coverage during political campaigns, asked for international assistance for civilian disarmament, and recognized the offer of the tripartite organizations to provide electoral technical assistance and electoral observation and accompany the materialization of the agreement. The agreement also recognized human rights obligations and Venezuela's signature of the Inter-American Democratic Charter, and called on compliance with those international commitments. While the agreement ended the table, it created a follow-up "enlace" (liaison) commission consisting of two representatives from each side, with the Carter Center and the OAS continuing to act as facilitators.

---

3. Although UNDP had not participated in any of the negotiations at the table, the OAS and Carter Center decided to invite the resident representative of the UN system to the agreement-signing ceremony as an original member of the Tripartite Working Group and as a strategic partner in the more broad-based efforts being undertaken in Venezuela.

4. Alfonso made the sign of the cross before signing, as if to say, "So help me God."

5. For the final agreement signed on May 29, 2003, see appendix A.

6. The Carter Center, *The Carter Center and the Peacebuilding Process in Venezuela*, 13–14.

Francisco Diez signing the agreement on behalf of the Carter Center, seated next to Secretary General Cesar Gaviria.
Courtesy of the Strengthening Peace in Venezuela Program.

Although the agreement neither set specific timetables nor included any specific concessions from the government, it did commit both sides to important principles and acknowledged that both sides saw an electoral process (recall referendum) as a "solution" to the political crisis. Even without an explicit role granted to the international community, the agreement opened the door for international actors to continue to encourage Venezuelans to pursue resolution of their differences through the communication mechanism of the liaison committee and through established constitutional procedures, and it eventually led to the August 2004 recall referendum.

The Strengthening Peace in Venezuela Program

In March and April 2003, the Carter Center, with support from UNDP, began to structure a more comprehensive and ambitious peacebuilding program. It was evident that the social divisions and fractures could not be healed through the work done at the negotiation and agreements table alone. At the same time, the Carter Center had gained a social and political space that allowed it to expand its range of activities. It knew, in particular, that a recall referendum in itself would not resolve the underlying conflicts in the country and could even contribute to greater tension due to the inherent divisive nature of an electoral process.

The workshops held by William Ury in October 2002 and February and March 2003 had helped identify several groups of persons interested in collaborating with Carter Center initiatives,[7] and with them the Carter Center identified three primary areas for action: training in constructive conflict management; working with the mass media; and generating a space to involve social and community networks.

Training

The first phase of the Comprehensive Training Program began with teacher training in constructive conflict management. The idea was that, once trained, the participants, supported by the Carter Center, would be in a position to hold constructive conflict management workshops and use consensus-building tools in their own spheres of activity and localities.

---

7. Néstor Alfonzo Santamaría, Gabrielle Guerón, and Mireya Lozada of the Universidad Central de Venezuela decided to actively join the Carter Center team as conflict resolution volunteer experts at first and later on as consultants to the program being sponsored by UNDP and the Carter Center. The team was completed with the arrival of Victor Hugo Febres, founder of the Los del Medio group, to work with the media.

The training was conceived not only as a useful tool for capacity build-ing but also as a means to forge alliances and coalitions that would serve to strengthen the conciliatory message and the institutional position of the Carter Center and its allies. It would thus provide a more solid foundation from which all "third siders" could operate in such a sensitive environment. The training activities opened three very valuable doors: first, they linked the Carter Center with organizations that already had a significant history and tradition of community work, such as the Red de Apoyo a Justicia y Paz (Network in Support of Justice and Peace), the Federación de Insti-tuciones Privadas de Attención al Niño (FIPAN, or Federation of Private Institutions for Attention to Children), the Escuela de Vecinos (Neigh-bors' School), and Fé y Alegría (Faith and Happiness), thus allowing the Carter Center to insert itself into already established social networks; sec-ond, they established bridges to professionals around the country, mainly in the states of Zulia and Lara, allowing the Carter Center to expand its reach in geographic terms; and third, perhaps most importantly, they put the Carter Center in direct touch with a large number of regular Venezuelans who, unlike the political actors, offered a variety of viewpoints regarding the reality of the country, thus revealing the wealth of nuances and cul-tural complexity of Venezuelan society that had been brutally simplified by political polarization.

The training sessions were multiplied over the course of a few months in very different places and arenas, particularly in schools, where a comprehensive program of education in the culture of peace and mediation was launched with the support of Minister of Education Aristóbulo Istúriz, among others.[8]

Mass Media

The media continued to both reflect and exacerbate the political and social polarization of the country. If one flipped between the state-owned televi-sion channel and any private station, it seemed one was living in two differ-ent worlds. The opposition newspapers were given to glaring, often alarmist headlines, and all opinion columns were mercilessly critical of the govern-ment, while the official agencies and publications operated like political propaganda mills rather than sources of information, singing the praises of the country's leader and attacking the opposition.

In addition to the high-level negotiations between the government and media owners described in chapter 3, the Carter Center also worked at the

---

8. In Venezuela, the Argentine educator and mediator Marta Paillet was a pioneer in this field.

intermediate level with journalists and editors through the Strengthening Peace in Venezuela Program. Workshops for journalists and editors were included in the visits of William Ury in February and June 2003, and together with Search for Common Ground,[9] the Carter Center designed a program of seminars to be taught by two Search for Common Ground experts who visited Caracas for a week in July 2003.[10] In addition, the Carter Center forged two lasting and important alliances in the field—namely, with the director of the cultural channel Vale TV, María Eugenia Mosquera, who had direct links with the owners of all the most important media outlets (in addition to plentiful political connections) and who provided support to all of the Carter Center's initiatives, and with a group of young journalists and communicators who had formed the group Los del Medio (The Media in the Middle). Los del Medio was concerned about the effects of the political conflict and the decline in standards in the journalistic profession.

With these and other sources of support, the Carter Center organized several talks and workshops, produced an educational short feature for television titled *The Third Side*, made small radio publicity spots on peacebuilding issues, and forged alliances with mid-level journalists and communicators to encourage the emergence of nonpolarizing stories.

In June, in parallel with the efforts at the intermediate levels, the Carter Center decided to again hold high-level negotiations between television-station owners and the government, with the latter represented once again by Minister of Information, Diosdado Cabello. Diez facilitated these negotiations and, after individual meetings with the relevant parties, two joint meetings were held at the minister's office using a 4+1 format (four opposition station owners and Cabello). These meetings proved helpful, as they defused the tension somewhat. It was agreed that each station owner would visit the minister individually in order to hold direct talks on specific issues.[11]

All of these activities opened up new channels of communications that allowed for more messages in the mass media that stressed the "third side."[12] The Carter Center believed it was indispensable to lend these peacebuilding initiatives a degree of "scale" and to collaborate, insofar as possible, in the construction of a social narrative that would serve as an alternative to that of the confrontation between Chavismo and anti-Chavismo.

---

9.   See the Search for Common Ground, www.sfcg.org/resources/training/resources_mediatraining.html.

10. These seminars enjoyed the support of the Ambassador Shapiro and were financed by USAID.

11. Only two meetings with Televen and Venevisión (by phone) actually took place, as Cabello, true to form, did not hold the scheduled rounds with RCTV and Globovisión.

12. Including in a radio program titled "Tolerance," which the Carter Center publicly supported.

Social and Community Networks

From the outset of the Strengthening Peace in Venezuela Program, the Carter Center sought to identify and contact networks of persons and organizations with whom it could join forces to build bridges between those sectors of society straddling the middle ground and between the capital and the interior of the country. It focused its efforts in creating three intertwined networks: a group of academicians in Caracas, a group of allies in the interior of the country, and a large group of NGOs and organizations.

The academicians. With the help of Universidad Central de Venezuela social psychologist Mireya Lozada, Diez began holding informal meetings with groups of academicians and intellectuals from different points on the ideological spectrum. Meetings were held over dinner (at the Carter Center's invitation) once every two weeks at the same discreet hostelry at which the center had worked with Ury and the media owners. Once a measure of trust had been established, the Carter Center suggested the creation of a consultative committee. The idea was to exchange visions, information, and opinions on an informal and confidential basis. At the outset, the conversations centered on generalities, but little by little they became more substantive and richer in content. The participants came from very diverse backgrounds and held a variety of opinions, forming an attractive reflection of the complex fabric of visions coexisting in the country. Almost all of their opinions were based on consistent and very well articulated narratives that were, at the same time, opposed in many ways. Most of them knew each other, some directly, others only indirectly. Everyone respected everyone else, and this made for some truly generative dialogues. This gathering of intellectuals evolved into the opinion group known as Aquí Cabemos Todos (There's Room for All Here), which was the title given to the group's first public document calling for dialogue and coexistence amid diversity.

From October 2003 to August 2004 the group issued six public communiqués that included the signatures of a considerable number of organizations and public figures.[13] Numerous initiatives had their origin in this space, and the personal relationships created during that period still persist.

The interior of the country. The Carter Center also wished to extend its activities to the interior of the country, where polarization found itself more nuanced by local realities than in Caracas. Once again, it resorted to William Ury, asking him to make a presentation in Zulia, Venezuela's second most

---

13. See The Carter Center, *The Carter Center and the Peacebuilding Process in Venezuela.*

important state and one in which the governor was an opposition leader;[14] the mayor of Maracaibo, the state capital, meanwhile, was a Chávez ally. For the holding of the event, the Carter Center secured the support of both individuals, as well as that of the local bishop, Monsignor Ubaldo Santana,[15] who was respected by all sides. The initiative triggered several activities that took place locally and integrated a "third-side" approach.

Likewise, the Carter Center forged alliances with groups and organizations in which some former students of the first training phase were involved and who came from other states. Working jointly with them, the Carter Center organized public activities and supported initiatives intended to promote a culture of peace.

The NGOs. As is the case almost everywhere in Latin America, the social and community movements, the numerous social advocacy groups, and the NGOs in Venezuela operate independently and often competitively, separated by the traditional fragmentation of society. This undermined the impact their initiatives might otherwise have had. At the initiative of one of the youths who was a member of the Strengthening Peace in Venezuela Program,[16] the Carter Center decided to create a "collective space" for networks and social organizations willing to foster peacebuilding actions. The group created Paz en Movimiento (Peace in Movement), which became public on September 21, 2003, International Peace Day, and whose membership would grow to include over one hundred groups and organizations.[17]

Members of the movement initiated a number of activities, such as the exchange of aggressive signs for more pacifist ones at the rallies held by pro-government and opposition forces, the creation of peace brigades for multiple activities, campaigns with titles such as "Massive Vaccination against Violence" and "Fair of Organizations Working for Peace," and peace campaigns and workshops given by the Spanish mediator Juan Gutierrez, who had been invited by the Carter Center to visit Venezuela.

Lederach: Synergy, Multilevel, and Multifocus

In May 2003, as the Strengthening Peace in Venezuela Program team began to gather momentum and demonstrate its capacity to take initiatives and

---

14. The governor was Manuel Rosales, who became the single opposition candidate to run against Chávez in the December 2006 presidential campaign.

15. In 2006 Bishop Santana became president of the Venezuelan Episcopal Conference.

16. Mediator Nestor Alfonso Santamaría, who described himself as a "peace activist."

17. For the press statement, see The Carter Center, *The Carter Center and the Peacebuilding Process in Venezuela*, 28.

Street photos created by the Strengthening Peace in Venezuela Program.
Photo by the authors.

Fair for Peace in the Central Square of Caracas.
Photo by the authors.

carry out activities, the Carter Center decided to seek the support of John Paul Lederach, whom it considered to be the foremost theoretician in the field of peacebuilding.[18] The Carter Center obtained support from the Polar Foundation, an organization linked to a large family business that was part of the opposition to Chávez, a very interesting network of grassroots community organizations capable of carrying out solidarity work, and Minister of Popular Economy Elías Jaua, with whom it had developed a very good relationship. Lederach agreed to come to Caracas in August 2003, and the Carter Center organized a public conference to which the opposition representative in the liaison mechanism, Asdrúbal Aguiar, and Elías Jaua were invited as panelists. Although each made comments from their own ideological point of view after hearing Lederach speak, they maintained a civil public dialogue. In addition, the Carter Center organized a two-day workshop with over sixty participants representing some twenty-five social organizations from different parts of the country, during which Lederach shared his knowledge and experience regarding the most efficient ways to advance a peacebuilding process based on community organizations and civil society.

Lederach's contribution was very important for the Carter Center, as it provided a theoretical-descriptive model for the management of social change that was sufficiently complex to encompass the Carter Center's different activities. The multilevel approach to conflict transformation espoused by Lederach emphasized the coherence between work on the elite-level (such as the table or the talks with the media owners and government officials), the intermediate level (such as the Strengthening Peace in Venezuela Program), and the community level (such as the training programs). Likewise, Lederach's concept of multifocus rapprochement lent sense and purpose to tasks in a variety of settings (the media, NGOs, schools, cities, community groups, universities, etc.). What had been a search first guided by intuition and good intentions and then informed by the work of William Ury thus acquired the significance of a mission with even deeper theoretical and empirical underpinnings. This inspired the entire Strengthening Peace in Venezuela Program team, which took on the main responsibility for opening up this space for synergy. After working with Lederach, the team had a much clearer idea of where it was going and why it was doing what it was doing. To use Lederach's words, the team's goal was to fight polarizations, build bridges between opposing forces, generate peace infrastructures at various levels, and plant the seeds for reconciliation.[19]

---

18. Lederach, *Building Peace.*

19. As these lines are written (February 2010), the program's founding members still continue to work for reconciliation through two civil associations, one named after the Strengthening Peace in Venezu-

The Appointment of Members to the National Electoral Council

By June 2003 the government was interested in the appointment of the new CNE in light of the regional elections scheduled for August 2004, while the opposition was divided between those who wanted to hold an immediate recall referendum against Chávez (media owners and the leaders with more media exposure) and those who preferred to wait until the government suffered additional attrition and the opposition could shore up its own strength for the 2004 regional elections and 2006 presidential elections (the more traditional parties).

Several attempts were made in the National Assembly to appoint the members of the CNE. A two-thirds vote of the assembly was required to elect the CNE's five directors and ten alternates. A tentative agreement was achieved on fourteen of the members, but the final member, the president of the council, had yet to be chosen. If the assembly proved unable to select that person, the decision would rest with the constitutional chamber of the Supreme Court of Justice, which would be asked to act due to the "omission" by the legislature.

By August, it was clear that the political actors could not agree and they would wait for the Supreme Court decision on the CNE board. The dilemma continued to be the selection of the fifth and final director. During that period, the Carter Center held parallel conversations with the opposition and the government, and in several of these discussions the name of Eleazar Díaz Rangel came up. Editor of the newspaper Últimas Noticias, he seemed acceptable to both sides. Although the newspaper was part of the Capriles chain and the property of an opposition family, Díaz Rangel was considered to be a moderate sympathizer of Chavismo.

The president of the Supreme Court, Iván Rincón, told the Carter Center privately that the constitutional chamber of the court would designate the entire CNE, after a process of "consultation" with all sectors. It had already made public a decision that gave the National Assembly ten days to appoint the council members, with an additional ten-day extension possible. If in that period no result was forthcoming, the Supreme Court would be fully entitled to select the electoral authorities. Thus, throughout August, the country witnessed the members of the Supreme Court's constitutional

---

ela Program and the other named Peacebuilders. In addition, many of the members of Aqui Cabemos Todos became the founders of the electoral observation NGO called Ojo Electoral. Ojo Electoral became the preeminent national election monitoring organization beginning in 2005 and continued as an active independent organization through this writing, with no links to the Carter Center and no support from the UNDP.

chamber calling in political and social actors to hear their views. The process was very open and the justices declared themselves in "permanent session." All sorts of theories and rumors were bandied about. Some stated that a pro-government justice would "fall ill," thus allowing the decision to favor the opposition, while others claimed that the government had "bought off" this or that member of the court.[20] Ultimately, the political muscle of the private media was demonstrated once again.

As these events were unfolding, Diez had breakfast with Miguel Angel Capriles, owner of the Capriles newspaper chain, which included Últimas Notícias, of which Eleazar Díaz Rangel was the editor in chief. Capriles was a man with whom the Carter Center regularly consulted due to his broad and balanced view of the Venezuelan political and economic scene. Diez mentioned the possibility that Díaz Rangel might be called upon to preside the CNE, and Capriles lamented that fact. Although he acknowledged that Díaz Rangel was the most serious and balanced candidate for the post, he did not want to lose a highly valued employee. Diez requested a meeting with Díaz Rangel in order to get to know him and propose a Strengthening Peace in Venezuela Program activity at his newspaper. The day Diez went to see him, Diez mentioned that he knew Díaz Rangel was a consensus candidate to preside the CNE. Díaz Rangel replied that he had been made an offer and would tender his reply that very day. Diez encouraged him to accept and assured him of the Carter Center's support, as his name had been expressly mentioned by important leaders from both sides of the political spectrum. Two hours after that meeting, Diez got a call from Supreme Court president Iván Rincón, who told him that he had had a very positive meeting with Díaz Rangel and that Díaz Rangel had accepted to lead the CNE, but that this was not yet public and had yet to be voted on by the constitutional chamber.

That night, Venevisión and Globovisión aired "special reports" on the personal and political profile of Díaz Rangel that were very critical and negative. As a result, Díaz Rangel's wife suffered an anxiety attack that, though with no lasting consequences, caused her to enter the hospital for high blood pressure. The next morning, the president of the Supreme Court called Diez again, this time to say that Díaz Rangel had ultimately declined the offer and that they were back to square one. Rincón was harshly critical of the television channels. According to Rincón, Díaz Rangel had told him: "If I am criticized

20. The Supreme Court at that time was considered to be about evenly divided between pro- and antigovernment justices. The constitutional chamber was considered to be more pro-government, while the electoral chamber was more pro-opposition. At different points over the next months, those two chambers would come into conflict with each other.

like this before even having been formally appointed, it is obvious it will be impossible for me to carry out my work, and the integrity of my family comes before all else." When Diez mentioned the episode in private to the directors of the television stations, Víctor Ferreres of Venevisión and Alberto Federico Ravel of Globovisión, they said that Díaz Rangel was unacceptable as president of the CNE because he was "a declared enemy of the media."

Finally, on August 25, 2003, the Supreme Court announced the names of the full CNE board of directors, as well as the names of the CNE's secretaries, mid-level officials, and advisory council. The new council reflected a fine balance, with the presidency going to Francisco Carrasquero, a little-known law professor from the Universidad del Zulia, the home state of the Supreme Court president.

Jennifer McCoy flew to Caracas to meet with the new CNE on its second day of work and to offer the Carter Center's assistance.[21] That last week of August, McCoy and Diez conducted a sweeping round of visits to the political leadership of both the government and opposition in order to verify the degree to which the new authorities were being accepted and to determine what contribution if any might be desired from the Carter Center. A very encouraging picture emerged, with most parties making generally positive comments about the CNE. Some members of the opposition and the government even talked about the possibilities for reconciliation.[22] In addition, the political actors encouraged the Carter Center to continue to expand its presence in Venezuela and to have a higher profile by monitoring implementation of the May agreement and observing any forthcoming electoral process.

The Onset of the Electoral Process

As the new CNE settled in, the opposition seemed happier with the outcome than the government. With the majority that the Chavistas enjoyed in the assembly, they had hoped for an electoral council clearly favorable to the government and were not at all pleased by the "balanced" decision taken by the Supreme Court. The new CNE had on its five-member board two members clearly connected to the opposition (Sobella Mejías of AD and Ezequiel Zamora, who had links to Enrique Mendoza, the governor of the state of Miranda and political head of Copei), and two who were obviously

---

21. The Carter Center was the first international organization to be received by the recently appointed CNE; the Carter Center also invited the UNDP to join it at the beginning of the meeting to offer the United Nation's electoral assistance.

22. For the press statement issued upon the conclusion of Jennifer McCoy's visit to Caracas, see The Carter Center, *The Carter Center and the Peacebuilding Process in Venezuela,* 35.

pro-government (Oscar Battaglini, a leftist university professor, and Jorge Rodríguez, who had a direct line to Vice President Rangel). The council's president, Francisco Carrasquero, was loyal to Iván Rincón, and as he was almost completely unknown, he did not generate strong resistance from either side. In fact, many commentators on both sides viewed the new CNE with relief, saying that it represented an equilibrium. At the popular level, graffiti appearing on Caracas walls reflected the hope generated by the new CNE: "CNE, give us peace."

Soon after the signing of the May agreement, it was clear that the new CNE's first move would be to issue an opinion regarding the signatures for a recall referendum presented by the opposition to the previous board. The political leaders had already accepted the idea that the CNE would declare these signatures invalid and would authorize a procedure for gathering new ones. The government, for its part, began to say with newfound zeal that it too would gather the signatures necessary to revoke the term of several of the opposition's most prominent legislators. In private conversations, government officials would wax enthusiastic, elaborating on their calculations that showed that they would be able to recall several opposition deputies in a number of states and reach a two-thirds majority in the National Assembly, which would allow them to pass any law they saw fit.

The Supreme Court had granted the new board the authority to issue legally valid enabling regulations for governing recall processes, as long as these regulations did not run counter to those established in the electoral suffrage law. This was necessary because the National Assembly had never drafted and approved a law for recall referenda following the creation of that provision in the 1999 Constitution. The five CNE board members decided to caucus behind closed doors for several days to discuss the decisions they needed to make. They agreed by consensus to declare the signatures presented earlier not to be valid, and to define the norms that would govern the new signature-collection process to petition for a recall referendum on the president of the republic and the deputies to the National Assembly.

The road to an electoral face-off was now clear, and both sides began once again to prepare to do battle. The atmosphere heated up and the new CNE became the center of attention. The election arbiter was to define how the struggle for power was to take place, and everyone began to look for the "green streets" that would allow them to influence that arbiter each step of the way[23]—that is, to ensure that the successive decisions would go their way. Po-

---

23. "Green streets" is a common expression employed in Caracas to describe alternate routes that allow for avoiding the daily traffic jams and is used when referring to lobbying efforts.

litical negotiations in the country concentrated on the five persons who were to take decisions by voting among themselves, and the CNE board members began to be subject to strong pressure from their own political sectors. Eventually, they were able to issue a consensual set of general rules intended to regulate the recall processes and thus the electoral phase got under way.

The Carter Center made clear its willingness to support the process by means of an electoral observation mission, but time went by and the CNE said nothing. Not until November did it issue a resolution inviting the OAS and the Carter Center to observe the signature-gathering process.

The International Context

Tensions were still high at the beginning of this period and spilled over to the diplomatic community. President Chávez accused three governments that had been critical of him in the past of intervening in Venezuela's internal affairs—Colombia, Spain, and the United States. Two days later, on February 25, 2003, the Spanish embassy and the Colombian consulate were bombed (without deaths). The OAS Permanent Council, the Group of Friends, and the Carter Center all publicly condemned the attacks, which occurred just one week after the table's signing of the "Declaration against Violence."

The Group of Friends remained active in the spring of 2003, trying to help push the Venezuelans toward an agreement. It met in March in Brasilia, issued a number of communiqués, and visited Venezuela in mid-May to personally urge a conclusion to the agreement. Two regional meetings also added pressure. The Rio Group meeting of Latin American presidents on May 23, 2003, provided an incentive for Chávez to finally conclude stalled negotiations in order to gain international legitimacy by reporting on a negotiated agreement with his opponents. Two weeks later, the annual OAS General Assembly meeting of hemispheric foreign ministers in Chile provided Gaviria the opportunity to report on his eight-month sojourn in Venezuela with a signed agreement and Chávez the chance to avoid more pressuring resolutions from the OAS meeting.

The Tripartite Working Group on Venezuela—the OAS, the UNDP, and the Carter Center—met in Atlanta in late June 2003 to discuss further engagement now that the table had concluded. The future role of international engagement was left vague in the May agreement. The agreement recognized that "the OAS, The Carter Center, and the United Nations have expressed their willingness to provide such technical assistance as the competent authorities of the Bolivarian Republic of Venezuela might request of

them for holding any type of electoral consultation," including election observation, but the agreement did not require this assistance.[24] The agreement
also opened the door to continued international engagement through the
follow-up liaison committee, which would be composed of two government
and two opposition representatives tasked with opening channels of communication, taking measures for the effective fulfillment of the provisions of
the agreement, and maintaining contact with the international facilitation
when the parties consider it necessary.[25]

The tripartite meeting identified four areas of contention immediately
facing Venezuela: the naming of a new CNE, continued tensions between
the government and private media, the need to disarm the civilian population, and the disarmament of the metropolitan police force. The Carter
Center said it would extend its representation in the country, with Francisco
Diez remaining to work with the follow-up liaison committee, on the media
issue, and on the "third-side" initiative. The Carter Center was also willing
to provide election observation, though not technical assistance. The OAS
determined that it would not continue any representation in the country
other than through its permanent representative, but that Fernando Jaramillo, Gaviria's chief of staff, would remain engaged with developments in
Venezuela and that the OAS would engage with the follow-up liaison committee as necessary. Both the OAS and United Nations would be available
to provide election monitoring and/or technical assistance, but the United
Nations made clear it would not do both, seeing a conflict of interest in those
two roles. The OAS was willing to do both as long as it was simply providing
equipment and training to the CNE and not actually carrying out any of the
national functions. The tripartite group finally agreed that if any invitation
to observe an electoral process arrived, the Carter Center and OAS would
conduct a joint electoral observation mission.

The international community maintained its high interest in the Venezuela process, and after the new CNE took office and the movement toward
a recall process gathered steam, the Group of Friends continued to issue
communiqués demonstrating that the international community was closely
following these developments. As tensions rose internally in September with
the CNE's rejection of the signatures presented by the opposition, Chávez
stepped up his rhetoric against the United States, strongly criticizing U.S.
ambassador to Venezuela Charles Shapiro and accusing the United States of
meddling in Venezuelan internal affairs.

---

24. The Carter Center, *The Carter Center and the Peacebuilding Process in Venezuela*, 23.
25. Ibid., 23.

Analysis and Lessons

The first lesson learned from this period is that the perceived needs of the actors generate the political will to reach an agreement. Chávez had initially called for and then accepted the presence of mediators to gain international legitimacy and strength, but after politically defeating the opposition in the Altamira "sit-in" and the oil strike, his only desire to close down the table and remove the international actors opened the way to an agreement. Once that phase was over, the government was in a position of relative strength and entered no further negotiations.

The second lesson is that personal relationships between the parties are a key element to consider when facilitating negotiations. In addition, to advance negotiations of any kind, it is crucial for the mediator to understand the pertinent aspects of the personal relationships between the parties. For example, negotiations between the government and the media got bogged down over and over again because Cabello personally detested Marcel Granier of RCTV. Something similar occurred in the relations between Nicolás Maduro and Asdrúbal Aguiar in the liaison mechanism, as well as between several of the delegates to the table. The OAS and Carter Center did not pay sufficient attention to this point. As mediators, the Carter Center team could have suggested spaces and ways for negotiation that might have allowed the actors to overcome these obstacles and pursue the satisfaction of their interests, or work out their personal issues directly in an appropriate manner.

The third lesson learned from this period is that in political conflicts involving all of society, it is necessary to take a long-term view, even when playing a short-term role. In the Venezuelan case, the political conflict did not reflect a temporary situation but rather the emergence of a fundamental process of social change over time. By its very nature as an international NGO presided by a former U.S. president with a small staff and no permanent country offices, the Carter Center usually defined its role as a transitional, high-level facilitator that is useful primarily in the short run. For this reason, its focus in Venezuela was originally aimed only at high-level negotiations and not at longer-term peacebuilding efforts. However, within the Venezuelan context, the Carter Center achieved a public position unrivaled by other national or international actors. It therefore decided to adopt a long-term view, to forge alliances with groups and organizations with a history in the country and a vocation to stay on (such as the existing national networks and the UNDP), and to favor dynamics in the working groups that would simultaneously optimize the Carter Center's contribution while rendering its role dispensable. Thus, from the stance of a mediator called upon to play a short-term role, it is possible to generate and support peace initiatives that can be self-sustaining.

6

Moving toward the Recall Referendum, November 2003–May 2004

Momentum toward the recall effort picked up speed in November 2003. The Carter Center was very much aware that the polarization and confrontation that was damaging the country's social fabric would not be resolved by a popular vote; on the contrary, it knew that the dynamic of the competition would further deepen the country's divisions and exacerbate the confrontation. In the absence of any other effort to accept diversity and strengthen the coexistence of opposites, the Carter Center launched the Strengthening Peace in Venezuela Program and decided to try one last negotiation effort to establish some mutual guarantees before the recall process began.

Petition drives to collect signatures for the recall began in late November. Although the focus was on recalling the president, the government decided to petition to recall some opposition deputies, and AD similarly decided, without consulting the rest of the Coordinadora Democrática, to collect signatures to recall government deputies. After signatures had been collected, the CNE would then be tasked with verifying the signatures, and citizen signers would then be given a chance to "repair" their signatures if they were questioned by the CNE. The process turned out to be cumbersome and full of delays, as the verification phase alone extended from the prescribed thirty days to more than one hundred days.

After receiving invitations from the CNE in November 2003, the Carter Center and OAS formed a joint international mission to observe the signature -collection and -verification process. Each organization mounted six short-term delegations to monitor the various stages and, in addition, from November 2003 to June 2004 maintained a longer-term field office and employed longer-term observers for this purpose. With the initiation of the signature-collection process, the OAS and Carter Center thus added the role of electoral observer to their previous role of facilitator and mediator. From past experience, the Carter Center knew that it would likely need to facilitate disputes about the rules of the game along the way and, indeed, this was the case throughout the Venezuelan recall process. The Carter Center and OAS mediated disputes among the government, opposition, media, and CNE, and pressed the CNE to refrain from causing nagging delays.

A Last Effort at Negotiation

In a private memo to the Carter Center dated September 30, 2003, Diez wrote:

> The greatest problem regarding the recall referendum is how the two sides are pre-paring themselves to "read" the results, whatever those may be, because the code ac-cording to which this electoral solution is to be interpreted calls for the elimination of the opponent, as has been the case since the beginning of this struggle, since April 2002, and as can be seen by the coup and the strike. The "electoral solution" is in no way a democratic solution. The opposition seeks the recall referendum as a means by which to take power and then be in a position to "eliminate" chavismo. They say so openly and everyone understands it as such. For their part, Chávez is after the failure of the opposition in the referendum as a way to eliminate every challenge to his "revolutionary" project and to consolidate power. Neither side is thinking about coexistence after the elections. That is the biggest challenge.[1]

The Carter Center thus felt it should at least try to get the opposing par-ties to reach some minimum agreements and give each other mutual guar-antees. The Carter Center's unconditional ally in this process, William Ury, was willing to travel again to Caracas, and Diez began to talk with actors on both sides about a "go-between" shuttle exercise with Ury in an effort to "reach consensus" on the rules of the game. This meant basic agreements on the development of the electoral process for both sides, acceptance of the results, and mutual respect during and after the process.

The Coordinadora Democrática was organizing to once again gather signatures intended to activate the recall referendum against Chávez. For the first time, the opposition had been able to unify a campaign command headed by the five most important political leaders. The Group of Five was made up of two "natural" candidates for the presidency on behalf of the op-position (Salas Römer, former presidential candidate of the Proyecto Ven-ezuela Party, and Enrique Mendoza, governor of the state of Miranda), the leaders of the two strongest political parties (Henry Ramos Allup of AD

---

1. For the full text of the memo, see appendix C, *this volume*.

and Julio Borges of Primero Justicia), and the "icon" of the resistance, former PDVSA manager Juan Fernández. The Carter Center hoped that finally it would be able to work with them as a single block. But when it met with the Group of Five to introduce its proposal of a negotiation exercise to be facilitated by Ury and the Carter Center, the group's members seemed reticent. Although they were willing to participate, they seemed very suspicious of each other. Mendoza and Römer studiously ignored each other, while Allup made fun of everyone else and Fernández and Borge went to great pains to disguise their disagreement.

In general, they seemed more concerned about jockeying for position among themselves in an effort to determine who was most important than anything else. With regard to the idea of holding discreet negotiations to ensure minimum guarantees for the upcoming electoral process, Ramos Allup suggested that Chávez invite the five of them to Miraflores for talks, while Salas thought that there should be no talks with the government, as this could be interpreted as a sign of weakness. Julio Borge ended the discussion by clarifying that it was simply a matter of talking to the Carter Center in a go-between exercise, and not a matter of meeting with the government. Finally, it was decided to designate Borge as the Group of Five delegate and that Timoteo Zambrano and Asdrúbal Aguiar, from the table's liaison mechanism, would join the group.

On the other side, the government kept to its usual style, with Chávez monopolizing the decision-making process and sending signals of support both to those supporters who were entirely against allowing a recall referendum and to those who were convinced it was necessary to hold the event and win it. Chávez's position was that of a permanent referee. This made it almost impossible to work with members of the government. After several attempts, McCoy and Diez were able to see Vice President Rangel and the government's strongman at the time, Minister of Information, Diosdado Cabello. Both reacted positively to the idea of opening a negotiation channel, but delegated the responsibility for coordinating the exercise to Nicolás Maduro, the representative in the liaison mechanism. When McCoy and Diez explained the proposal to Rangel, he replied that "you have my green light to set this up, but you can't say you've got my green light." Cabello added that he did not think the opposition would sit down for serious talks, as he had information regarding preparations by extremist groups to carry out acts of violence during the signature-collection process. The Carter Center undertook a number of efforts to set up a sequence of meetings, but the government never appointed its representatives. Nor did Chávez's office respond to the Carter Center's repeated efforts to set up a telephone conversation with Carter until finally, two days before Ury was scheduled to arrive in Caracas in November 2003, Maduro asked the Carter Center to put everything on hold because he could offer no guarantee that the effort met with Chávez's approval. In addition, an account had appeared in a weekly magazine according to which a secret meeting between the Group of Five and the government was being "cooked up" under the auspices of the Carter Center, and this had alarmed opposition leaders. That aborted the last effort at direct negotiation.

The Petition Drive

From then on, interaction between the sides focused on the electoral contest and on gaining the favor of the referee, in this case the recently appointed CNE, in order to wrest some advantage from the opponent. Working jointly with the local OAS representative, the Carter Center organized a couple of meetings with members of the liaison mechanism and the CNE board, but these were formal in nature and lacked substance. The CNE began to function around the axis created by directors Ezequiel Zamora (opposition) and Jorge Rodríguez (government), who were developing a very good negotiating relationship.

The Carter Center's previous work with different levels and sectors in the society now bore fruit in terms of access to the CNE political dynamics. Media owners and political party leaders with whom it had worked provided a direct channel to Ezequiel Zamora, who had always been open to international observation. Simultaneously, one of the members of the Strengthening Peace in Venezuela Program hosted a private dinner for the Carter Center team and Rodríguez. Based on these informal meetings with Zamora and Rodríguez, it was possible to build relations of trust that allowed the Carter Center to work smoothly with them.

The political actors on each side began to restructure their political organizations in preparation for the electoral battle. On the opposition side, the Coordinadora Democrática had the growing leadership of Governor Enrique Mendoza and the technical support of the NGO Súmate (Join in!), which provided human volunteers to collect the signatures and process them in a sort of parallel verification effort.[2] The government, in turn, decided to

---

2. Súmate was a new organization that had been created by young upper-class professionals, many of whom were educated abroad and media savvy. They began collecting signatures during the first oil strike, but when the incoming CNE took over, the signatures were discarded. In the period described here, they had a large number of volunteers, excellent equipment, and good number of technicians willing to once again set out to organize the gathering of signatures.

establish a campaign "commando" at the National Assembly, placing Ismael García, a deputy from an allied political party, in charge of the group. This group had enthusiasm, but not extensive technical skills.

The government approached the initiation of the recall process with trepidation. Even though it was the solution to the political conflict long advocated by the government, once the moment arrived for the signature collection to begin, the government adopted a strategy of obfuscation and tried to avoid a recall by introducing delays and invalidating signatures. If the CNE ended up certifying sufficient signatures for the recall, the delay strategy would give the government more time to shore up its support through economic growth, massive social spending, and the registration of new voters and naturalized citizens.

Collection of Signatures

The first move from the government after the CNE announced the rules for recall referenda was to petition for the recall of opposition deputies. This was motivated by a desire to increase its razor-thin majority in the National Assembly, mobilize its own supporters against the opposition's drive, and diffuse the impact of the recall by extending it from a single person—Hugo Chávez—to multiple elected officials. The CNE decided to hold the government signature collection first on November 14–17, 2003. The weekend was peaceful and well-attended, allowing the country to breathe a visible sign of relief and setting a precedent that the observers could point to in calling for similar calm during the opposition's signature collection two weeks later. The fact that President Chávez and Vice President Rangel went to sign gave heart to opposition leaders who thought that Chávez's and Rangel's participation would legitimize the entire process and make it difficult to question it.

The opposition weekend was indeed peaceful, but President Chávez chose the strategy of alleging a "megafraud" before the four-day signature drive came to a close. This accusation put additional pressure on the CNE during the subsequent signature-verification period. It also angered Gaviria terribly that Chávez would destroy in one public comment the efforts Gaviria had made over the past year to produce the recall scenario. Chávez accused Gaviria and the OAS (without mentioning the Carter Center, even though the Carter Center and OAS had made a joint statement about the acceptability of the signing weekends) of intruding on sovereignty. The OAS therefore determined to walk softly so as to continue its access in the country.[3]

---

3. Jennifer McCoy, personal notes, December 2, 2003.

Verification of the Signatures

After the recall-petition signatures were delivered in December 2003, the CNE implemented a process for verifying them that was quite complex and that took not the prescribed one month to complete but nearly four. Disputes during this period revolved around the tension between efforts to detect fraud and efforts to honor signers' intentions. The government stressed the first concern and the opposition the second, charging that pro-government members of the CNE were unfairly invalidating signatures in order to keep the number below the 2.4 million required to trigger a presidential recall vote.

The government's obfuscation strategy became clear in January 2004 during the verification process when CNE decisions began to be made 3:2 in favor of the government's desired outcome. This was in contrast to the first four months of the CNE's existence, when the five CNE directors assured the Carter Center that they were working harmoniously and making many decisions on the recall regulations unanimously. The Carter Center knew that they were negotiating among themselves, as they were the fulcrum of the national political conflict, and that the results were cumbersome compromises.[4]

President Carter scheduled a trip to Venezuela for the end of January 2004, with the hope that the verification would be completed by then and that he could help both sides accept the final determination of whether sufficient valid signatures had been gathered to trigger the recall. This was always one of the challenges—having to plan far enough ahead of time to accommodate Carter's busy agenda, without knowing the exact pace of Venezuela's political evolution. In this case, the verification was far from complete when Carter arrived. He used his trip to emphasize that the process needed to be brought to a close by the end of February (allowing the CNE a few days beyond the nominal deadline for technical delays) and that the voters' intention should outweigh excessive technicalities. His statement that there should be "no tricks" in the verification was repeated many times by the opposition in subsequent months.

President Carter took advantage of his trip by meeting with Chávez as well. Diez had arranged a meeting between Carter and some social workers, who shared powerful stories about the impact of Chávez's message of hope and empowerment through his social programs (the so-called missions) for

4. McCoy's personal notes from November 25, 2003, include this entry: "CNE—all asserted they're working together as team. Clearly they are negotiating on the part of the two sides and coming to resolutions, representing the interests of both sides. They could work more effectively and professionally if they didn't have to fulfill the roles of negotiators AND arbiters, but at least they're making most decisions by unanimity. They claim to be working as a team at least, and not doing a bad job."

Carter with Gaviria in a press conference at the CNE.
Courtesy of the Carter Center archives.

the residents of the slums. Carter opened his meeting with Chávez with his positive impressions about the social programs and said that he would ask CNN to send reporters to write stories on the missions, to which Chávez responded enthusiastically. Carter then turned to the recall issue, advising that Chávez accept the recall and ensure that it be transparent; he added that it could be a means of demonstrating Chávez's popular support and relegitimating his mandate. Although Chávez responded by citing potential fraud in the signatures, his public comments about the process changed after Carter's visit, becoming much more positive toward the possibility of the referendum.

The verification period beginning in January 2004 was the most contentious part of the entire process, with the rules being devised—and changed—as the verification proceeded. The CNE made one significant and highly controversial decision after it discovered that multiple signatures on the same petition sheet (*planilla*) had similar handwriting within the signers' data. This discovery of similar handwriting on petition sheets presented the largest bloc of signatures questioned by the CNE that could potentially prevent the recall, and represented a significant dilemma for the international observers. The opposition contended that due to the lack of clear regulations, many signature-collection workers (who were party members rather than CNE employees) at the signing centers had helped signers by filling in their basic data and then giving them the forms for signature only. Thus, many petition sheets (each with ten lines for signatures) had the same handwriting for the basic data. Because of the similar handwriting on them, these sheets were referred to as "flat sheets" (*planillas planas*)—a reference to exams copied by one student from another.

Although Carter Center observers had the witnessed signature-collection workers filling in this data, the Carter Center also knew that a provision allowing for roving petition collectors had fewer safeguards and that it would have been theoretically possible to invent signatures. Indeed, some petition sheets shown to the observers actually looked as though the signatures themselves, not just the basic data preceding the signatures, were in the same handwriting. Further, an opposition CNE director had previously admitted to the observers that signatures collected in a prior effort by the opposition (at the conclusion of the 2003 strike) were partially fabricated.

The "flat-sheets" problem led the CNE to introduce new verification criteria in the middle of the process and put into "observation" all of those signatures within the "flat sheets." This decision required a second round of verification of the names that had already been reviewed, and ultimately resulted in more than nine hundred thousand signatures from opposition voters, and more than a million signatures from Chavista supporters requesting the recall of opposition deputies, being questioned and going to the "repair" (*reparos*) period in May.

The announcement that the signatures included into the "flat sheets" would not be immediately validated unleashed a fury among opposition members. Tensions heightened and rumors of coups and violence again circulated. On February 27, 2004, a massive protest was held outside the site of the G-15 summit meeting, and the *guarimba* (violent protest) began. This was the most violent protest to date, with radical sectors of the opposition blocking roads and burning tires, bringing the eastern half of the city to a standstill. (Ironically, the protestors remained in the opposition stronghold, affecting the opposition's own supporters more than anyone.)

The OAS–Carter Center Joint Mission

The OAS–Carter Center joint mission publicly disagreed with the "flat-sheets" decision, as well as with other decisions in which the CNE questioned more than 1 million of the 3.4 million signatures gathered by the opposition to recall the president. According to the division of labor previously agreed upon with the OAS, the Carter Center was in charge of conducting a random sample of the verification procedure to test for bias by CNE review-ers. The Carter Center attempted to determine whether its own observers' assessments produced the same number of validations, rejections, and ob-servations as the CNE workers when following the CNE's own published criteria. The Carter Center included in this assessment an analysis of the handwriting by checking certain predetermined letters for similarities. It did find instances of similar handwriting during the process but in much smaller numbers than the CNE had found—specifically, it found nearly 300,000 fewer cases of similar handwriting than the CNE, or 23 percent versus 31 percent of all signatures in the presidential recall petitions.

The OAS–Carter Center joint mission issued three public statements in early 2004 trying to influence the CNE on this issue.[5] The first state-ment on February 13 followed President Carter's call to privilege the intent of the citizen over "excessive technicalities." The second statement on February 24 made public a proposal that had been privately made to the CNE involving a method to statistically check the extent of the problem of similar handwriting. The third statement on March 2 criticized the deci-sion announced that day by the CNE to pass all of the names with similar handwriting either in the basic data or in the signatures themselves to the May repair period. While expressing disagreement with the decision, the Carter Center and the OAS simultaneously sought to find a mechanism to salvage the process. They urged that negotiations continue to ensure that the repair period would offer a sufficient venue for citizens to either confirm a signature as their own or reject it as fraudulent.

A major reason why the Carter Center criticized the decision rather than condemn it and walk away was because McCoy and Diez knew that if the decision were appealed to the courts, it was highly likely that the Supreme Court would throw out the names with similar handwriting based on a par-ticular interpretation of a vague regulation, thus making it impossible for the required number of signatures to hold the recall to be met. The president of the Supreme Court had said as much to Francisco Diez when he was explain-ing the Supreme Court's interpretation of the law to Diez. Based upon the observers' reports, Diez insisted on differentiating between similar signatures (a few cases) and similar handwriting in the signers' personal data (almost a million cases). This meeting between the president of the Supreme Court and Diez, who expressed the Carter Center's point of view about the "flat sheets," and the strong opinion of the president of the Supreme Court about the need to eliminate all of the "flat sheets" would have later consequences.

---

5. The Carter Center, *The Carter Center and the Peacebuilding Process in Venezuela*, 41–43.

Because the OAS was inclined to stay and it was important for the OAS and the Carter Center to maintain a joint position, the Carter Center felt it could not withdraw alone in protest. Although the Carter Center did not condone fraudulent signatures, it felt there were more than sufficient safeguards in the verification process to protect against them, and that the CNE's decisions were prejudiced against the intent of the petition signers for the recall. The Carter Center's goal was to protect the rights of citizens who wished to petition for a recall. It thus hoped to be able to ensure that the true intent of the signers could be recognized through adequate procedures during the repair period. At no point did the Carter Center advocate to the opposition to either withdraw or continue. It believed that to be a decision for the political parties alone to make.

Facing Criticism from the Government

Although the government had initially favored the Carter Center over the OAS, the active Carter Center role in attempting to facilitate better conditions for the rights of citizens soon led to it becoming the target of virulent government criticism. Francisco Diez, as the Carter Center's "face" in Caracas, became the subject of most of the attacks. For example, in the middle of February, as the "flat-sheets" controversy was heating up, McCoy and Diez went to see President Chávez, who warned Diez that he was overstepping his bounds as an observer and becoming too interventionist. Chávez literally said, "It is as if I invited a friend to spend a few days in my house and suddenly I found him in the door of my bathroom watching my wife take a shower!"[6] Three times in that conversation Chávez warned Diez to be careful. It was clear that the conversation between Diez and the president of the Supreme Court was well known by President Chávez.

Leaving the meeting shaken and depressed, Diez and McCoy talked of the dilemma of combining the role of facilitator with that of observer. Diez, in particular, as a mediator and the field representative of the Carter Center in Caracas, felt trapped between the role of facilitator, as someone trying to help the parties generate options that satisfy the basic interests of all of them, and the role of observer, as someone who judges and reports on what he sees without intervening. He felt personally threatened and believed that he had lost his effectiveness in Venezuela. In that context, the Carter Center planned for Diez to take two weeks off to visit his ailing father in Argentina.

---

6. From the authors' notes.

The CNE also began to publicly criticize the Carter Center, issuing a public statement accusing it of being biased toward the opposition. Meanwhile, the OAS continued to be the subject of irritation to the CNE and to the government, and by the end of the repair period, the CNE was openly calling for the OAS chief of mission to be replaced.

Trying to Advance the Process

In anticipation of the completion of the verification process by February 29, McCoy returned to Venezuela on February 25, the day after the CNE announced that it would send all signatures with similar handwriting to the repair process. The Carter Center privately took the position, and communicated it to Jorge Rodríguez, that if acceptable conditions for the repair process were not provided, it would have to withdraw from the process, even though such a move would be disastrous for the country and a terrible disappointment for the Carter Center's team.[7]

The preliminary results were delayed to March 2. The system had become so complicated, with multiple levels of review and changes of rules, that the CNE's internal system was unable to keep track of the numbers. The CNE told the Carter Center that it was delaying the complete results of the verification process to give the Carter Center time to facilitate negotiations with the political parties on the procedures for the repair period.

The Carter Center had set up a February 29 meeting at the CNE with opposition representatives to discuss the repair period, but the day ended with dueling press conferences. After Diez and McCoy, four CNE directors, and opposition representatives had waited at CNE headquarters two and half hours for the fifth director (representing AD), it became clear that her delay was not due to traffic congestion but rather to her preparing a political statement to read before the press directly on her arrival. Diez and McCoy concluded it was a deliberate attempt to obstruct the negotiations, and an insult to them. They told the CNE that they could not conduct the negotiations in those circumstances. A comical sequence of press conferences ensued between the team and CNE president Carrasquero. As McCoy and Diez left the building, Carrasquero descended to the media area to give a press conference explaining what had happened, adding that the Carter Center was withdrawing its mission from the country. When McCoy and Diez heard this on the car radio, they were shocked; the car's driver immediately turned around so that they could return to the CNE. With the approval of CNE director Jorge Rodríguez, Diez and

---

7. McCoy, personal notes, February 27, 2004.

McCoy both spoke to the press at the CNE to explain publicly that in fact the Carter Center was not withdrawing its mission (to the applause of CNE staff and journalists), and that the Carter Center's representative, Francisco Diez, was returning to his home country only for a few days. Incensed that he had been made to look bad, Carrasquero returned to the cameras to say he had not lied about Diez leaving the country. The private television stations delighted in showing the sequence of dueling statements between the Carter Center representatives and the CNE president. Diez indeed left the country for his planned two weeks leave and McCoy extended her stay in Caracas for two more days to begin the talks between the CNE and the political parties.

Containing the Violence

In addition to trying to mediate the signatures dispute, the Carter Center continued to work with Paz en Movimiento, which helped common citizens in the face of violent protests and a dramatic increase of tensions. Using the networks of dozens of NGOs, the Paz en Movimiento circulated a set of concrete recommendations about how each family could protect itself from the violence and stop confrontations from escalating in tense social and political situations.[8] This simple action led more people and groups to join Paz en Movimiento and on March 14 the organization published its first major document, *Our Greatest Challenge: Constructing Peace.*[9]

As fears rose of a general wave of violence, Paz en Movimiento issued more public statements and organized workshops in an attempt to lower the tension. Although some sectors of the opposition seemed to want to provoke a violent reaction from the government, the government refrained and the protest died out on its own.

Negotiating the Repair Process

When the CNE finally issued a preliminary finding on the number of valid, invalid, and "questioned, but repairable" signatures on March 2, the opposition had to decide whether to participate in the repair process. The procedures for the repair phase had not been written before the end of the verification period, so discussion immediately turned to the conditions for this phase (how many signatures would be validated, rejected, or sent to repairs; how many centers for repair would be opened for how many days; etc.). With negotiations arranged

8. See the text in The Carter Center, *The Carter Center and the Peacebuilding Process in Venezuela,* 46–47.
9. Ibid., 48.

by the international facilitators, the opposition named two experienced negotiators to represent them. On both sides, extremists wanted nothing to do with
the negotiations. Extreme government supporters believed that the opposition
was untrustworthy and had already cheated, and that they should not enter an
electoral competition while the mass media was controlled by the opposition.
Extreme opposition supporters pointed to the "flat-sheets" issue as proof that
the CNE could not be trusted, that it was in the hands of the government, and
that the only recourse remaining was civic rebellion.

The CNE announced yet another set of preliminary numbers on March
7, and it soon became clear that the opposition would not conclude negotiations on the repair period until it had a definitive answer on the number of
signatures that had been validated, rejected, and sent to repairs.

Spurring the Process Along: The Carter-Gaviria Letter to the CNE

The Carter Center and OAS decided to send a private letter from Carter and
Gaviria to the CNE on March 10 expressing their concerns and criticisms
of the verification process and their views of the minimally acceptable conditions necessary to hold the repair period. These conditions included allowing
a large number of signatures under "observation" by the CNE and those that
had been rejected that could be confirmed or denied by the citizens themselves in the repair period, establishing the number of centers needed for the
process, and forgoing the use of new electronic roll books. They hoped in this
way to indicate privately to the CNE the limits of their willingness to condone a problematic process, and to communicate through the CNE directors
what it considered reasonable conditions for the government's and the opposition's participation. The Carter Center was very conscious of the risks of
the letter being made public, which would likely cause the CNE to become
defensive in the face of the criticism and to adopt a harder line in the negotiations, but it felt that the possible benefits outweighed the potential risks.

The story of the delivery of the letter itself illustrates how pure logistics
can potentially derail a mediation effort! From Atlanta, McCoy negotiated
the text of the letter by phone with Carter at his home in Plains, Georgia,
and Gaviria at his home in Washington, DC. After the letter was finalized
and signed later that night, it was sent to the Carter Center's office in Caracas. A Carter Center staff member was sent to retrieve the fax at 11 p.m.,
only to discover the fax machine was out of ink! The next morning, when
Diez tried to hand deliver the letter personally to CNE president Carrasquero at a previously scheduled meeting with the opposition, it turned out

the meeting had been cancelled and no one was at the CNE office to receive the letter.

In the middle of this drama, McCoy spoke by telephone with Jorge Rodríguez at the CNE, telling him she was going to send a letter outlining the Carter Center's concerns and suggestions. Although he expressed a willingness to follow through on the proposals, he was so concerned about a critical letter becoming public that he asked the Carter Center not to formally deliver the letter. Gaviria rejected the idea that the delivery of a letter from the observers would threaten the CNE in any way and said the OAS and Carter Center should either hurry up and send the letter or drop it entirely.

As the Carter Center considered dropping the letter, another technical mishap occurred. Because of a bad phone connection between Diez and McCoy, McCoy understood that Diez had already delivered the letter to the CNE president, and so she instructed her assistant to e-mail a copy of the letter to President Chávez, implementing a basic negotiating tactic of informing the person whom the mediator is trying to influence. Chávez actually received the letter *before* the CNE, then, and thus the Carter Center had no choice but to follow through with sending it to the CNE. Diez finally succeeded in getting the letter to the CNE president and informed the other directors of its existence so that they could directly ask the CNE president for copies. This was meant to minimize the risk of the letter being leaked. Miraculously, the letter was not leaked and it seemed to have had the desired effect of breaking open the logjam, though it would take another month to finalize the rules.

The following day, on March 12, McCoy traveled to Washington, DC, to join the OAS in updating the Group of Friends ambassadors on the process. She and Gaviria discussed the delays in the repair negotiations. Gaviria feared that if the delays were not resolved soon, the entire process would break down and violence could ensue. Indeed, both McCoy and Gaviria believed this was another make-or-break moment in Venezuela.[10]

Resolving Remaining Differences

The repair negotiations bogged down for two different reasons. First, the opening of the nomination period for gubernatorial and mayoral candidates for the upcoming regional elections distracted the parties' attention. Second,

---

10. McCoy wrote in her personal notes on March 12, 2004: "If the negotiations break down over finishing the recall referendum procedure, there are no alternatives left. I would see only a depressed and alienated opposition and an increasingly bold and belligerent government, with the possibility of localized violence escalating to major violence."

the Supreme Court's electoral chamber, dominated by pro-opposition justices, ruled that the petition sheets containing similar handwriting should all be validated, while its constitutional chamber, dominated by pro-government justices, ruled that the electoral chamber had no jurisdiction to make such a ruling since the constitutional chamber had appointed the CNE.

With this division in the Supreme Court, it seemed that Venezuela had lost another institution with the capacity to act as arbiter, and that both the CNE and the Supreme Court had been politicized and divided. Gaviria believed it might take a personal intervention by himself and Carter to break the logjam, but he also knew that every time the international facilitators arrived, the Venezuelans tended to negotiate with them rather than each other.

When the CNE finally announced the procedures on April 14, without complete accord from the opposition, the Carter Center and OAS released a statement calling on all concerned to resolve remaining differences quickly, and President Carter sent a private letter to President Chávez. In a breach of confidence, the government published the letter on the Ministry of Information Web page, highlighting the positive aspects of the letter and neglecting its critical aspects.

Finally, on April 23, the CNE announced the details of the repair period, with Jorge Rodríguez unilaterally lowering a bit the number of signatures that could be repaired. This was a splash of cold water for the opposition, and in particular its negotiators, who lost face among the opposition. The Coordinadora Democrática had to make a very difficult decision. Only those who had previously signed the petitions could go to the repair period. The opposition needed 2.4 million valid signatures to invoke the recall referendum, and only had 1.9 million signatures in hand with this recent announcement by the CNE. It needed to obtain a net increase of 525,000 signatures during the repair. Making matters worse for the opposition, the 1.1 million signers whose signatures had been questioned needed to turn out to the repair centers and reconfirm their signatures on the specified days. Súmate advised the Coordinadora Democrática that the needed mobilization would be nearly impossible.

On top of this, the government had made public the list of signers and many had reported that they were being "punished" for signing—being refused government services such as passport renewals, foreign exchange for travel, etc. The opposition feared that the threat of intimidation would likely lead many to refrain from turning out for the repairs. Finally, the government introduced the notion of the "repentant signer," arguing that citizens should be able to "change their minds" and withdraw their signatures during the repair.

The international observers assiduously refrained from contact with the opposition, wanting the Coordinadora Democrática to make its own decision about whether to participate. In order to avoid pressure from the press and contacts with the opposition, the Carter Center brought Diez to Atlanta for meetings. Five days later, on April 28, the Coordinadora Democrática announced it would participate in the repair. After it agreed to participate, the international observers announced that both Gaviria and Carter, along with teams of international observers, would be present to ensure the integrity of the process.

The government and its supporters seemed taken aback that the Coordinadora Democrática had decided to participate, with some Chavistas telling the Carter Center's team that they had expected the opposition to drop the recall idea and focus instead on the gubernatorial and mayoral elections scheduled for September. With the opposition's decision to go to repair, the government entered a debate between those who believed they should avoid the recall referendum at all costs, and those who thought it better to face the process and relegitimize Chávez's mandate. The government itself reacted in two ways: first, it initiated a round of judicial procedures against opposition leaders, including detaining a mayor and opening a case against Súmate for receiving funds from the U.S. National Endowment for Democracy; second, it sought to "win" the repair phase with a strategy of calling on signers to change their minds and withdraw their signatures through the so-called repent option.

The Repair Process

The presidential recall repair finally took place on May 28–31, 2004, under clear and transparent rules agreed upon by the CNE and the political parties.[11] The OAS and Carter Center sent a joint mission of 120 observers led by Carter and Gaviria, knowing that it would be crucial that both sides accept the results.

The opposition faced an uphill battle in locating and turning out previous signers to confirm their signatures, particularly in light of the reported discrimination against petition signers by government offices and the government's active campaign for signers to "repent" and withdraw their signatures. The op-

---

11. The repair period for the signatures collected by the government to recall opposition deputies were held the previous week and resulted in nine of the fourteen petitioned deputies being subject to recall. The recall vote for deputies was never held as all actors focused on the presidential recall.

position feared that many would not want to bring attention to their position as petition signers, or that they would be subject to government pressure or inducements to change their mind and withdraw their names. The joint international observer mission publicly criticized the "repent" strategy, arguing that the original intent of the repair period was only to allow citizens to confirm their signature if questioned, or to withdraw their signature if it was falsely included on the list. Jorge Rodríguez became so incensed at this statement that he angrily declared in a press conference that he would not meet again with Francisco Diez until Diez withdrew the observers' statement.

On the last day of the repair process, the CNE mysteriously stopped counting signatures. Carter and Gaviria decided in the early evening to visit the CNE to see what was happening. After the Carter Center called the CNE to determine that the CNE president Carrasquero and Rodríguez were still at the CNE, Carter and Gaviria immediately traveled there by motorcade with all of the security and flashing lights due a former U.S. president and sitting OAS secretary general. As the motorcade arrived, the protocol chief called to say that Carrasquero was not there but that the vice president (one of two opposition members of the CNE) would receive Carter and Gaviria. The vice president confirmed that the counting had stopped for unclear reasons and he agreed to show Carter and Gaviria around. While walking through the CNE building, with television cameras following Carter and Gaviria and broadcasting live, Diez received agitated calls from Carrasquero and Rodríguez, both of whom said they had seen them on television and that they were not authorized to move around the building. Diez replied that the CNE vice president had offered the tour and that should be sufficient authorization. Asking why the count had been suspended, he received no satisfactory answer. Informed by Diez, President Carter made a calming statement to the press and the motorcade departed. Five minutes later, Rodríguez appeared on television from the same CNE press location that Carter and Gaviria had just vacated and criticized the unacceptable conduct of the international observers. It was obvious that Carrasquero and Rodríguez had left the CNE to avoid seeing Carter and Gaviria. Nevertheless, the count resumed later that night.

The following morning, the Carter Center team had its previously scheduled appointment with President Chávez and explained what had happened the night before, noting the bad humor the CNE president was in regarding Carter's and Gaviria's visit. President Chávez called the CNE president in the team's presence and personally asked him to meet with Carter to resolve the differences.

The authors briefing Gaviria and Carter about the electoral observation mission. *Courtesy of the Carter Center archives.*

At the meeting with the CNE president, another CNE board member, Oscar Battaglini, who arrived late and had consistently been the most concerned about international intervention in Venezuela's internal affairs, had a heated discussion with President Carter about the proper role of international observers. After Battaglini complained about the Carter Center's "improper intervention," Carter told him sternly that the Carter Center had acted throughout according to international principles of election observation and that he knew that Battaglini was the member who had most obstructed the team's work. Battaglini looked at the floor and could not meet Carter's gaze, nor respond. The opposition vice president who had guided the team on the tour the previous night smoothed over the meeting and the issue was resolved. Battaglini was subsequently put in charge of international observation for the recall vote itself, imposing a number of serious restrictions.

In the end, 700,000 signers confirmed their signatures and nearly 100,000 withdrew their names, producing a final result of more than 2.5 million confirmed signatures, surpassing the required 20 percent (2.4 million) of registered voters to trigger a recall referendum. The CNE announced official results on June 8, scheduling the recall vote for August 15, 2004.

The International Context

Throughout the recall process, the diplomatic community in Caracas was very supportive of the joint OAS–Carter Center mission. The international community had generally favored the recall referendum as a means to help resolve the Venezuelan political conflict and answer the question about the mandate of President Chávez, and a voting process seemed to most to be an appropriate constitutional and democratic method to determine that question. The Group of Friends issued periodic statements supporting the international mission, calling for nonviolence, and urging more rapid movement during the slow verification process. In the United States, interest was keen and multiple academic and policy conferences were held to discuss the Venezuelan conflict.

Although international pressure was not sufficient to speed up a process that eventually took ten months, it was instrumental in bringing to a close the question of whether a recall would be held at all. The OAS annual meeting of foreign ministers (the General Assembly) was scheduled to meet June 6–8 in Quito, Ecuador. The Venezuelan government knew that the United States and other members of the Group of Friends were planning a debate about Venezuela at the General Assembly. As a result, when it had become clear that the opposition had actually succeeded in achieving sufficient signatures and that the OAS and Carter Center would attest to that fact, the government quickly changed tactics and accepted its "defeat." The CNE announced preliminary results on June 3, before the General Assembly began, effectively preempting any debate over Venezuela. Chávez immediately began his campaign, going on live national television to launch his new battle cry, labeling his campaign strategy going into the referendum the "Battle of Santa Ines."[12]

The opposition took a breather after the intense negotiations and repair process, and the international observer mission withdrew to await an invitation to observe the final phase of the recall process—the campaign and recall referendum itself.

Analysis and Lessons

The first lesson learned from this period is the need for clear, timely, agreed-upon rules during electoral processes. Venezuela entered the recall process without a clear set of rules on how to conduct the exercise, which in a climate of distrust exacerbated suspicions and paranoia. Although the Supreme Court's designation of the CNE board initially was greeted with

---

12. As explained to the authors, the Battle of Santa Inés was one in which Bolívar allowed his enemy to enter Bolívar's own terrain, making him feel victorious, and then counterattacked him from a strategic position and defeated him.

relief and acceptance by all sides, the five-member board quickly became the fulcrum of the political conflict. Both the government and the Coordinadora Democrática viewed board members as representatives of their interests, with the consequence that every decision of the CNE represented a negotiation over the larger conflict. As the CNE devised the regulations for the signature-collection process, the negotiation process produced a hybrid process controlled completely by neither the CNE nor the political parties.

The CNE had failed to devise a clear set of rules for the verification before it began and then changed the rules in the middle of the process by questioning more signatures. This produced dismay among the observers, and violence from the opposition. In contrast, the negotiations over the conditions for the repair period was a much more transparent process with clear rules, and the results were accepted by both sides.

The second lesson learned during this period is that changes in the perceived strength of each side affect the willingness of each side to enter into real negotiations. As long as the government felt strong, it did not urge its "representatives" on the CNE board of directors to seriously negotiate clear, fair rules for the signature-verification process, preferring instead to maintain a margin of discretion to impose its own will on the process. However, as the international observers took an increasingly active role in criticizing the process, the opposition felt strengthened. It always believed that it had sufficient signatures but lacked the weight to have those signatures recognized during the verification process. The January 2003 visit by President Carter and several visits by McCoy, the ongoing presence of Diez and OAS mission chief Fernando Jaramillo, and the Carter-Gaviria letter about minimal conditions for the repair period all played a role in putting increasing pressure on the government.

By March 2004, the perceptions of strength had changed to the point that the parties and the CNE were willing to enter into negotiations, and they asked the third parties to facilitate the negotiations. With this international assistance and pressure, the repair period was finally held under satisfactory conditions and both sides could accept the results.

The third lesson learned during this period is that third parties must make tough choices when two or more of their core values are in conflict. In this case, the Carter Center was faced with the decision about whether to withdraw in protest over CNE's treatment of the "flat sheets." It faced a trade-off between preserving the process to determine the will of the people with regard to recalling public officials and protecting the rights of each and every individual citizen who signed. By accepting the CNE's arguments about the "flat sheets," some individual signers were sacrificed (i.e., their signatures would be rejected irrevocably), but the majority would have the opportunity to affirm their signatures in the repair procedure and potentially trigger a recall referendum. In short, by staying and facilitating negotiations to arrive at a compromise, the third parties were thus able to ensure a more transparent and fair process, even while some signers would be negatively affected. Of course, the risk of this compromise was that a referendum would not be triggered, and that the third parties would not definitively know whether there truly were insufficient voters calling for a referendum, or whether those individual signers who had been "sacrificed" would have made the difference. In the end, the presidential recall went forward, despite the disqualification of some of those signers, while many of the recall petitions against opposition deputies failed to gain sufficient signatures as even more Chavista signers were disqualified for similar handwriting. No one seemed to care about those citizens' rights, however.

The fourth lesson learned during this period is that the roles of mediator and observer are distinct, and should be kept distinct. As the recall vote grew nearer, some Venezuelans and particularly other international organizations began to raise the question of whether an international organization could and should simultaneously attempt to mediate and monitor, given that these roles are based on possibly contradictory principles. In the case of Venezuela, the Carter Center team debated this question among itself in 2003 before it accepted the invitation to observe the signature collection. As noted in chapter 2, this dilemma raises two points.

First, there is a potential conflict of interest when an actor who has served to mediate a conflict then also serves to monitor and judge its outcome. At the time, the Carter Center did not view this as a conflict of interest. It realized that judging an outcome is not the same as helping the parties to negotiate agreements about the rules for a process of signature collections that would not yet result in an outcome (as an outcome would occur only if a recall vote took place). The Carter Center knew its role would not change in nature through the signature-collection process, and it viewed the recall process as the continuation of the political conflict and its attempted resolution. In brief, it viewed its mandate to include facilitating the implementation of, and monitoring compliance with, the agreement that it had facilitated.

Second, a mediator will have difficulty maintaining the trust of both parties when he or she must simultaneously evaluate and "judge" the actions of those parties. In the case of the recall process, the Carter Center initially sought to resolve this dilemma by separating Francisco Diez from the observation mission and focusing his efforts instead on the Carter Center's other activities, such as the "third-side" initiative and the mediation with the media. But as the recall process grew more contentious, it became obvious that the Carter Center needed to play a mediating role to help the actors to resolve disputes over the rules, and Diez became more involved in the recall process as a facilitator of the negotiations, even as the Carter Center, in its observer capacity, had to make evaluations and at times had to publicly criticize the process, potentially risking the trust of the actors. As the public face of the Carter Center during much of this period, Diez thus became the target of criticism, particularly by the government.

7

Campaign for the Recall Referendum, June–July 2004

W ith the announcement that the recall would indeed be held, Chávez went into high campaign mode—approaching the campaign as a military battle and immersing himself in an electoral context in which he thrived. Meanwhile, the opposition was exhausted after the long ordeal of getting the recall petition confirmed and disoriented by Chávez's high energy, and the international observers had to await a new invitation from the CNE for this phase of the process. After the experience of the signature-verification and -repair period, the CNE became much more rigid in relation to the observers, who had to negotiate hard to get minimally acceptable access to observe the recall vote.

Reactions to the Recall Announcement

The Government

Chavistas had approached the repair phase with trepidation, fearing both Chávez's wrath if they failed to stop the recall, and fearing loss of power, position, and protection if the recall succeeded. Remembering the persecution of Chavista officials during the short-lived April 2002 Carmona government, Chavista officials and supporters literally saw the recall referendum as an all-or-nothing affair, with everything to lose. Now that the recall had been announced, they remained uneasy.

Speculation abounded as to what strategy the government would choose to respond to the referendum.[1] If the referendum went forward and the president lost, the Supreme Court would have to rule whether he could run in the consequent election (an illogical consequence of a recall vote). Some speculated that

---

1. Gordon Streeb, memo based on interviews in Caracas, Carter Center, June 7, 2004.

Chávez would instead resign in order to trigger new elections in which presumably he could run. Others feared that the government would pursue a strategy of delaying the recall vote until after the August 20 deadline, or of scheduling it so close that the results could be delayed until after that date. August 20 was the deadline after which any successful recall vote would simply mean that the vice president would serve out the remainder of the presidential term—that is, the vote would not trigger new elections.

The recall referendum date was set for August 15 (though the opposition preferred a week earlier to ensure time to count the votes). The Carter Center's team debated which strategy the government would take to defeat the recall referendum, assuming it came to pass. According to the constitution, to successfully recall an official, the number of "yes" votes needed to be (1) more than the number of "no" votes cast in the recall and (2) at least one more than the absolute number of votes by which the official was elected in the first place. In this case, given that President Chávez had won the 2000 election with 3,757,773 votes, those who wanted to recall him needed at least 3,757,774 votes.[2] The government could thus choose a strategy of intimidation in which it tried to depress turnout in order to defeat the referendum under the second condition, or it could campaign in a positive way to encourage its supporters to vote "no" in larger numbers than the opposition and thus defeat the first condition. It soon became clear that the president chose the latter strategy, while the opposition spent valuable time debating whether to choose a potential presidential contender before the recall, and how to organize itself for the campaign.

Chávez approached the recall referendum with enthusiasm, immediately shifting to high campaign mode, a mode in which he excelled. He did change the campaign command, replacing the "failed" Comando Ayacucho—a group of political party leaders supporting President Chávez named after the famous Bolívar battle against Spanish domination—with a new group of campaign managers in the Comando Maisanta. This new group was led by Chávez himself and included political and social leaders selected directly by him, with a hierarchical structure going from the presidency to the electoral districts and finally to the so-called UBE (electoral battle units), of which there was one for each of the voting sites defined by the CNE. He also entered the battle himself, traveling the country, announcing the opening of new "missions" and social programs, and spending lavishly on campaign spots and posters. With rising oil prices, he spent additional oil

---

2. OAS, "Carter Center and the OAS on the Recall Referendum in Venezuela," August 17, 2004, 9.

revenues rather than deposit them in the country's oil stabilization fund as a safety valve to protect against lower oil prices in the future. His strategy was to shore up his popular support through popular spending, enlarge the pool of potential "no" voters, and maintain his influence within the CNE.

Public opinion polls indicated that his strategy was having an impact. Two opposition polls showed Chávez's support rising in June, while the U.S. firm Greenberg and Associates showed a dead heat among likely voters, with 48 percent each for "yes" and "no."[3] An unpublished opposition poll by DATOS in late June actually showed Chávez ahead 51 to 39 percent, which really scared the opposition.[4] Three weeks before the referendum, Chávez's job approval rating had risen to 55 percent based on economic growth, the mission programs, the fact of the referendum as a democratic tool, his effective campaigning, and growing registration rolls.[5]

Three months before the recall, the government enacted the second prong of its strategy to enlarge the pool of potential "no" voters. "*Misión identidad*" (identity mission) used mobile vans to quickly process citizenship applications of long-term foreign residents and provide *cédulas* (national identification cards) for poor Venezuelans who had never received them. This "mission," in combination with the new registrants following the November 2003 petition signing, added a little over 1 million new voters to the roles.[6] When the Carter Center asked an opposition leader if he was worried about these new voters, he said not at all—that most of them would vote against Chávez.

The Opposition

The Carter Center expected the opposition to be triumphant and euphoric at the announcement of the recall referendum. Instead, it seemed exhausted after the long battle over the signatures, and disoriented by Chávez's enthusiastic about-face. The Coordinadora Democrática formed a large, cumbersome campaign coordinating committee, which had a difficult time deciding on strategy. The Group of Five opposition leaders could not agree on the

---

3. McCoy, trip report, July 1, 2004.

4. McCoy, personal notes.

5. McCoy, in conversation with Greenburg and Associates official, August 5, 2004.

6. For an analysis of the growth of the voter list and complaints about it, see the Carter Center, *Observing the Venezuelan Presidential Recall Referendum: Comprehensive Report* (Atlanta, GA: The Carter Center, February 2005), 56, 74–76, www.cartercenter.org/documents/2020.pdf. The Carter Center concluded that although 2.5 million new people had attempted to register between November 2003 and July 2004, only 1.2 million of them were eventually added to the rolls, corresponding roughly to the natural growth rate of the voter list in previous elections.

best timing to announce a presidential candidate should the recall succeed and trigger new elections,[7] much less agree on a candidate. Henrique Salas Römer eventually broke with the other four leaders and stopped attending meetings of the Group of Five. In the end, they decided to defer the decision of a candidate until after the referendum, and Miranda governor Enrique Mendoza served as the most visible face of the opposition in his role as campaign manager.

The impact of these decisions was extremely detrimental to the opposition. The unknowns about an alternative future to Chávez failed to give confidence to those "*ni–ni*" (neither-nor; specifically, neither Chávez nor opposition) sectors in the center of public opinion. One Chavista campaign poster captured the dilemma brilliantly as it depicted an individual on the edge of a cliff, with a big hand pushing from behind and the legend reading: "Don't fall; vote NO." The "yes" campaign itself seemed dispirited, with very little campaign advertising visible in the cities, in great contrast to the government's "no" campaign. The Carter Center was later told by Mendoza that he learned after the vote that the commitments he had received from the AD, the most structured political party within the Coordinadora Democrática, to get out the vote under the campaign 10x10 (a pyramid of ten people each looking for ten additional voters and so on), using money he personally had raised from various sources, had not been fulfilled. According to Mendoza, AD had spent the money on other things and had lied to him about its efforts, because there was very little actual organizational work going on.[8]

As the polls began to show a reversal, with Chávez's support growing in the polls and the opposition's declining, opposition members cited three factors that continued to give them hope: (1) the undecided usually go with the opposition in a vote; (2) there would be a "hidden" vote from those afraid to tell pollsters they intended to vote against the president; and (3) a moderate turnout at historic levels (55 percent) would help them, while a larger turnout would help Chávez (as additional voters, mostly from lower social classes, would be Chavistas).

Reconciliation amid a Campaign?

The Carter Center knew that once the recall date was announced, all energy would go toward winning this new battle. It also knew that both sides

---

7. The Group of Five was composed of Henrique Salas Römer, Enrique Mendoza, Julio Borge, Juan Carlos Fernandez, and Henry Ramos Allup. See chapter 6 for a description of the group.

8. Mendoza, in an interview with Diez, Caracas, November 2005.

viewed the referendum not as a simple measure of the president's continued legitimacy, but as another battle in the war to permanently defeat the other. The logic of any election is a divisive logic, forcing citizens to choose sides. Generally speaking, there is an expectation that the day after the vote, a new national consensus would emerge and the country would accept the results and move forward, always with the knowledge that the losers' fundamental rights would be respected by the victors and that the losing side would have another chance to compete for power in subsequent elections.[9] In the Venezuelan case, however, there was uncertainty and fear on both sides that rights would not be protected, and that the losing side would not necessarily have another chance to compete for power in the future. Thus, "contingent consent" was not assured.[10] The recall was yet one more symbol of the war to control the levers of power in the country, and perhaps the very soul of the country.

As indicated in chapter 6, the Carter Center team knew that the recall vote would not solve the underlying conflict and that it would probably deepen the polarization within the country.[11] Although the team knew the chances of success were low, it felt it had to make one more effort to achieve mutual guarantees, and it began to explore the possibility of a dialogue effort before the referendum and to plan for various postreferendum scenarios for dialogue and reconciliation. At a minimum, it knew that mutual reassurances would be required to protect the rights and basic interests of the losing side and the ability of the winning side to govern. During planning sessions at the Carter Center, the team tried to envision various outcomes, whether a close vote or a wide margin, with each side winning and losing.[12] It put in

---

9. Laurence Whitehead, "Closefly Fought Elections and the Institutionalization of Democracy," *Taiwan Journal of Democracy* 2, no. 1 (July 2006): 1–11.

10. Guillermo O'Donnell and Philippe C. Schmitter, *Transitions from Authoritarian Rule: Tentative Conclusions about Uncertain Democracies* (Baltimore, MD: Johns Hopkins University Press, 1986), 59–60.

11. In testimony before the U.S. Senate on June 24, 2004, McCoy pointed this out: "We should not lose sight of the fact that the *referendum itself will not solve the underlying divisions within Venezuelan society*. It will help to resolve the question as to the level of confidence that the Venezuelan people have in the government of Hugo Chávez at this moment, and it will provide for the citizens to express their will in this unprecedented exercise of participatory democracy. But it will not resolve the fundamental differences with regard to the future direction of the country. *Resolving those differences will take a renewed effort of dialogue* and direct communication among political and social actors to understand one another's grievance. It will take a concerted effort at social reconciliation to heal the trauma that divides cities, neighborhoods and even families." Jennifer McCoy, "The Venezuela Recall Referendum Process," prepared testimony for the hearing of the Senate Subcommittee on Western Hemisphere, Peace Corps, and Narcotics on "The State of Democracy in Venezuela," Washington, DC, June 24, 2004.

12. At different points in 2003 and 2004, the Carter Center conducted internal scenarios analyses to plan its efforts and exit strategy, defining criteria for remaining engaged and for pulling out.

place plans to have President Carter stay in Caracas for several days after the recall vote to begin a dialogue process toward a governability accord no matter what the outcome of the vote.

Earlier, at a conference on Venezuela at Georgetown University in May 2004, McCoy had discussed with Arturo Valenzuela, former U.S. assistant secretary of state for Western Hemisphere Affair and then director of Georgetown's Latin American Center, the possibility of inviting government and opposition leaders to Georgetown in July to discuss an agreement for a postreferendum governability accord. Although the Carter Center knew it would be very difficult for competing political leaders to enter into discussions during a campaign, it believed that it was crucial to begin some discreet conversations between the two camps to discuss what would happen the day after the recall vote and to seek mutual reassurances.

The Carter Center consulted with both sides during a trip by McCoy to Caracas on June 30–July 1. Within the Coordinadora Democrática, AD leader Henry Ramos Allup wanted dialogue over electoral conditions but preferred to wait for other issues until after the recall. He did acknowledge, however, that the judicial question would be important during the campaign in the wake of intimidation arising from political detentions (e.g, Súmate leaders under indictment and opposition Mayor Henry Capriles under pretrial detention) and invasions of private property and party headquarters. Primero Justicia leader Julio Borges agreed that a preagreement before the referendum would be good to reduce the stakes of the referendum and make it less confrontational. According to Borges, the dialogue should not involve the principal leaders but rather interlocutors with some political weight. Governor Mendoza, privately, was the most open to dialogue and was preparing for both victory and defeat. He thought a discreet dialogue in the second half of July, as both sides began to get scared about losing the recall, would be appropriate, and he identified three themes for a potential governability accord: decentralization, popular participation, and poverty. He feared that leaks would politically damage anyone who participated. So he proposed starting the process with nonpolitical interlocutors who might meet at Georgetown and focusing at first only on electoral issues.

President Chávez told the Carter Center that he would authorize his top deputies to participate in a dialogue on the conditions for the recall vote, and that a dialogue on judicial issues and fighting poverty after the recall would be important. His concern about the judiciary was the opposite of that of his opponents—he was concerned about weak or corrupt judges unable to prosecute criminals, including, in his view, the oil strikers, and said that the new judicial law under discussion in the National Assembly should strengthen the judicial system. He feared, however, that any prerecall dialogue involving himself directly would give the impression that he was negotiating his departure. He promised to consider the offer of discreet meetings at Georgetown. In the end, the government never responded and the initiative withered.

Meanwhile, the Carter Center had to prepare for the expected invitation from the CNE to observe the final phase of the recall effort—the campaign and August 15 vote. It decided to continue with its previous efforts at mediation between the government and the media and to strengthen the "third-side" public space with its intermediate-level reconciliation efforts.

The Third Parties during the Campaign

After the repair period ended in early June, the OAS functionally withdrew from the country, leaving the Carter Center alone to pursue its conciliation efforts through the Strengthening Peace in Venezuela Program and renewed negotiations with the media, this time involving the public and private media directors and the CNE. One of the things Carter discussed with Chávez at the end of the repair period was the need to have balanced media access and treatment during the recall campaign. Chávez agreed at that time to have William Ury return to Venezuela in late June to begin discussions with the media. In the meantime, a meeting took place that shook all of Venezuela and many outside of Venezuela: a private meeting between media magnate Gustavo Cisneros and President Chávez, facilitated by Jimmy Carter.

Carter-Cisneros-Chávez Secret Meeting

Chávez had publicly labeled Gustavo Cisneros as public enemy number one, and his followers put up color posters around the city accusing Cisneros of masterminding the April 2002 coup and using his television station to continue antigovernment propaganda. In the spring of 2004, government harassment of the Cisneros family and its property and television station had increased, and included a raid on one of Cisneros's farms in reaction to the nearby discovery of a mysterious military training camp for young Colombian soldiers whom the government accused of being brought into Venezuela illegally by the opposition in May.

Carter had a personal relationship with both men, and throughout the Carter Center's efforts in Venezuela since 2002, he had tried to get them together, believing that a better mutual understanding between them could help lower the tensions in the country. At the time of the repair period in late May 2004, Cisneros was particularly concerned about the safety of his family in Venezuela, given Chávez's statements that singled him out, and he was thus ready to meet with Chávez. Carter privately proposed the meeting to Chávez right after the repair process concluded and Chávez agreed to a meeting, perhaps motivated by the knowledge that he would need an arrangement with the private media to get out his campaign message for the recall. A June date was planned and arrangements were made to hold a very discreet meeting on the island of La Orchila in a government residence. At the last minute, Chávez asked for the location to be changed to the military headquarters in Caracas, Forte Tiuna, claiming he had to stay in the city for pressing matters. Cisneros and Carter reluctantly agreed and they arrived at the main airport, Maiquetia, in Cisneros's plane, ready to board a helicopter to travel directly to Forte Tiuna.

News of the meeting soon leaked as airport workers recognized Cisneros and Carter. The airport workers notified one newspaper reporter who broke the story, and the rest of the media became incensed that the Carter Center had not informed all of them at the same time. It took McCoy another twenty-four hours to get approval from both Chávez and Cisneros for a brief statement acknowledging the meeting, and each man then followed with their own interpretation of events.

The meeting itself was conducted with only the three of them present, with Carter facilitating. The results of the meeting as acknowledged by Chávez and Cisneros included a mutual recognition of their respective positions as a legitimate president and as a business owner with a significant interest in the country;[13] a commitment to honor constitutional processes and support discussions to be led by William Ury between the government and the news media in preparation for the recall referendum; and agreement on the need for a national dialogue after the recall vote. Chávez and Cisneros also agreed on two liaisons to facilitate communication between them, and a few weeks later the government purchased advertisements on Cisneros's television station. After the recall, the station dramatically toned down its political rhetoric and returned to its original focus as a station of popular soap operas and children's shows.

News of the meeting shocked Venezuelans, causing confusion among Chavistas about why their leader would meet with the principal "*golpista*"

---

13. A colleague mediator from Argentina, Gachi Tapia, was asked by the Cisneros team to give advice to him prior to this meeting. She stressed the importance of "recognition" as a powerful tool in negotiations. See the discussion regarding theory in chapter 10.

and leading to absurd conspiracy theories among the opposition that the three men had negotiated the outcome of the referendum. In reality, it was simply a conversation, an exchange of views about the polarized state of the country, and a chance to talk about how to make the recall happen and how the country could move forward after the recall in a more unified spirit.

Making it public, nevertheless, served Chávez's purpose of neutralizing Cisneros's leadership among opposition forces, because the most radical opposition members considered him a traitor. On Chávez's side, although some sectors were shocked, no one challenged Chávez's decision. Chávez himself framed it as a need for preserving the people's rights. He explained, "I would negotiate with Lucifer if needed to defend the people and the revolution."

Negotiations between the Media and the CNE

The CNE had announced that it would issue a regulation about campaign coverage by the media. With Ury's pending late June visit already approved by Chávez and Cisneros, the Carter Center approached the private media owners, the public media, and CNE director Jorge Rodríguez. Diez offered to work with them on a draft text about the rules the CNE planned to issue to regulate media coverage during the campaign, and all accepted his and Ury's mediation.

After six drafts, produced through a "single-text" methodology,[14] the public and private media owners, in consultation with two CNE directors, agreed on "points of consensus to support a transparent and balanced campaign," which could serve as an input to the CNE.[15] An important and innovative point in Venezuela was that the CNE would "contract" space in each media outlet and distribute it equitably to the "yes" and "no" campaigns.[16]

The CNE approved the media regulation at the beginning of July. Directors of two of the most vocal opposition stations—Cisneros's Venevisión and the twenty-four-hour news station Globovisión—told McCoy on July 1 that the meetings with the CNE directors had been excellent and that they were ready to start implementing the media agreement. The two directors also agreed that RCTV's broadcasts of personal attacks on CNE director

---

14. The "single text" methodology implies that the mediator writes a first draft of an agreement after extensive talks with each side. The mediator will then work separately with each side to develop the agreement further until a single coherent text is reached that is approved by both parties.

15. See text of the agreement in The Carter Center, *The Carter Center and the Peacebuilding Process in Venezuela*, 69–70.

16. Unlike the legal codes in most of the continent, Venezuelan law had no provision for the public financing of campaigns or for required access to the media.

Jorge Rodríguez were counter to the media agreement. RCTV had alleged that Rodríguez bought an expensive new apartment with illicit funds and broadcast the address of the apartment, inviting harassers. Even opposition CNE director Ezequiel Zamora defended Rodríguez and chastised RCTV director Marcel Granier. By the middle of July, three of the four opposition television stations were broadcasting the political ads of the "yes" and "no" campaigns and the CNE voter education spots, abiding to the agreement, with the sole exception being RCTV.

Probably the most sensitive aspect of the negotiated agreement was a monitoring mechanism of media behavior. During the negotiations, Ury and Diez were trying to figure out how the agreement could be enforced, when out of the blue came a call to McCoy from a Norwegian professor offering a proven method of media monitoring. Stein Ove Grosund and his Swedish colleague Tomas Anderson had developed and used a methodology to train students to code television news and advertisements in order to measure neutrality of coverage and equality in ad placement. The Carter Center incorporated into the observation project the Nordic team, which immediately began training Venezuelan students (Chavista and anti-Chavista) to code not only news but also talk shows, as part of the agreement called on public television talk shows to invite opposition spokespersons and private television talk shows to invite government spokespersons.

By the end of July, after the Carter Center reported the first results of the media monitoring project to the private and public media, there was a dramatic improvement in neutrality and balanced coverage across the board.[17] Media access and coverage had been the government's biggest concern, and the private channels were showing the government's ads as promised. The public stations, on the other hand, still showed some pro-government bias and the *"cadenas"*—obligatory government speeches—continued, leading the private stations to air more anti-Chávez programs to balance out the pro-Chávez "cadenas."[18] Two days before the referendum, the final meeting between the CNE and the broadcast media directors occurred, with Carter Center facilitation. The CNE asked for help in maintaining equilibrium over the next three days, as well as a commitment not to air results or exit polls before official results. The public station and three of the private stations agreed to this request. RCTV did not make a commitment because its legal representative was not present.

---

17. For results, see the second report of the monitoring group in The Carter Center, *The Carter Center and the Peacebuilding Process in Venezuela*, 71–74.

18. McCoy, memo, July 27, 2004.

The Strengthening Peace in Venezuela Program

With the support of the UNDP for some activities and other partners and donors for others, the Carter Center continued working with the Strengthening Peace in Venezuela Program to generate a nonconfrontational public space. In an attempt to normalize the role of journalists in this polarized context, one initiative brought in foreign experts for a journalism training program on covering electoral processes. Another initiative led to an agreement with the Venezuelan newspaper that had the largest circulation—*Ultimas Noticias*—to include an eight-page insert on the two Sundays prior to the referendum that presented ideas and basic guidelines for peacebuilding, conflict resolution, and tools for citizens to defend their rights.

Finally, the group of intellectuals who had formed Aquí Cabemos Todos worked intensively in the weeks leading up to the referendum to communicate a message of national unity, tolerance, and reconciliation. It convened discreet political dialogues, invited social organizations to meetings, and issued an important press communiqué shortly before the referendum. One excerpt from the communiqué in which Diez actively worked with the members of the group captures the essence of the message: "We believe that the recall referendum can contribute to building the peace only if its results are accepted and attitudes of retaliation, persecution, and revenge against those not favored by the vote are avoided. Recognizing the losers as valid and legitimate interlocutors is a necessary step toward the coexistence of those holding divergent points of view."[19]

The Carter Center used one of the formal meetings between the media directors and the CNE to allow the group to present the communiqué in a televised context. It was a powerful expression of a nonpartisan group of intellectuals expressing the exhaustion of many Venezuelans with the political conflict.

The Problematic Invitation to Observe the Recall Referendum

Jorge Rodríguez had privately told Francisco Diez near the end of the repair period that the CNE would not accept an OAS mission for the recall itself. The CNE had already pushed for OAS chief of mission Fernando Jaramillo to be replaced, even before the repair process was over, and now Venezuela moved to block the OAS from sending an observer mission. This would have been a personal defeat for Gaviria, who was ending his ten-year term as secretary general in September of that year. Chávez told Jennifer McCoy

19. The Carter Center, *The Carter Center and the Peacebuilding Process in Venezuela*, 78.

Aqui Cabemos Todos press conference with the CNE directors. Seated from left to right: Jennifer McCoy, Jorge Rodríguez, Mireya Lozada, Eziquiel Zamora, Sobella Mejias, and Walter Pecly. *Photo by the authors.*

at the end of June that he had been very close to ejecting the OAS from the country during the repair period, but that Gaviria had come to see him and worked it out.[20] For the recall vote, he hoped that the Carter Center would be more diligent in its search for fraud and that the OAS would name a diplomat to lead its mission rather than secretariat staff.

In the first week of July, with no invitations yet issued by the CNE to observer organizations, Gaviria arranged to meet CNE president Carrasquero discreetly to discuss the form of OAS observation. Rodríguez was concerned, however, that Carrasquero would end up in a dispute with Gaviria and he asked Francisco Diez to help. Diez met Gaviria at the airport and put him on the phone with Rodríguez to discuss the terms so that Rodríguez could "prepare" Carrasquero. As in many other situations, the Carter Center was "facilitating" the dialogue between the OAS and the government representatives, in this case the CNE directors close to Chávez. The CNE wanted a mission headed by a diplomat, not Jaramillo or Gaviria. In the end, Gaviria agreed to name a diplomat as chief of mission and agreed to attend the recall vote as secretary general.

As the CNE geared up for the recall referendum and the OAS temporarily departed from the country, the Carter Center engaged in discussions about conditions for electoral observation. In late June, the CNE approved a new regulation with additional restrictions for international observers, appointed a subcommittee to liaise with international organizations, and named the hard-liner Oscar Battaglini (with whom President Carter had had the run-in in May) to head that commission. Battaglini announced his vision of international observation: observers would come to the country two days prior to the event, would be escorted by the CNE to locations previously chosen by the CNE, and would be limited in numbers. McCoy traveled to Caracas at the beginning of July to explain to the CNE that while Battaglini's vision might be suitable for invited guests, the professional and independent international observer missions of organizations like the OAS, the European Union, and the Carter Center operated very differently. Such missions included long-term observation of the campaign and preparations, complete freedom of movement within the country, access to the technological aspects of the process, and sufficient credentials for the number of observers the organizations deemed necessary.

Diez had begun negotiating an agreement with Jorge Rodríguez that would give the Carter Center all of the access it needed to the technological components of the process. McCoy finalized and signed that agreement

---

20. McCoy, trip report.

during a mid-July trip, when the Carter Center finally received on July 15 its formal invitation from the CNE, one month before the recall vote. She had a positive meeting with Battaglini and seemed to come to agreement with him on the Carter Center's needs for a professional and independent observation mission. The Carter Center's technical consultants and observers immediately began their work (the mission director had been in the country since July 1, anticipating the invitation).

Meanwhile, the OAS was negotiating a new chief of mission and Gaviria chose the Brazilian ambassador to the OAS, Walter Pecly. The Brazilian government of Luiz Inácio Lula da Silva was known to be friendly, though not blindly so, with Chávez and also to resist an interventionist approach. It would be Pecly's first observer experience. He arrived in Caracas with the goal of winning the confidence of the CNE and soon developed positive relationships with most of the actors in the country. When it came time to negotiate the OAS agreement with the CNE, however, he was alone in the country with his political advisers, without the electoral experts of the OAS. The agreement he signed in the second half of July was more restrictive than the one the Carter Center had previously signed with Jorge Rodríguez, and in particular seemed to limit the ability of the observer missions to make public comments.

The CNE then informed the Carter Center that its agreement with Rodriguez's operational division was not valid, and that it must sign an agreement similar to the one signed by the OAS. Battaglini was so incensed about the Carter Center's agreement with Rodríguez that he wrote a scathing letter to President Carter and began to publicly criticize the Carter Center. CNE president Carrasquero also wrote a letter of complaint to President Carter and called in Diez to bawl him out. Thus, the differences among the directors once again became public. Further, Battaglini began to treat the Carter Center differently than the OAS, arguing that since it was an NGO, it would be limited to fewer observers than the OAS, and fewer than it had requested. The roles had been reversed—now the OAS was the "friend" of the CNE and the Carter Center the "enemy." The Carter Center's team surmised that some of Chávez's advisers feared Carter's influence over Chávez and were behind Battaglini's attempts to restrict the Carter Center's ability to observe and his efforts to invite a number of international "personalities" to dilute the international message.

McCoy and the Carter Center's new election director in Caracas, Edgardo Mimica, spent much valuable time in July negotiating and pressing on the conditions the Carter Center needed to observe the recall. The CNE ran hot and cold throughout July and early August, in some meetings seeming to be convinced by the Carter Center's arguments about its methodology and need for independence, but then issuing new requirements or trying to impose new restrictions.[21] It was quite nerve-racking because the Carter Center had to book flights and transport its observers to the country, without knowing if they would even be awarded credentials to observe! Carter Center election observers are all volunteers who receive no compensation other than for their travel expenses, which are paid for by funds that the Carter Center raises entirely outside of the country being observed. The Carter Center's observers are experienced election monitors and country experts, many of whom had participated in numerous election observation missions throughout the world, whether with the Carter Center, the OAS, the European Union, or the Organization for Security and Co-operation in Europe. Likewise, OAS observers are volunteers with long experience in election observation. In the end, the CNE gave the Carter Center the number of credentials it sought, complete freedom of movement in the country, and access to the relevant technological components, with the exception of the central tabulating computer. It also tolerated the Carter Center's public comments.[22]

The European Union sent an exploratory mission to Venezuela in early July but concluded that the time was too short and the conditions too restrictive for it to consider an observer mission. In reality, the CNE was not inclined to invite it at any rate. In contrast to the Carter Center and OAS, the European Union had had no presence during the earlier phases of the recall process and would be starting fresh in the country only six weeks before the vote. Nevertheless, it was a difficult decision for the Carter Center to accept the CNE's invitation and negotiate in the minimal conditions it needed. The Carter Center was in the midst of discussions with the United Nations and other observer organizations to develop a set of principles for election observation, including not only a code of conduct to guide observer

---

21. In one surreal sequence of conversations, Carrasquero told McCoy in mid-July that he would resolve with Battaglini the issue of the number of observers to meet the Carter Center's needs. He then told President Carter by phone in late July that the OAS chief of mission had accepted a lower number of observers than the Carter Center had previously agreed with Gaviria as its minimum, and President Carter told Carrasquero the number was insufficient. Carrasquero then told Diez that President Carter had accepted the CNE's limits! He had either just lied twice, or had a serious case of psychological cognitive dissonance.

22. The Carter Center did not believe access to the tabulation computer site was necessary, since it would not be able to see inside the computers, and since it had statistical means to verify the tabulation of voting results. On the other hand, the CNE did disrupt the work of the Carter Center's long-term observers spread throughout the country during the campaign, arguing in late July that they were not authorized to meet with local election workers. The Carter Center got around that restriction by putting in writing to Battaglini all of its plans for meetings.

behavior in a country but also the minimum conditions needed to be able to observe. As a result, the Carter Center felt that it should comply with those emerging principles and thus worked hard to negotiate the minimally acceptable conditions it finally got from the CNE.

Although the Carter Center considered withdrawing at various points, Gaviria insisted it was very important that both the Carter Center and the OAS be there for the recall, even if his own hands were tied since his chief of mission had already signed the restrictive agreement. The Carter Center worried that its withdrawal would create incredible tension in the country. It agreed with Gaviria on two nonnegotiable conditions for continuing its observation: freedom of movement and sufficient numbers of credentials for its observers. If the OAS and Carter Center delegations arrived and were prevented from deploying around the country two days before the vote, the OAS and Carter Center would withdraw. As for the restrictions on public statements, Gaviria interpreted that to refer to his chief of mission and not himself, and that if things went badly he would ignore the restrictions.[23]

The Carter Center negotiated a clause in its own agreement with the CNE that stated that it would give the CNE its final report before making it public and that the Carter Center would give the CNE weekly confidential reports with its observations and recommendations, but that it always maintained its right to inform the international community throughout the electoral process. As a courtesy, the Carter Center also gave the CNE copies of its press releases before issuing them publicly, even if just an hour before.

Electoral Issues of Concern during the Campaign

Both sides were nervous and expressed various concerns before the recall vote. The opposition leaders denounced numerous unfair conditions and proclaimed that the playing field was not level. Nevertheless, in the weeks leading up to the recall vote, they did not seriously consider in public or in private conversations with the Carter Center withdrawing from the race. (The Carter Center was later told by others that the opposition was split over whether to continue with the process or to sabotage it, as its internal polls showed Chávez with an increasing likelihood of defeating the recall.)

The issues of concern to each side in the lead up to the recall vote included the new voting machines and thumbprint machines purchased by the CNE, the voter's list, election-worker substitutions, and access to the media. In

---

23. McCoy, memo to President Carter, July 27, 2004, author's private collection.

addition, the international observers were concerned about late regulations and contingency plans.

New Machines

The CNE had contracted with a little known company named Smartmatic in November 2003 to build new touch-screen voting machines to replace the previous optical scan machines produced by the U.S. company ESS and operated by the Spanish company INDRA in the 1998 and 2000 elections. In addition, the CNE proposed to use new machines to identify voters through their thumbprints. These machines were produced by the same U.S. company, Cogent, that produced the U.S. fingerprint machines used at immigration counters in U.S. airports. The goal was to build a national database of voters and prevent double voting. The main concern expressed by the opposition was that the thumbprint machines would slow down the vote.

Although the new technology appeared impressive, the Carter Center felt that introducing new technology in the midst of a tension-filled electoral process, with deep distrust among the political actors, and on short notice, was extremely risky. It would be difficult to build confidence in the process and could produce a volatile situation, especially if the vote were close.

When the recall was convoked by the CNE in early June, the opposition called for a manual vote while the CNE insisted on an electronic vote, citing the 1997 electoral law requiring automated voting. Concerns about the voting machines were expressed both by the government and the opposition. Nonetheless, in the days immediately prior to the August 15 vote and after simulations with the machines, neither the government, nor the opposition, nor the international observers expressed serious reservations about the voting machines. The only serious dispute was whether the machines should first print the results and then transmit them electronically to central headquarters, or transmit them first and then print them. The CNE decided, with the consent of the directors representing the opposition, that the machines would simultaneously transmit and print the results, meaning in effect that the printing would conclude after the transmission.

The opposition thus accepted the voting machines but called for a parallel count of the paper receipts produced by the machines. The final compromise agreement was to hold a "hot audit" of 1 percent of the voting machines, to be identified by a statistical sample drawn in the afternoon of the recall vote, which would allow a comparison of the paper receipts with the electronic tallies and thus confirm or question the validity of those results.

Voter's List

The electoral registry had been an issue for several months prior to the re-call due to concerns that the number of eligible voters had grown too large too fast and that the number of dead people on the list was too large. The national NGO Súmate performed two audits of the voter list, one based on the August 2003 cutoff of registration prior to signature collections in No-vember 2003, and one in July 2004 based on the cutoff of registration prior to the recall referendum. The first audit found less than 2 percent error rate in names, ID numbers, and deceased still on the list. The CNE did work to clean the names of the deceased from the list, leading the second Súmate audit in July 2004 to show error rates of less than 1 percent, well within international norms. A technical adviser to the Coordinadora Democrática even called for citizens to take advantage of the express registration to vote, saying that 3 million citizens were still not registered to vote and that the opposition should abandon its "paranoia" about the express ID process, since those citizens would politically behave like the rest of the country (implying that they would not necessarily vote Chavista). He reiterated that the audits of the opposition to date indicated no fraudulent activity.[24]

The primary concerns expressed by the opposition prior to the recall focused on unrequested changes of location of voting booths (or "migra-tions") for some voters and problems in registering Venezuelans abroad. The issue was whether opposition voters were being deliberately moved to new, unknown voting locations, potentially too far away to reach on voting day. The CNE reported that it had received complaints from a little less than 1 percent of registered voters regarding their address and voting location, and had resolved the majority of them. Súmate's second audit concluded that about 0.5 percent of voters had either been relocated or were not found at the addresses reported. A Carter Center analysis found that of the 64,000 unexplained relocations, only 30 percent corresponded to voters who had signed the recall petition and thus the problem did not appear to be targeted to Chávez opponents.[25]

Election-Worker Substitutions

A third issue arising prior to voting day was the indication by some directors of the CNE that poll workers who had signed recall petitions (against the president or against legislators) should be replaced since they had already

---

24. *El Nacional,* June 20, 2004.
25. The Carter Center, *Observing the Venezuela Presidential Recall Referendum,* 58.

exhibited partisan bias. The opposition argued strongly against this provision, and in the end, the CNE decided not to replace such poll workers. Nevertheless, credentials to poll workers who had been chosen by lottery from among registered voters, and who had already received training, were delivered only in the five days prior to the vote. Carter Center observers received many complaints from citizens who claimed that they had been chosen and had received training, but that when they went to retrieve their credentials, they were not on the list. In addition, the CNE confirmed that some municipal-level election officials were changed in the two weeks before the vote, without explanation.

Given the level of suspicion and the direct complaints the Carter Center received, both President Carter and Secretary General Gaviria were prepared to raise these issues about election workers in their meeting with the CNE directors on the eve of the recall referendum. Directors with opposition and government sympathies reassured Carter and Gaviria that no poll worker had been replaced because of partisan loyalties. The opposition directors specifically said that the issue of last-minute replacements of municipal officials had been satisfactorily resolved, with about 200 of 2,000 municipal officials being replaced for expressing a political opinion, as is normal. This report thus left the international observers with no basis for complaint.

Electoral Regulations and Contingency Plans

In addition to the above concerns, the international observers also made observations and suggestions on another issue of concern prior to the recall: the late issuance of regulations and contingency plans. Contingency plans are essential for a stable electoral process, and only clear rules, known beforehand, can guarantee a peaceful process. Like the signature-verification process, the CNE was making up the rules as it went along, since no referendum law existed. Several late regulations clearly had an impact on the perceptions of the process once the vote was concluded. One of those had to do with contingency plans if the voting machines failed. In the weeks leading up to the vote, as the population grew more nervous, no one knew whether a failed machine would mean switching to manual votes, suspending the vote, or shifting the entire system to manual if a certain number of machines failed. Given the lack of confidence and distrust among the parties to begin with, this kind of uncertainty fueled rumors and anxiety.

Another issue was the military vote. Due either to a failure in communication or to security reasons, the CNE did not receive from the military the location of individual soldiers, information needed to add them to the printed list of voters for each voting precinct. Consequently, the CNE gave blank voting lists to the precincts, fueling speculation that either people would be able to vote multiple times on the blank lists, or that the secrecy of soldiers' votes would be violated.

The issue that caused the biggest problem, however, was the confused and late regulation over the "hot audit." The regulation was issued only three days before the vote and did not even state clearly that the "yes" and "no" votes should be counted, leading some centers to count only the total number of votes! The poll workers, the military, and the parties were unclear on the procedures, leading to a poorly executed audit that nearly derailed the entire referendum, as will be explained in chapter 8.

The International Context

Throughout this period, the international community paid close attention to Venezuela, although the OAS issued no further resolutions or declarations prior to the recall. The United Nations followed the process closely and Secretary-General Kofi Annan kept in touch with both Gaviria and Carter. Annan wanted the OAS and Carter Center to take the lead and reach out to the United Nations as a last resort. In addition, Annan communicated to Chávez the importance for dialogue.[26] The U.S. Senate held a hearing in June about the recall, at which McCoy testified. In early July, the CNE sent Carrasquero and Rodríguez to Washington, DC, to inform the policy community about its preparations for the recall.

The Carter Center communicated frequently with the OAS and foreign governments to inform them about its perceptions of what was taking place in Venezuela, explain the problems with the international observation, and seek their help in encouraging the Venezuelan government to be more accommodating to the requirements of observers. McCoy talked with the Brazilian and Mexican Foreign Ministries prior to Chávez's meeting with Presidents Lula and Vicente Fox in early July, to explain the constraints the CNE intended to impose on the observers and why that was unacceptable to the Carter Center. It was especially important for the Brazilians to understand the Carter Center's model of election monitoring and the international principles it followed while negotiating with the United Nations and others, since a Brazilian diplomat was named head of the OAS delegation.

---

26. UN Department of Political Affairs official, in conversation with McCoy, August 3, 2004.

In the meeting with Lula and Fox, Chávez told them that he was receptive to making the observer regulations more flexible but that he recognized there was one radical member of the CNE. He was pleased that the OAS mission would be headed by a Brazilian ambassador and mentioned he would like to have the United Nations present as well. He also mentioned his respect for President Carter.[27]

The Brazilians sent a team of "e-voting" experts in July, invited by the Foreign Ministry, to make a private assessment of the Venezuelan voting machines. The delegation included the inventor of the Brazilian touch-screen voting machines, which had already been used in Brazil for several elections without paper receipts and with apparent public confidence.

The CNE invited many international personalities who were interested in the process and mostly sympathetic to the revolution to attend the recall referendum. In addition, the Costa Rica–based election institute CAPEL organized a delegation including other election officials from Latin America that followed the prescribed CNE observation program.

Analysis and Lessons

The first lesson learned from this period is that third-party actors must understand the meaning that each party in the conflict is giving to an event, and strive to influence and change that meaning in a way that will help each party to move toward a mutually acceptable solution by reducing the stakes involved. In this case, each side perceived the recall referendum as another opportunity to eliminate the other. It was thus a fundamentally undemocratic view. This was in stark contrast to the reading of the international community, which by and large favored an "electoral solution" to the conflict as a peaceful, constitutional, and democratic means of answering the question of whether President Chávez enjoyed the needed popular support to continue his mandate.

The Carter Center knew that neither side could envision a means of coexistence after the recall vote. Chavistas clearly perceived that if they were ousted, they would not only lose their position but also their freedom, their property, and perhaps even their lives; at the same time, many opponents clearly perceived that Chavismo was installing a repressive regime that would deprive them of their property, freedom, and way of life. The Carter Center believed it was fundamental to try to influence those perceptions before the recall referendum and to help both sides reframe the referendum more as the

---

27. Brazilian official, in telephone conversation with McCoy after the meeting, July 8, 2004.

international community was looking at it. The Carter Center thought it had an opportunity because each side believed it could win, but also knew it could lose. It therefore sought to make clear to each side that, if it lost the vote on August 15, it would not lose everything; in other words, the Carter Center sought to reduce the stakes of the recall vote.

The second lesson learned during this period is that attempts to reduce the stakes before an electoral process are constrained by electoral competition. The Carter Center thought that if there were no talks toward mutual reassurances before the recall, there would be none after, because the confrontation would escalate as the winner tried to assume complete power and the loser, not completely eliminated, would resist. Its efforts failed, however, as both sides perceived that any approach to the other side would be seen as a weakness before the final "battle" of August 15 and thus reduce their electoral support. Even when the Carter Center tried to run a secret "go-between" exercise, the menace of a leak prevented both sides from entering into it.

The third lesson learned during this period is that multiple decision points are presented to third parties during the course of an election observation to either continue or withdraw from the process. Each point requires careful consideration, even if with incomplete information. During this time period, the Carter Center faced two decision points: first, whether to accept the anticipated CNE invitation to observe; and second, whether to stay in the country after the CNE initially refused its conditions.

On the first decision point, the Carter Center staff considered the dilemmas presented by the conflicting roles of mediators and observers discussed in chapter 6. Given the fact that the process had become 100 percent electoral in nature, they made their decision from the point of view of an international election observer. They believed at the time that no other organization, outside of the OAS and Carter Center, could or would observe the process. They knew the European Union would send an exploratory mission, but they also knew that time was too short and the conditions too restrictive for the European Union to accept. Besides, they knew the CNE did not really want EU involvement and would not acquiesce to its requests to make an invitation attractive. Finally, the opposition parties asked the Carter Center staff to stay as a guarantor of a fairer process. The Carter Center believed that it could make the process acceptable and encourage all sides to accept the outcome; after all, this was its normal role as international observer in countless disputed electoral processes around the world.

The second decision point was when the Carter Center faced the intransigence of CNE director Battaglini in the face of its demands for a larger group of observers with complete freedom of movement. The Carter Center could have called his bluff and pulled out in the third week of July, but it accepted Gaviria's argument that doing so would be devastating for Venezuela. The Carter Center also realized that the CNE had hardened its position after the repair period, when the international observers had pushed the CNE very hard on the conditions for the signature collection, and thus that it would have to work diligently to combat that hardened position.

Further, as William Ury told the Carter Center, the CNE was embarrassed by Carter and Gaviria's unscheduled visit to the CNE during the repair period and needed to save face. This analysis likely applied to Battaglini personally as well, considering the dressing down he received from Carter in May. The Carter Center therefore employed a mission director whose manner was soft and accommodating to deal with Battaglini. It also tried to protect its position by agreeing with Gaviria to withdraw if the two nonnegotiable positions were not met before the recall: credentials for all of the Carter Center's observers and complete freedom of movement. In the end, the Carter Center's conditions were met and it was able to observe the elections unfettered.

8

The Recall Referendum and Aftermath, August–September 2004

The recall referendum finally occurred on August 15, 2004, with long lines of voters and high enthusiasm mixed with tension. The contentious aftermath, however, in which Chávez opponents would challenge his victory, affected Venezuelan politics for the next three years.

Election Eve

While the international observers of the Carter Center and the OAS fanned out around the country in the two days before the referendum, the delegation leaders held political meetings in Caracas. In a meeting with former president Carter and OAS secretary general Gaviria the day before the referendum, President Chávez was serene and promised to accept the results, whatever the outcome. He expressed concern that the Coordinadora Democrática would not await official results and would announce its own results early. He also noted that in light of the media agreement reached, he had suspended the "cadenas" and public acts the week preceding the referendum. Carter told Chávez:

> Tomorrow is the clearest test yet of your status in the country. In a series of miracles, you have survived a coup, strikes and perhaps tomorrow's vote. The divisions in Venezuela are a concern to the world. Your government has complied with the constitution in every test, but your public statements and animosity aggravate the divisions. You have won many tests, but not been successful in reuniting the country. There are some radicals in the opposition, but many good Venezuelans who voted against you and just want harmony. I hope and expect you will be gracious if you win and will reach out to join the country in reunification.[1]

---

1. McCoy, personal notes from the meeting, August 14, 2004.

Chávez replied that he would be magnanimous and reach out to his opponents if he won. He explained that his first government had been inclusive, but that when he had to fire some individuals for doing business from government offices, they left their positions and went to the opposition.

On election eve, the Coordinadora Democrática told Carter and Gaviria that it would wait for the official results before making announcements of its own. A prominent opposition member linked to the media privately told the Carter Center that the last-minute polls showed the "no" vote (not to recall the president) was ahead 51 percent to 48 percent, but that projections of the undecided vote would tilt the result to 48 percent to 52 percent, leading to a "yes" vote victory. As discussed in chapter 7, most polls, including opposition-commissioned polls, had shown Chávez's popularity rising in 2004, with the projected "no" vote equaling or overtaking the "yes" vote by late June. The Carter Center's own internal poll of field staff workers on the eve of the election showed that all but one predicted a "no" victory.

Voting Day

The morning of election day found eager voters in long lines ready to vote as early as 5 a.m. The CNE was prepared for 80 percent of registered voters to vote, but any percentage above that number would severely strain the system. Despite the massive turn-out early in the morning, the voting machines worked without issue and the crowds remained calm. By late morning, the long lines had grown restless because of slow voting, which many assumed was caused by the new fingerprint registration machines. Along with the U.S. firm Cogent, which provided the automated fingerprint identification system, the CNE had contracted with the Israeli satellite telecommunications company Gillat to provide telecommunications services. Cogent set up and ran the central data center, provided the scanners, and trained the operators in the voting centers. The purpose was to capture fingerprints digitally by satellite and create a national database for the future as well as identify any double voting on that day.

The Coordinadora Democrática had raised concerns ahead of time about delays in the voting that would be caused by these machines. In fact, the long lines were not caused exclusively by the fingerprint registration machines—they occurred even where there were no such machines. Instead, they were caused by the multiple steps that the voters had to take and the fact that in one-third of the precincts, as many as 2,000 voters were assigned to a single voting table and had to line up in one line to be processed, even when that

Carter-Gaviria-Chávez meeting
Courtesy of the Carter Center archives.

table had three voting machines to accommodate them. Generally speaking, voting centers, such as schools, might have ten voting tables, each ideally with 600 voters, and thirty voting machines. As was traditional in Venezuelan elections, the military was assigned the role of keeping order and protecting the security of the ballot boxes and voting machines.

By 1:30 p.m., the CNE had issued instructions to election workers to organize the lines of voters in each center by the voting table in which they were assigned. They decided to have voters go through the fingerprint machine step after they voted in those centers where the fingerprint machines seemed to be holding up the vote and to even abandon the fingerprint machines if they were too problematic. Soon after, the Carter Center spoke with the opposition, which wanted the voting hours extended to ensure everyone would get to vote, and then with the CNE, which agreed. The CNE extended voting until 8:00 p.m. to ensure that voters could go home to eat and rest and would not have to stand in line to be counted by the original closing at 4:00 p.m. Anyone in line at closing time is allowed to vote by Venezuelan law.

By midday, the Carter Center was getting reports from the Coordinadora Democrática that its exit poll showed 55:45 in favor of the "yes" vote, and around 1:30 p.m. the exit poll showed a result of 57:43. Its exit poll was carried out by Penn, Shoen and Berland, a notable U.S. polling firm. Because Penn, Shoen and Berland had not been able to contract a Venezuelan polling firm to conduct its exit poll, it contracted Súmate, the NGO that had been advising the Coordinadora Democrática and that had organized the collection of signatures for earlier recall petition efforts.

Tensions were high throughout the day as rumors swirled. Both sides claimed exit polls showing themselves well ahead. At 2:50 p.m., in a bizarre move, the CNE directors played a tape that they had been given of an impersonation of the CNE president's voice announcing a "yes" victory at 8 p.m. that evening, and said this was a grave crime that would be investigated. The Coordinadora Democrática replied that the tape was simply part of a comedy show made weeks earlier, with CDs having circulated for days in the streets, and that the CNE chose that moment to play it up as a serious matter in order to discredit what the Coordinadora Democrática saw as the forthcoming "yes" vote victory.

One hundred twenty international election observers for the Carter Center and the OAS were deployed throughout the country, while in the capital the delegation leaders visited polling sites as well as the major components of the process. President Carter visited the headquarters of CANTV (the privately owned telephone company that would transmit the election results through its lines), the data center of the fingerprinting system located at the new public Bolivariana University, and the situation room at the CNE, which monitored the functioning of the voting tables and reported any malfunctioning voting machines or other problems. All of these sites reported a generally well-functioning process, with any glitches being quickly corrected.

The Carter Center also met with various political actors and consultants throughout the day. At 4:00 p.m., it met with a group of private media directors and owners who reported that they expected to reach the required number of 3.75 million "yes" votes to recall the president only after 8 p.m. They were worried about nighttime dangers and feared that voters still in line at 8 p.m. might not be allowed to vote. They reported on two different exit polls, one showing a "yes" lead of 20–22 percent and another of 16 percent.

At 5:00 p.m. at CNE headquarters, the directors confirmed to the Carter Center that anyone in line at 8 p.m. would be able to vote; that 5 million had voted up to that point with a potential of 7 million more eligible voters; and that they were predicting only a 20 percent abstention rate. By 8 p.m.,

Voting line on referendum day.
Courtesy of the Carter Center archive.

the CNE had decided to again extend the time for voting, this time until midnight, due to continued long lines. While the opposition was concerned about getting to its magic number of 3.75 million votes, the government also wanted a high turn-out vote so that the "no" vote would outvote the "yes" vote. It viewed the extension of the hours as a chance to turn out more government supporters. As described earlier, the fingerprint machines were ostensibly intended to modernize Venezuela's antiquated identification system (which still relied on manual thumbprints on hard copies of identification card applications). The machines would digitize thumbprints of those who voted in this referendum, providing a massive leap to a nationwide automated identification system. At the same time, they would be able to detect double voting and thus deter that particular kind of fraud. An unpublicized attribute of the system was that it allowed the CNE directors in charge of it to monitor turn-out in specific precincts and estimate levels of pro- and antigovernment turn-out throughout the day.

By 9 p.m., Súmate's exit poll results from 20,900 voters showed 60:40 in favor of "yes" with a 0.6 percent margin of error. A private media director told the Carter Center team that crossing four exit polls showed a 59:41 result in favor of "yes" with a 3 percent margin of error, while the government was reporting a 53:47 vote in favor of "no." Throughout the day, each side used exit polls to persuade observers that it was winning and to influence perspectives on the final official vote results.

At 1:25 a.m., the CNE directors invited international delegation leaders from the Carter Center, OAS, and Capel to accompany them to the "totalization" room to receive the first results.[2] They reported on 75 percent of the automated vote (63 percent of the total, since some rural precincts still had manual voting) and the results were 58:42 in favor of "no." The Carter Center leaders were shocked, no doubt having been influenced by the continual reports throughout the day from the opposition whose exit polls showed almost exactly the reverse. On the way out of the room, the OAS mission chief received a call reporting on the first results of the joint OAS–Carter Center quick count.[3] These were in line with the official results and, indeed, predicted an even larger "no" spread of 59 percent to 41 percent.

---

2. In actuality, one of the pro-government and one of the pro-opposition directors had already seen the results, though they pretended this was the first unveiling.

3. A "quick count" or rapid parallel vote tabulation is a projection of the total voting results based on the actual results observed at individual voting tables in a statistical sample. OAS statisticians designed and drew the sample and told the international observers the morning of the election which voting table they should observe the vote count for that night. After the count, they called in the results to headquarters. This quick count is a tool used by election observers to corroborate official results, or to

After learning of the results at the CNE, the Carter Center and OAS delegation leaders returned to the hotel and called the leaders of the Coordinadora Democrática and media directors to meet with them at about 3 a.m. The delegation leaders shared the information and the fact that their quick count confirmed the CNE results. The opposition leaders said that their quick count also confirmed a "no" victory, but they continued to cite the exit polls showing almost exactly the opposite result. The mood was completely glum, with some opposition leaders expressing deep skepticism about the veracity of the results, and others saying that since they had previously said they would accept the results as long as the international observers endorsed them, it would look bad to renege now that they had lost.

One opposition leader suggested another audit that would compare the paper receipts in the same sample drawn for the opposition's quick count, expressing doubt about the "hot audit" sample. The delegation leaders explained to the Coordinadora Democrática and media leaders the process used to draw the sample for the "hot audit," which the opposition technicians had participated in and approved, and indicated that the international observers had observed 10 of the 192 "hot audit" sites and that the results seemed to be matching the electronic tallies.[4] However, the delegation leaders did note that the "hot audit" did not seem to be taking place as planned in all the locations, because there was either confusion about the rules or people were just tired and going home after the very long day. President Carter then called President Chávez and told him he had seen the CNE's preliminary results and asked Chávez not to claim victory before the CNE had made a public announcement. Carter also noted the importance of calming passions and not gloating in victory.

At 4:00 a.m. on August 16, the CNE gave its first televised report, with 94 percent of the voting machines reporting. They reported that 58 percent of the votes were "no" and 42 percent were "yes." Shortly thereafter, President Chávez came on television for his victory speech, claiming a victory for the Venezuelan constitution and inviting all Venezuelans to recognize the constitution, which allowed for this unprecedented exercise. He proposed a "new Venezuela" and a national project in which all could participate and said he felt like the president of all Venezuelans.

---

raise questions if significant discrepancies are found. It is different from an exit poll, which asks voters departing polling places how they voted and then estimates results.

4. The Carter Center and the OAS had jointly decided to draw their own sample of voting sites to conduct an independent quick count, and thus did not send their observers to the sites of the CNE's "hot audit." For that reason, their observers only viewed a few of the "hot audit" sites when they coincided with or were near the Carter Center's and OAS's own specified locations.

Following Chávez, Henry Ramos Allup of the AD spoke in the name of the Coordinadora Democrática and categorically rejected the results, claiming that its own count gave results of 59 percent in the "yes" column and 41 percent in the "no." Thus began the rejection of the results by the opposition leaders, and the questioning of the electoral processes by many others, that would consume Venezuela for months and even years.

After the early morning results were announced by the CNE, Diez and McCoy began receiving insistent phone calls from Jorge Rodríguez asking when the Carter Center, as the international observer from whom the world was waiting to hear before accepting the results, would endorse them. Months later Rodríguez told Diez and McCoy that he was receiving pressure from the military, which said that it would put tanks on the streets to claim victory if the results were not confirmed soon. As a normal practice, the Carter Center waits to hear from all of its observers and to complete its own tests (including quick counts and other samples) before giving any press conferences, and in this case it was particularly important to wait until all data was in, particularly given the opposition's questioning of the results. The Carter Center also had not been able to obtain from the CNE the results of the "hot audit." In the interim, the Carter Center team planned to get a few hours of sleep and reconvene in the late morning with Gaviria and the OAS mission chief, Walter Pecly, along with the other former presidents forming part of the Carter Center observer delegation.[5]

The Day After

After early morning celebrations around Chávez's victory speech, the streets emptied out and there was an eerie calm in the capital. The Carter Center team had a staff meeting with Carter at 11 a.m. The discussion focused on determining what pieces of information the Carter Center had and what questions remained—for example, were the machines really recording and transmitting the votes accurately, since the "hot audit" was not providing the information needed, and how could the contradictory exit polls and quick counts be explained? In debating whether there was sufficient information to make a conclusion about the basic results, and whether any additional information would be forthcoming, the Carter Center determined that all the previous opinion polls, the OAS–Carter Center quick count, and the Carter Center's own perceptions of the probable results, all indicated a government

---

5. The Carter Center delegation included former presidents Raúl Alfonsín of Argentina, Belisario Betancur of Colombia, and Rodrigo Carazo of Costa Rica.

victory and that the single dissonant piece of information was the opposition exit poll. The Carter Center thus resolved to try to get additional information from the "hot audit" and about the exit poll methodology.

Gaviria arrived to the meeting at 12:30 p.m., and he gave his view that the Coordinadora Democrática knew it had lost, based on its own copies of the tally sheets, but that it did not know how to tell its supporters that it was wrong. The only possibility the Coordinadora Democrática leaders could conceive of was that of electronic fraud. The Carter Center was extremely worried that if the international observers did not make a definitive announcement soon, there would be violence in the streets as Chavistas would come out to defend their president. It was agreed that Gaviria and Carter would give a joint press conference at 1 p.m. indicating that their own joint mission tests and evaluation were consistent with the CNE's preliminary report, that they had found no evidence of fraud but would be willing to investigate claims of fraud, and that the CNE should help in allaying the concerns of the opposition.

At the press conference, to these points President Carter added: "It is the responsibility of all Venezuelans to accept the results and work together in the future." The clarity of this statement, contrasting with the vagueness of Gaviria's statements at the same press conference, directed the fury of the opposition toward President Carter and the Carter Center for having accepted the results. Soon after, Carter went with Gaviria to see Chávez to encourage him to be magnanimous toward the opposition and to offer the Carter Center's help in facilitating reconciliation in Venezuela.

In the meeting, Chávez noted that there were some constructive opposition members, and that the governor of Zulia, Manuel Rosales (who would later contest Chávez for the presidency in 2006), had recognized the opposition's loss in Zulia. Gaviria said that the media directors were ready to meet with Chávez, and Chávez agreed that William Ury should return to Venezuela to help reconcile the government and the private media. He also wanted to reinitiate meetings with the private sector that had stopped during the referendum process, so the Carter Center offered its help on developing an antipoverty dialogue with the private sector.

A Second Audit

As the afternoon of August 16 wore on, the Carter Center received information that the "hot audit" of the night before had indeed failed, while opposition members presented to the Carter Center the mathematical oddities they were finding in the voting patterns. In turn, the Carter Center began to press the CNE for another audit of the paper receipts from the voting machines in order to address any lingering questions among Venezuela's citizens. On the morning of August 17, the Carter Center consulted with Súmate, which was instrumental in advising the Coordinadora Democrática on technical aspects of the vote. Súmate had already confirmed that its own quick count showed a "no" victory of 55 percent, but it was suspicious of the machines. It too agreed on the need for a second audit of the voting machines and at first wanted the sample to be its own exit poll locations and its quick count of 300 machines. However, the Carter Center argued that the sample should be randomly drawn, which would more accurately reflect any problems. The Carter Center agreed with Súmate on a proposal for a new audit with a sample that would be nonstratified and that would use a simple Excel program (Random) to draw 150 voting tables and 50 substitutes, with members of the opposition, government, and CNE conducting the audit and with an international observer at each location.[6]

In a series of meetings with CNE directors and opposition leaders over the next two days, the Carter Center and the OAS proposed the second audit and facilitated negotiations of the terms. The opposition, however, would not seriously consider the proposal for the second audit. It failed to send its technical people to the CNE for the planned meeting on the terms and said instead that it would send them to the hotel to meet with the international observers. When the Carter Center team returned to the hotel, it found the same two interlocutors it had dealt with going back to the negotiating table, neither of whom was an electoral expert or understood statistics. Rather than discussing the proposal for the audit or offering an alternative proposal, they presented another fraud theory—a mathematical concern about the pattern of results that was actually a completely normal pattern.

By late Tuesday, August 17, it was clear the opposition did not want to participate in the second audit. It presented additional "suspicious" patterns of voting results, including a cap on the number of "yes" votes in certain voting tables that it suspected was programmed into the machines. It also contended that since the machines and voting materials were in the control of the military in each region after the vote, the machines could have been tampered with by the time of the second audit. The Carter Cen-

---

6. Súmate also wanted to compare a portion of the *"chorizos"* or sausage rolls—the long rolls of individual vote records for each voting machine, each identified with a random string of thirty-two numbers and letters. The Carter Center argued, however, that auditing these strings of numbers would be infeasible in the short term. It discussed the possibility of examining 15 percent of the chorizos in detail.

ter and the OAS proposed that they deploy observers to each military barrack guarding voting materials, and that only then would the sample of voting tables to be audited be drawn in the presence of the opposition and government. The individual machines and boxes of paper receipts would then be located and pulled out, in the presence of the observers, and transported to a central location in Caracas for the audit. In this way, it would be completely infeasible for soldiers to coordinate an effort to change out the paper receipts in all 20,000 voting machines around the country to match the "false" results reported by the CNE, and with no one leaking the information!

Although the CNE and the government agreed to this proposal, the opposition continued to resist. Continued efforts by the OAS and the Carter Center to convince it that a statistically random sample with all of these safeguards would indeed demonstrate any manipulation of the voting results at the level of the machines were unsuccessful. After one more unsuccessful attempt to convince the opposition on Wednesday morning, the Carter Center and the OAS went to the CNE to finalize the plan without the opposition. At that meeting, the technical experts from each organization decided the details for the second audit. (One of these details would long be pointed to by some opposition factions in an attempt to discredit the process, as will be discussed.) Meanwhile, the OAS and the Carter Center had to scramble to assemble a team of observers who could stay in Venezuela four days longer than planned for by the observation mission. Within both the Carter Center and OAS teams, sufficient numbers of volunteers offered to extend their stay.

At the August 18 meeting to discuss the terms of the audit, Jorge Rodríguez stated that this additional audit was not necessary in light of the preelection audits of the voting machines and the various certifications. He said that the CNE was entertaining the observers' proposal only because of the rumors spread by the Coordinadora Democrática and the insults in the media and that this was the last effort the CNE would make to convince the people they live in a democracy. He announced that the manual vote count (based in primarily pro-Chávez rural areas) was 70 percent "no" and 30 percent "yes," even further widening the gap. He clarified that the second postelection audit about to be undertaken would not be to measure inconsistencies between the paper receipts and the electronic tallies, since the paper receipts were not a legal instrument of the vote and could be damaged. Instead, the *"chorizo"* (the long scroll recording individual votes) was the legal vote and the CNE proposed to look for patterns of fraud by comparing the paper receipts, the chorizo, and the acta (electronic tally). His largest fear was either that the paper receipts could have been manipulated by voters intentionally destroying them rather than placing them in the ballot boxes, or that expected small inconsistencies between the paper receipt count and the electronic count would be blown out of proportion.

To demonstrate fraud, intentional manipulation of results needs to be shown and this is done by showing patterns of voting results that systematically advantage one side or disadvantage the other. By comparing the discrepancies between paper receipts, the chorizo, and the acta, one could determine whether the average discrepancy for the "yes" votes was significantly different than the average discrepancy for the "no" votes. In fact, the CNE expected some discrepancies but thought that they would be randomly distributed among the "yes" and "no" votes.

The observers then began to discuss the methodology with Rodríguez. He agreed on a procedure that essentially followed the procedure that the Carter Center and Súmate had agreed to two days earlier. First, international observers would travel to each departmental military barrack where the voting materials were being stored under guard of the military. The observers would be present at those sites when a new sample of 150 voting tables (and 50 substitutes) would be drawn that afternoon at 6 p.m. in the presence of the political parties and the international observers. The observers would watch the military locate and pull out the voting boxes of materials for each of the voting tables identified in the sample. Each voting table had up to three voting machines and all machines would be audited. The observers would then accompany the voting boxes to Caracas to a warehouse where the audit would take place. They would sleep there until the audit would begin at 8 a.m. on August 19. Each CNE auditing team would work only when there was a Carter Center or OAS observer present, and the teams would count the "yes" and "no" votes in each box.

The one difference between this procedure and what had been discussed with Súmate involved the computer program that would be used to choose the sample. The first audit on August 15 was done with a Pascal Delphi program, approved by the opposition and checked by the international observers. Although the possibility of using an Excel Random program to draw the sample had been discussed with Súmate, the CNE proposed using the Pascal Delphi program again since it had already been tested and approved by the political parties and the international observers. At that meeting, McCoy asked both the OAS and the Carter Center technical experts whether they believed either program would make a difference and they said no. Knowing that the opposition had already decided not to participate in the audit, the Carter Center and the OAS agreed to the CNE proposal for the program and were present that afternoon when the sample was drawn. The program required a four-digit seed to be provided to initiate the program. On Sunday, during the initial audit, a Coordinadora Democrática observer and a government observer had each provided two of those digits, but for the second audit, because the Coordinadora Democrática had declined to participate, the CNE asked the OAS and Carter Center observers to each provide two. The OAS observer declined on the basis that the OAS was only there to observe, not to participate in the process; consequently, the Carter Center observer also declined. The CNE operator then had to choose the four digits, in the presence of the observers, to initiate the program.

The sample was drawn and the lists were sent to the military barracks, while the Carter Center and OAS simultaneously called their observers and provided them with the list of boxes to be pulled from each location. The Carter Center and OAS observers stayed with the boxes, riding on military trucks or flying in military planes back to Caracas overnight so that the audit could begin the following morning.

The CNE workers, international observers, and witnesses from the Comanda Maisanta (government party campaign leaders) gathered in a large warehouse on the outskirts of Caracas for a massive three-day operation. The sample of 150 voting tables produced an audit of 336 voting machines, since many voting tables had more than one machine. CNE workers painstakingly inspected each box of voting materials, pulled out and separated all the paper receipts into piles of "yes" and "no," and counted them meticulously. Anytime an international observer needed to take a break, the work would halt until the observer returned.

The operation lasted until Saturday, August 21, at which point the CNE announced in a press conference the results of the audit: the average discrepancy for the "no" vote was one-third of one vote per machine, and for the "yes" vote one-half of one vote per machine. In other words, there existed no pattern of significant difference in patterns between the "yes" and "no" votes. Extrapolating those results to the national results, the discrepancies between the paper receipts and the machine tallies represented less than one-tenth of 1 percent.

In all, sixteen observers from the Carter Center and twenty observers from the OAS watched as CNE auditors sorted and counted over 135,000 voting receipts. International observers contributed 1,700 hours of work over three days, and CNE auditors, government party witnesses, and a group of

Recounting audit boxes coming with the military.
Courtesy of the Carter Center archives.

European observers also put in a great number of hours in order to complete the task at hand.

McCoy and Gaviria held a press conference in which they confirmed the results, explained the international observer's role, and once again reviewed all of the checks on the entire automated voting system. Although President Carter and Walter Pecly had already left the country, Gaviria and McCoy made clear that both the Carter Center and the OAS would continue to investigate any evidence of manipulation presented by the opposition and that, at that time, there was no evidence to refute the CNE's results.

In the weeks after the recall vote, the Carter Center indeed continued to receive complaints from the Coordinadora Democrática about suspicious patterns in the voting results. Both the OAS and the Carter Center had their own statisticians on staff for the mission, and they investigated and refuted all of the initial concerns presented by the opposition. However, the Carter Center wanted second opinions as well. On the very first day after the referendum, McCoy sought an independent statistician's assessment of the mathematical patterns and called William Ury for help. To provide extra time, she asked him to identify someone on the West Coast of the United States (Caracas is four hours ahead of the Pacific Standard Time). He found a statistician at Stanford University, completely uninvolved in Venezuela's politics, who confirmed the Carter Center's own statisticians' opinion that the patterns of repeated "yes" results (which were alleged to show an artificial cap programmed into the machines) were actually within the realm of statistical probability.

The Carter Center continued to employ independent statisticians, voting machine experts, and political scientists to assess new allegations and mathematical "proofs" presented by Venezuelan mathematicians over the next several months. One of the most publicized was the "black swan" paper presented by two opposition Venezuelan scholars in the United States—one an economist at Harvard University and one a mathematician at the Massachusetts Institute of Technology.[7] Their scholarly credentials provided a great deal of credibility to their report, and the Carter Center took it quite seriously, though the U.S. press covering the issue never reported that the two scholars were Venezuelans opposed to the Chávez government. The "black swan" paper alleged that the second audit sample, drawn on August 18 as earlier described, was manipulated to include only "clean" voting machines whose paper receipts had not been tampered with, while other voting machines excluded from the sample had in fact been tampered with to produce an incorrectly high "no" vote.

The Carter Center convened a group of independent experts to assess the "black swan" paper and other mathematical studies that had emerged over ensuing months. These experts included a noted critic of electronic voting machines from Johns Hopkins University, an econometrician from the University of Utah, a political scientist who specializes in voting patterns from the University of California at Berkeley, and the aforementioned statistician from Stanford. They found no statistical evidence of fraud in any of the studies they examined.[8]

The International Observers

After the recall vote, the Carter Center mission quickly shifted from scenarios of reconciliation to damage control about the results. As described

---

7.   Ricardo Hausmann and Roberto Rigobón, "In Search of the Black Swan: Analysis of the Statistical Evidence of Fraud in Venezuela" (unpublished manuscript, September 2004).

8.   See their report, as well as the Carter Center reports and explanations of the second audit, in the Carter Center, *Observing the Venezuelan Presidential Recall Referendum*, 127–34.

Carter Center observer Nealin Parker observes CNE workers counting the
paper ballots during the August 18 audit.
Courtesy of The Carter Center.

in chapter 7, it had planned for President Carter to remain in the country
three days after the recall vote to initiate talks between the government and
the opposition about how to move forward with national reconciliation in
light of whatever results occurred on August 15. However, given the opposition's questioning of the recall vote results, the bulk of the Carter Center's
energy was spent addressing the opposition's concerns and observing the
second audit.

The pitfalls of working in a severely divided country manifested themselves once again during the negotiations over the second audit. For the
evening of August 17, the Carter Center had previously planned a dinner
for President Carter with several of the top business leaders in the country
as an attempt to find mechanisms of reconciliation. By that time, however,
the Carter Center staff were engaged in discussions about conducting a
second audit. McCoy and Diez spent most of their time at the dinner on
the phone negotiating the terms of the audit and arranged a meeting with
Jorge Rodríguez for later that night to discuss the details. Upon leaving
the dinner, McCoy and Diez received a call from the Carter Center's chief
of mission, who was already at the meeting with Rodríguez and indicated
that the meeting was awkward and that their presence was needed imme-

diately. It turns out that the meeting was being held at Rodríguez's house, at the same time he was hosting a party for the CNE to celebrate the close of the intense ten-month recall referendum effort! McCoy and Diez thus unknowingly entered a party and waited in a bedroom to discuss the audit with Rodríguez. When neighbors in the condo commented on the party to media personalities, McCoy and Diez became the subject of opposition talk-show hosts' ire the following day for "attending" the party.

The OAS had a somewhat divided response to the recall referendum, with the chief of mission presenting his preliminary report to the press in Caracas on Thursday, August 19, and endorsing the recall results. To the Carter Center's surprise and without explanation, he then departed the country. The Carter Center was later told that he had not wanted to participate in the second audit without the participation of the opposition. Ambassador Pecly presented his verbal report to the OAS Permanent Council in Washington, DC, on August 25. Secretary General Gaviria, meanwhile, remained in Caracas for the conclusion of the second audit and final press conference with McCoy on Saturday, August 21, again corroborating the results of the recall referendum. Gaviria had told the Carter Center team in a preelection meeting on August 14 that the electoral system was functioning properly but that the opposition was legitimately concerned because it did not participate in the preparation of the system. The international observers provided the internal checks that were absent due to the constitutional transition and the government's supermajority.[9] Gaviria continued to publicly present the various tests that had been performed, while also acknowledging the opposition's concerns.

The OAS mission reports on the recall referendum were themselves somewhat confusing, as the chief of mission for the signature-verification phase (Fernando Jaramillo) wrote one report, never publicly made available, while the chief of mission for the referendum phase (Walter Pecly) published an early report endorsing the recall vote. Secretary General Gaviria's report on the two-year OAS mission to Venezuela to facilitate the negotiation and dialogue table and observe the signature collection and recall referendum vote went through two versions, with the second toning down some of the criticism of the process that had appeared in the first version. Since his term as secretary general was ending September 15, 2004, he did not have time to include any analysis of the Coordinadora Democrática's fraud allegations in his report, but he did express his concerns about larger institutional matters, in

---

9. McCoy, personal notes, author's private collection.

particular the dangers of expanding the Supreme Court without a supermajority of the National Assembly.[10] He also published a report on his ten-years
of service as secretary general of the OAS upon his retirement in September
2004, which included a discussion of the Venezuelan episode.[11]

The Carter Center presented its conclusions in several documents as well.
McCoy published an article in the *Economist* on September 2, 2004, de-
scribing the three types of tests that the Carter Center and the OAS had
performed to check each phase of the automated voting system: (1) the projection of total results from a sample of the electronic results received by the
central CNE computer to test the aggregation of the results; (2) the quick
count projection from the sample of electronic voting machine results to
test the accuracy of the transmission; and (3) the second audit of the paper
receipts to test the accuracy of the individual voting machines. The Carter
Center published its initial conclusions of the entire process, including the
criticisms of the signature-verification process, in late September 2004, and
its final report on the entire year-long process, which included six different
observer delegations, in February 2005.

Francisco Diez ended his two years in Caracas in September 2004, returning to Buenos Aires. When the Carter Center originally invited Diez to
represent the Carter Center in July 2002 to facilitate a national dialogue, it
thought the assignment might last two months. It ended up lasting twenty-
six months in an intense roller coaster of emotions as the dynamics of this
volatile, complex conflict unfolded. The Carter Center engaged an electoral
consultant to follow the postreferendum dispute process from Caracas, while
it continued with the expert panel from Atlanta to investigate the electronic
fraud allegations. It maintained its office in Caracas, from which Ana Cabria
Mellace, an Argentine mediator trained by Francisco Diez, worked with the
Strengthening Peace in Venezuela Program until February 2005, when the
Carter Center presented its final report to the Venezuelan authorities and
political actors.

The International Context

Following the referendum, the international community generally expressed
relief and a desire to move on from the intense focus on Venezuela. There
was reluctant acceptance of the results by some, primarily within the U.S.
government and Congress. Within Latin America and the OAS, there was

---

10. César Gaviria, in conversation with McCoy, September 9, 2004.

11. César Gaviria, *The OAS in Transition, 1994–2004* (Washington, DC: OAS, 2004).

no movement to intervene further in Venezuela, whether in taking an active role to foster reconciliation or to assure that the rights of the minority would be respected.

Carter called U.S. secretary of state Colin Powell on August 16 to tell him of the referendum results, and Powell said he would issue a statement endorsing the findings of the OAS and the Carter Center. Although many in the State Department were not happy with the results, the United States had said many times prior to the recall that it would look to the report of the international observers to make its own determination (and in so doing caused some resentment within the CNE). The State Department had little choice, therefore, but to accept the results. In a visit by McCoy to Washington, DC, on September 9, 2004, she found the State Department largely accepting of the results, though she did encounter some questions about the fraud allegation. Although she received even more questions from Congress, the broader Washington, DC, community accepted the results.

On August 26, the same day the CNE announced the final official results, the OAS passed Resolution 869, recognizing Chávez as the legitimate winner of the recall referendum and concluding that the referendum process adhered to the principles of the Inter-American Democratic Charter.

Analysis and Lessons

The first lesson learned during this period is that the outcome of the recall referendum was the result of the strategies of the government and the opposition and of external contextual factors. To begin, repeated delays in scheduling the referendum hurt the opposition's chances. Venezuela's GDP had contracted more than 9 percent in the first half of 2003 due to the oil strike and widespread disorder. This decline reduced the popularity of the government. However, the economy began to recover as the world price of petroleum climbed to $29 per barrel in August 2003 and $41 per barrel in August 2004. President Chávez used the resulting windfall to channel more money into his popular "missions"—programs he personally controlled that distributed resources directly to the urban poor in the form of medical clinics, subsidized food markets, housing, and adult education programs. In addition, the government initiated a broad national-identification campaign, naturalizing immigrants (including many illegal immigrants) and issuing identification cards to those (mostly poor) who previously had none. Government officials expected that these newly naturalized citizens would overwhelmingly vote "no" on recalling the president, while the opposition expected large numbers of them would vote "yes" and therefore did not express great concern about these government initiatives prior to the referendum.

In contrast to the well-coordinated efforts by the government, the opposition formed a unified electoral command only in the final two weeks of campaigning for the recall. Part of this delay derived from prolonged but ultimately unsuccessful negotiations to select a unity presidential candidate to challenge the president should the recall referendum succeed. Such disarray and bickering among opposition forces left voters with no clear alternative to the Chávez presidency. In addition, a weak grassroots organizational effort hampered the campaign.

The different ways in which the government and the opposition approached the recall reflected their differing time horizons. The government took the longer view, systematically consolidating its power and riding out challenges in order to survive and press the Bolivarian Revolution forward. The opposition, in contrast, was gripped by the desire to remove the government immediately. Its strategy echoed the television-influenced approach to politics in which the immediacy of the moment commands all attention and the media decisively shape political messages and public opinion. This shorter horizon ruled out efforts to organize at the grassroots level in ways capable of winning voter trust and changing the accountability of institutions (the courts, the CNE, and the offices of the attorney general, comptroller general, and ombudsman), all of which were led by government sympathizers.

With all of these factors at work, the president's approval ratings rose steadily in the months leading up to the August 15 referendum. The share of voters who told pollsters that they would vote to recall the president dropped from 69 percent in July 2003 to 44 percent in the first week of August 2004. Correspondingly, approval of President Chávez steadily increased, from 31 percent to 56 percent over the same time period. The final results of the balloting in the recall referendum—with 59 percent voting to retain Chávez and 41 percent voting to remove him—were consistent with these trends.[12]

The second lesson learned during this period is that the recall referendum could not solve the country's underlying political conflict. The recall referendum as a means of conflict resolution raised expectations that could not be met. Militants in each camp desired that the referendum would signal the other's total defeat. The less partisan simply wanted it to solve the crisis. But

---

12. Datanalisis, *Encuesta Nacional Omnibus 2004*. Polling that the U.S. firm of Greenberg, Quinlan, Rosner did for the opposition found similar numbers and the same trend line. Data from both polling firms were provided to the authors.

a yes-or-no referendum question is an inherently divisive process in which voters are asked to vote against an elected official rather than to make an affirmative choice among candidates. It thus offers poor prospects for resolving deeper issues of the kind troubling Venezuela. Nonetheless, many, including the Carter Center, hoped that a recall vote could at least let the country gauge how much support Chávez and his agenda enjoyed and then peacefully move forward on the basis of that information.

9

Government Consolidation of Power, 2005–10

After the defeat of the presidential recall referendum, the opposition shattered and its leadership dissolved. Political leaders were divided over whether to participate in the elections of governors and mayors scheduled for October 2004, and with the continued allegations of vote fraud, abstention among opposition voters was high and the government won the vast majority of seats. The next opportunity for national political contestation would be the National Assembly elections in December 2005, followed by presidential elections in December 2006.

In the meantime, the government focused on consolidating control over remaining institutions. In 2005, President Chávez announced his new economic strategy of "twenty-first-century socialism" and, with his reelection in 2006, began to lay plans for deepening and radicalizing the Bolivarian Revolution through another constitutional reform. Extensive reforms were defeated in December 2007, marking the first vote Chávez lost in his nine years of office, but twelve months later he proposed a single amendment to allow for the indefinite reelection of the president.

The third parties disengaged from Venezuela after the recall vote. The OAS, with the resignation of its new secretary general only three weeks after his inauguration in September 2004, was in turmoil. Although Francisco Diez departed Venezuela in September 2004, the Carter Center continued to support the country's peacebuilding networks and renewed its offer to the government to help the country reach consensus on controversial issues, such as media regulation and fighting poverty.

The OAS and the European Union sent observer missions to the December 2005 and December 2006 elections, endorsing the results each time, after which the CNE stopped inviting large election observation missions.

After Chávez defeated the internal opposition, the U.S.-Venezuelan dispute took a dominant place in U.S. foreign policy in the hemisphere, while Chávez, in turn, focused on the United States as a new threat and began to prepare for an alleged U.S. invasion that he warned would possibly come through Colombia.

The Aftermath of the Recall Vote

Chávez's victory speech after the recall referendum intimated a new chance for Venezuela, where all could participate in a national project. Nevertheless, the opposition refusal to accept the results gave Chávez an excuse to refrain from consulting with them on his national project, and he refused to recognize the Coordinadora Democrática any longer. He promoted dialogue with those who would work with his revolutionary project, and his government had talks with private-sector representatives and media owners. But the government also took advantage of the victory to further consolidate its control: it renewed a series of judicial accusations against opposition members, moved forward with plans to expand the Supreme Court, passed laws to further regulate the media and increase penalties for political dissent, and created a new ministry to implement the controversial land reform decreed in the land law of December 2001.

The judicial pressure on opponents to the government included charges filed against some four hundred opposition members who had allegedly signed the "Carmona decree" of the short-lived 2002 coup government, and charges of conspiracy against three leaders of Súmate for accepting a U.S. grant allegedly to work for the opposition to defeat the government.[1] There was some speculation that the Carmona decree charges were aimed at disqualifying some opposition candidates from running for reelection in the October 2004 regional elections, as the popular governor of Zulia (Manuel Rosales) and a popular mayor of a Caracas suburb (Enrique Capriles Radonsky from Baruta) were on the list. In the end, they were not prevented from running and being reelected. The Súmate trial was repeatedly delayed

---

1. During the two-day Carmona government in April 2002, many supporting citizens had entered the presidential palace and signed what they thought was a guestbook. In addition, the military-appointed president, Pedro Carmona, had issued a decree abolishing the Congress and Supreme Court and establishing the Carmona government's own credentials, which some guests may have signed as well. Some of the opposition political leaders and one of the Súmate leaders were on that list. Separately, Súmate was accused of conspiracy to overthrow the government with foreign support based on a grant from the National Endowment for Democracy, a federally funded U.S.-based organization, to provide for voter education and encourage participation in the referendum. The initial charges against Súmate leaders were filed in June 2004, but the courts did not pursue them until September 2004.

and suspended, but the charges remained hanging over the leaders' heads, serving as an implicit threat to them and other dissenters.

A law authorizing changes to the Supreme Court had been approved in a controversial vote by a simple majority of the National Assembly prior to the recall referendum, but the government decided to wait until after the heated recall environment to implement it. In December 2004, the National Assembly expanded the Supreme Court from twenty to thirty-two members, ostensibly to reduce the backlog of work of the magistrates. This action changed the partisan balance of the court from one perceived as evenly divided in 2004 to one with a clear pro-government majority in 2005. The new chief justice, in fact, declared he was part of the revolution and removed a number of judges for apparently political reasons.

Control of the private media was enhanced with the social content law that had been approved in December 2004. The stated aim of this law was to reduce the violence and pornography to which children were exposed on television, and to increase the amount of Venezuelan programming on television. Critics claimed, however, that the law muzzled the private media and impinged on free speech. Media directors feared that broadcasts of political protests, including any violence that might ensue, would be deemed by the Ministry of Communications as violating the law. Severe administrative fines and sanctions included in the law seemed to push the private media to voluntarily reduce the government critiques prevalent in private television and radio programming. This change from the media's previous confrontational tone was quite notable.

In addition, the subsequent changes to the penal code in early 2005 increased jail time for insulting public, military, and intelligence officials. These changes went counter to rulings by the Inter-American Court of Human Rights that defamation and public insults should not be punishable at all with imprisonment; they also seemed to be a backward step with regard to Venezuelan law. Venezuelan judicial reforms in 1997 had prohibited pretrial detentions and moved to an accusatory trial system as in the United States, but the new draft penal code removed political protest and libel of government officials from this prohibition on pretrial detention, as well as made illegal certain kinds of nonviolent protest such as *cacerolazos* (pot banging). The media law, combined with changes to the penal code, thus worked to curtail political dissent and served as a means for the government to confront and weaken a sector it had long held to be the drivers of the opposition—the private media.

In the months following the recall referendum, even before the social content law was passed, it was clear that the private media had softened its position and moved to more entertainment programs, more balanced news coverage, and less political programming. Some of the most conflictive talk-show hosts disappeared from the airwaves, and many of the private media sought government ads. Meanwhile, the public media continued to be very pro-government in its coverage.[2]

The October 2004 municipal and gubernatorial elections gave the government another opportunity to consolidate its control, as it won 21 of the 23 governorships and 270 of the 335 mayoralties. With its defeat of the recall referendum and victories in the October regional elections, the government recognized that it had survived all of the challenges presented by its opponents over the previous three years, and that it had to begin focusing on governing the country and providing services to the people. Chávez instructed his ministers to go into overdrive to tackle corruption and inefficiencies and to use the rising oil revenues to respond to the needs of the people. His urgency to produce results precluded the "luxury" of consultations, building consensus with opponents, and planning, and his view was that those who wanted to join in the "revolution" were welcome, but that he would not waste time trying to bring recalcitrant elements on board.

Meanwhile, the opposition reacted to the recall results with disbelief and denial. The nearly mirror image reversal of the results from the Penn, Schoen and Berland–Súmate exit poll disseminated throughout voting day led to profound suspicion among many opponents of Chávez. Leaders of the Coordinadora Democrática and the private media reinforced those suspicions with their allegations of fraud.

Even though these same media leaders and Coordinadora Democrática leaders had told the Carter Center prior to the referendum that the polls were trending in favor of Chávez, after the vote they immediately began to search for possible bases of fraud to explain their loss. The allegations of fraud in the electronic voting machines failed to be corroborated by the parallel vote tabulations, the second audit, or the independent panel of experts, as described in chapter 8.

In September, the opposition began to focus on a second possible explanation of their defeat: inflated voter rolls. The opposition claimed—for the first time—in September and October 2004 that 1.8 million newly registered voters (or about 12 percent of all those on the rolls used for the August recall and the October elections) lacked proper addresses and were thus

---

2. Diez, trip report, November 21, 2004.

suspect.[3] The CNE claimed that this figure was actually less than 2 percent and that such lacunae did not make those voters ineligible, particularly because the absence of proper addresses in the slums would be registered as missing values in the voter list.

A Súmate audit several weeks before the August recall had found less than 1 percent of the registered names with problems in their addresses. With regard to the growth of the voter list, a Carter Center analysis found that even though the CNE had collected over 2 million applications for voter registration between November 2003 and July 2004, only 1.2 million were added to the rolls, corresponding to the historic rate of growth of the voter list. Nevertheless, given the controversies and lack of sufficient opposition oversight over the voter list, the Carter Center strongly recommended that an independent, external audit be conducted of the voter list before future elections.

The net political results of the fraud allegation strategy were devastating for the opposition. First, its refusal to recognize Chávez's victory gave the president the excuse to move forward with his own agenda and ignore the opposition's. Second, the fraud allegations created much confusion and cynicism among opposition voters in the run-up to the October gubernatorial and municipal elections, in which opposition parties fielded candidates. Voters heard the message that they could not trust the CNE and the voting machines, and at the same time, that opposition candidates were campaigning for their votes.

As a result, in the year following the recall referendum, the population continued to be polarized, even though the opposition lacked any sort of leadership, and the roots of the conflict continued to revolve around a power struggle for control over the state and its resources and competing images of the country (pro-West vs. anti-imperialist Chavismo).

The National Assembly Elections

The next national electoral contest after the recall referendum—the National Assembly elections—took place on December 4, 2005. President Chávez and his allies won all 167 seats in the National Assembly. This outcome completed the marginalization of those who had governed Venezuela between 1958 and 1998. The lopsided outcome came after the opposition decided to boycott the election during the week leading up to it.

---

3. This claim was made by one opposition party—Copei—and by the newly formed committee of governors and mayors who were negotiating the conditions for the October 31 regional elections.

In the months prior to the election, the opposition had continued to question the electoral process due to the absence of an internationally verified voter list, a hole in the law allowing the majority party to win a number of seats higher than its proportion of votes, and continued suspicions about the electronic voting machines.[4] Consequently, the CNE agreed on additional preelectoral audits and election-day recounts of the paper voting receipts, and invited the OAS and European Union to send observers to monitor the elections. Nevertheless, opposition supporters were especially distrustful of the new technology introduced during the 2004 recall vote, which included checking fingerprints to determine if a prospective voter was legally entitled to cast a ballot. The opposition became convinced, without any way to prove it, that with this system the government would be able to know how individual electors voted and that this information would be used against them in the future.

Additional negotiations facilitated by the international observers resulted in the CNE meeting the stated conditions of the opposition to continue its participation—primarily removing the fingerprint machines and adding safeguards for the electronic voting machines to guarantee the secrecy and accuracy of the vote. Nevertheless, to the surprise of the observers, the opposition parties withdrew one by one in subsequent days, apparently in reaction to continued lack of citizen trust in the process, and projections that they would win at most 20 percent of the seats.[5] After the elections, the opposition charged that the 75 percent abstention rate delegitimized the entire process.

The OAS and European observers verified in a public news conference after the election that the voting had been honest and that President Chávez's allies had indeed captured all 167 seats in the National Assembly. However, they also stated that distrust of the CNE was widespread and urged the government to name a new council in which all Venezuelans could have greater confidence. President Chávez reacted with some irritation to this recommendation, but in general the government and the opposition made little effort to engage each other in the aftermath of the National Assembly elections. Both withdrew to contemplate the course of events in 2005 and plan their strategies for the presidential election year of 2006.

---

4. For an explanation of the electoral law loophole allowing parties to run "twin candidates" (known in Venezuela as *morochas*) on the party slates and on the single-member district districts, see McCoy and Myers, ed., *The Unraveling of Representative Democracy in Venezuela*, 301–02.

5. Some opposition leaders opposed the boycott and even voted, but the political parties all felt the pressure to join the boycott and eventually did so. After their anemic showing in municipal council elections, their goal before the boycott had been to gain one-third of the seats in the National Assembly, enough to prevent the government coalition from approving constitutional reforms and organic laws.

The Presidential Election

In mid-2006, the main issues of discussion in the country besides the up-coming elections centered around concerns about personal security (Venezuela's homicide rate had risen to one of the highest in the world) and unemployment.[6] Chávez faced significant vulnerabilities, including the notion that his social programs could be reaching the limits of their capacity to improve the living standards of their recipients and growing complaints among his own supporters about the incompetence, corruption, and mismanagement of his government.[7] The collapse of the bridge connecting Caracas to the port and airport on the coast in January 2006 shocked the country and was emblematic of the long-term government neglect of infrastructure (both under Punto Fijo and Chávez). The rising crime rates, the lack of jobs, and an open corruption scandal within the Chavista movement, in which a Supreme Court magistrate accused government ministers of corruption, frustrated many. Despite these concerns and those over restrictions of political, civil, and property rights, President Chávez's approval ratings oscillated between 60 and 70 percent in 2005 and 2006. High and rising oil prices, and perhaps his government's continued very noisy dispute with the United States, buoyed his ability to increase public spending and ride the wave of anti-imperialist nationalism.

The opposition eventually united behind a single candidate for the 2006 presidential election—the popular governor of oil-rich Zulia state, Manuel Rosales. It did not expect to defeat Chávez, but it saw the value in mobilizing opposition supporters to participate in the electoral process once again, to demonstrate that there was more than one political view in the country, and to organize for the future. In the end, Chávez won by a striking 62 percent in an election endorsed by the European Union and OAS,[8] but Rosales demonstrated a new maturity from the opposition, recognizing his

---

6. McCoy, trip report, May 27, 2006.

7. For further analyses of these issues, see Steve Ellner, *Rethinking Venezuelan Politics: Class, Conflict, and the Chávez Phenomenon* (Boulder, CO: Lynne Rienner Press, 2008); Jennifer McCoy, "Engaging Venezuela: 2009 and Beyond," in *The Obama Administration and the Americas: Agenda for Change,* ed. Abraham Lowenthal, Theodore Piccone, and Laurence Whitehead (Washington, DC: Brookings Institution Press 2009); and Ana Maria San Juan, "Referendum del 2D en Venezuela: Balance y Perspectivas" (unpublished report prepared for the Carter Center, December 7, 2007).

8. Electoral conditions improved during the 2006 elections primarily through the mutual agreement of certain rules and policies before the campaign began in August. Nevertheless, the lack of regulations for the use of state resources during reelection and the difficulty of the CNE to regulate access to the media continued to be an issue for Venezuela. Pressure from government ministers on public workers to vote for the president and the partial use of the thumbprint machines over the objections of the opposition candidates may have contributed to some level of fear among or intimidation of voters that is very difficult to measure.

defeat and the legitimate reelection of the president and promising to act as a constructive opposition leader. Chávez made a conciliatory speech, giving hopes for a new reconciliatory stage in Venezuela politics. Those hopes were quickly dashed, however, as the government decided to become even more radical in 2007.

A Deepening of the Revolution

The Chávez government first began to define a new economic model in 2005, a model it described as "twenty-first-century socialism." It initially included co-management of enterprises between managers and workers, cooperatives, and a mixed economic system of private and state capitalism, implementing for the first time some of the decree laws issued in 2001. In practical terms, the government began to reshape the economy through two major initiatives: a controversial land reform and changes in the country's petroleum policy. Implementation of the 2001 land reform act became a high priority in 2005 as the National Land Institute sought to identify unproductive private lands and required large estates to show proof of title going back as far as the War of the Federation in the 1850s.[9] In collaboration with regional governors belonging to the government party, the central government challenged the titles of selected private estates and expropriated lands it deemed idle. Portions of these estates were to be redistributed to landless rural workers or to those already squatting on the land. President Chávez also proclaimed that his power to expropriate unproductive land included industrial food processing plants the government deemed to be insufficiently productive.

Petroleum policy sustained the strategy of tightly controlling petroleum supply in order to support high oil prices, which continued to rise through 2006. In turn, the high price of crude oil on the international market led Venezuela to rewrite its contracts with foreign oil companies, requiring from them the payment of larger royalties on the production of viscous or heavy oil from the Orinoco Tar Belt and giving the state majority control in joint ventures. In addition, President Chávez opened talks with China and India to explore construction in Asia of a new facility capable of refining heavy Venezuelan oil. This reflected the president's desire to develop an alternative market for Venezuelan petroleum to the United States, where the Houston, Texas, Lake Charles, Louisiana, and Delaware Valley refineries remained,

9. A former agriculture minister from the pre-Chávez era told McCoy that land titles in Venezuela had been unclear since the 1960s land reform, when the government distributed some of the best land to military and public officials, who in turn leased it or lent it to others to farm. It was even more difficult to demonstrate land titles back to the nineteenth century.

along with those located in Curaçao, the only ones in the world capable of refining Venezuelan crude oil on a large scale.

After Chávez renewed his mandate in the 2006 presidential elections, he moved rapidly to deepen the revolution. Rather than reach out to his opponents and reciprocate the gestures of recognition from the losing candidate, he immediately began to concentrate even further on his personal control of the country by seeking and receiving decree powers from the National Assembly, creating a single official political party—the Unified Venezuelan Socialist Party (PSUV)—and devising constitutional reforms.

To implement his vision of "twenty-first-century socialism," Chávez announced his intention to withdraw Venezuela from the International Monetary Fund and World Bank, initiated a state takeover of a majority share in the country's heavy oil projects (previously dominated by foreign oil companies), and nationalized with compensation companies in strategic sectors of the economy over the following two years, including telecommunications, electricity, steel, and banking. Negotiations with foreign oil companies resulted in four of six companies accepting the new terms of state majority joint venture control, while two companies (Exxon and Conoco-Phillips) refused to accept this arrangement, filed arbitration claims, and withdrew from Venezuela. In terms of organization of the productive sector, "twenty-first-century socialism" in 2007 envisioned a mixed system including social property, collective property, individual property, and private (enterprise) property, but the government soon shifted from its previous ideas of cooperatives and worker-management schemes (cogestión) to the idea of "social production companies."

The president also moved to revamp the organization of political representation, announcing his intention to form a single official party, the PSUV, while still allowing opposition parties. Somewhat surprisingly, some of the government-allied parties declined to join the new party, causing some commotion. Although they declared themselves to still be in favor of the revolution, the president stated they would now be considered opposition.

The government also began to change the country's political structure, creating a parallel system to the elected mayors and governments. Communal Councils of up to four hundred families each were formed across the country and could receive funding directly from the executive to carry out neighborhood projects. This was interpreted either as a positive move to create more citizen empowerment and local control over budgets or as a negative arrangement that would encourage corruption, displace elected local governments, cause the state to abdicate its responsibilities, and create a direct link between the president and local communities.

The most controversial move the government made in 2007 was to refuse to renew the license of the RCTV, the most vocally oppositionist private television station, which had legally expired that May. The government justified its decision on both technical grounds, asserting nonpayment of taxes, and political grounds, asserting that the station and its managers had supported the 2002 coup and urged citizens to overthrow the government. The television station claimed it was political recrimination because it had been critical of the government. The move unleashed a torrent of international criticism from media associations and human rights groups. Even those who recognized the overtly political role that RCTV had played in 2002–04 argued that accusations of "coup-mongering" should be tried in the courts rather than administratively through this mechanism.[10]

Perhaps most importantly, the government's move reawakened a student movement that had been dormant for nearly twenty years. Student activists took to the streets, in a specifically nonpartisan manner, to protest the infringement on free speech and political dissent, refusing to align with opposition parties in organizing marches. This movement would prove even more important in December 2007 when the president put his constitutional reform proposals up for a vote.

The Battle over Constitutional Reform

With his renewed mandate, the president not only began initiating the described economic changes but also established a commission to begin writing constitutional reforms behind closed doors. The presidential proposal became public in August when it was sent to the National Assembly (still controlled by the governing party), which then added another bloc of reforms when it presented the proposal to the public in November, one month before the referendum. Although the reforms contained some "carrots" such as a shortened work day, a voting age lowered to 16, and social security for informal workers, the most controversial reforms included the following:

- allowing the indefinite reelection of the president (but not governors and mayors) and the extension of presidential terms to seven years;
- geographically reorganizing national territory and reducing the role of elected governors, as the president would name vice presidents over regional territories and channel funding through them;

---

10. Both the Carter Center and the Washington Office on Latin America made press statements along these lines that criticized the move.

- renaming and redefining the military as a "popular, patriotic, and anti-imperialist" force and creating a popular militia under the president's control;
- creating a new branch of government called the popular power and centralizing the communal councils;
- reducing civil liberties and due process under states of emergency;
- reducing citizen political participation by increasing the signature requirements to petition for recall and repeal referenda;
- reducing the independence of the Central Bank and, without clear definitions, creating additional categories of property to include social, cooperative, public, and private property.

Early in the fall of 2007, opposition political parties seemed disorganized and could not decide whether to participate in or abstain from the constitutional reform approval referendum; these divisions continued up to the December vote and they were unable to enact a coherent campaign against the constitutional reforms. Amid these divisions, new leadership emerged to challenge the government from unexpected sources. First, the student movement that had been born in protest of the closing of the RCTV in May reemerged to oppose the constitutional reforms. The students played an important role in galvanizing the public to vote against the reforms and not abstain. In addition, the largest of the government-allied parties (Podemos), which had earlier refused to join the president's new party, now openly rejected the reforms. Finally, the recently resigned defense minister, General Raul Baduel, came out publicly against the reforms, arguing that it concentrated too much power in the hands of the president. He was considered the most important military official still supporting Chávez. His views, and his standing within the military, reflected divisions and uneasiness among the Chavistas over the reforms.

Overall, criticisms centered both on the process and the substance. The process questions included the lack of public consultation in the writing of the reforms, the short time for public discussion and inequity in campaign resources, and the very legitimacy of requesting such fundamental changes to the constitution through a reform process rather than through electing a constituent assembly. The substantive questions centered on the overall consequences of the reforms: an increase in the centralization of power within the figure of the president, an increase in the socialist character of the state without clear definitions, and a reduction in the participatory nature of Venezuela's democracy, which had been one of the hallmarks of the Bolivarian Revolution.

Although President Chávez tried to make the referendum a plebiscitary vote on his own rule, in the end, the public voted on the constitution itself. Even though Chávez continued to enjoy approval ratings of over 60 percent, many of his supporters uneasy about the reforms appear to have abstained from voting as an expression of their continued support for him. Opponents of Chávez appear to have adhered to the call to vote rather than to abstain, and after a day with reports swinging wildly about the nature of the results, the final vote was an extremely close 51 percent to 49 percent in defeat of the reforms. This was the first electoral defeat of Hugo Chávez in his political career, across a dozen votes in nine years.

The reasons for the defeat included both mistakes by the government and dissatisfaction of the people. The government failed to understand the depth of dissatisfaction arising from its performance. Crime was the number one priority of the population, followed by unemployment and then a host of public service concerns including health, education, housing, and garbage collection. Poor public maintenance was reflected in lines of workers forming outside public office buildings waiting for a single working elevator to get to their offices. The new bridge to get to the airport was still not complete, two years after its collapse. Economic concerns included a 20 percent inflation rate and growing shortage of basic food.

The public appeared to blame the president's ministers rather than himself for the lack of progress, and the president fed that perception as he berated his ministers on his *Aló Presidente* program and changed his cabinet frequently. Nevertheless, by the time of the referendum, the vote became in some sense a punishment of the government for focusing too much on politics and too little on governing. Political reasons were also at play. Polls indicated that citizens supported social democracy (or democratic socialism), but not socialism without democracy, and they opposed continuous reelection. Other political/electoral mistakes included the fact that President Chávez himself spent much of November out of the country rather than in the country campaigning; the government responded harshly to its internal critics and to the student movement; and the government's own governors and mayors refused to mobilize their electoral machines since they would lose personal power, being one of the principal victims of the regionalization reforms.

The president's reaction was slow in coming as he wrestled with how to handle the defeat, with the CNE delaying a final announcement of the results until early in the morning following the referendum. Nevertheless, Chávez accepted the defeat and said his movement would undergo a process of review and correction of course. An interesting debate among Chavistas ensued to analyze the political, economic, social, and electoral reasons for the defeat.[11]

The government and its supporters turned the defeat into a victory by pointing out how the defeat proved the democratic credentials of the president and the autonomy of the CNE. The president also immediately began preparing for the November 2008 elections for governors and mayors, since his constitutional reform to create new regional vice presidencies appointed by the president had just been defeated. Chávez moved to speed up the creation of the PSUV and hinted that he would pursue a coalition with his former allies who had refused to join the PSUV. The opposition, meanwhile, announced that it would form a united slate of candidates to challenge the government candidates.

Further Radicalization

The defeat in the constitutional referendum was a wake-up call for the government, and initially it appeared the government would focus on improving government performance and perhaps engage in self-criticism and internal ideological debates. Food shortages were addressed aggressively over the course of the next year with a plan for food sovereignty that included expropriating national and foreign property and food industrial plants that did not comply with the government mandates for producing basic foodstuffs under federal price controls. Although these policies, along with massive imports, caused food shortages to abate, they raised concerns about respect for private property rights.

Social missions continued and the communal councils were given opportunities to create local public work projects. The effectiveness of these policies, however, appears to have been mixed. Although there is general consensus that poverty and unemployment was reduced and that more people had access to potable water, the impact of the adult literacy mission and the program that placed Cuban doctors in the neighborhoods has been difficult to measure and subject to debate. Serious housing shortages continued, and the homicide rate continued to be one of the highest in the region.[12]

Chavistas were divided between those favoring a stronger role for the state in carrying out the needed reforms (the top-down approach) and generally more positive about political parties, and those advocating more radical democracy and a bottom-up grassroots approach focused on social

---

11. San Juan, "Referendum del 2D en Venezuela."

12. McCoy, "Engaging Venezuela."

movements and citizen democracy.[13] These positions were reflected in the divergent evaluations of the social missions and communal councils which were perceived as either duplicative, inefficient, and dependent on the state, or as important empowerment tools that represented the beginnings of radical democracy.

This and other divisions concerning the strategy of revolutionary change (for example, questions over the speed and end goals of the revolution) existed within Chavismo but were never given an open hearing or space for ideological debate and clarification. Even during the creation of the PSUV, such an ideological debate failed to occur. The lack of space and even tolerance for internal debate and dissension is one of the strongest criticisms of Chavismo and could prove to be a fatal weakness over the long term.[14] At the same time, the unwillingness to define the long-term goals of the revolution and the lack of ideological debate has allowed Chávez to personally manage the competing currents within the movement through occasional back stepping and pragmatic actions, even while he has appeared to veer closer to the hard-line view as time goes by.

The elections for governors and mayors in November 2008 were hard fought. Dissatisfaction with government performance resulted in the governing party's loss of the five largest states and several major cities. The most striking results were in the Caracas urban areas, where official candidates lost in the races for mayor of the greater metropolitan area and mayor of the eastern half of Caracas, which includes the largest poor neighborhood of the country. This was the first time the government had lost these votes, and the loss came despite running some of the president's closest confidants as candidates and the president campaigning personally on their behalf. Though not necessarily a rejection of Chávez personally, the vote reflected the frustration of the people with the inability of the government to solve the pressing problems of soaring crime rates, lack of water and paved roads, unemployment, and inflation.

The ability of the opposition to use these victories to deliver better government services and thus launch competitive bids for national-level offices would depend, however, on national revenue sharing and the cooperation of the federal government. The Chávez administration had already rolled back some of the decentralization reforms of the previous decade and decreased the autonomy of municipal and state governments. Within five months of the vote, the National Assembly passed a law transferring control of ports,

---

13. Ellner, *Rethinking Venezuelan Politics.*
14. See San Juan, "Referendum del 2D en Venezuela" and Ellner, *Rethinking Venezuelan Politics.*

airports, and highways from states to the national government. Even more blatant was a law creating a new presidentially appointed head of government of the Caracas district, marginalizing the opposition-elected mayor of the metropolitan area.

This trend toward recentralization was defended by Chavistas as combating neoliberalism and its advocacy of small states, as well as opposition governors and mayors who wanted to privatize certain services. But this trend was characterized by others as undermining the constitutional provision for the decentralization of power and a blatant attempt to reduce the role of opposition leaders and their chances to move toward national office. The latter charge was reinforced by efforts in early 2009 to reopen corruption charges against several prominent opposition and dissident leaders, including former presidential candidate and Zulia governor Manuel Rosales and dissident General Raul Baduel.[15]

The world financial crisis hit Venezuela full force in September 2008, with oil prices plummeting from a high of $150 per barrel to about $30 per barrel. Venezuela's 2009 budget was initially calculated at $60 per barrel, so the downturn was expected to increase pressure on the budget deficit in a country where 50 percent of the government budget and over 80 percent of export earnings comes from oil revenues.[16] The financial pressures and the mixed outcome of the November 2008 regional elections motivated the government to accelerate its plans to accomplish the reforms defeated in 2007 and to further implement its socialist program.

Some of the defeated constitutional reforms were implemented in a package of twenty-nine decree laws issued by the president just before his eighteen-months of delegated powers expired in July 2008; others were enacted by the National Assembly. A final reform—continuous presidential reelection—was proposed by the National Assembly at Chávez's urging, with a referendum to approve it on February 15, 2009. Although previously defeated in 2007 and not receiving high public opinion favorability two months before the vote, Chávez proposed in January to include all elected offices in the proposal. This change, combined with aggressive campaigning (and inequitable campaign conditions and convoluted wording for the referendum question, which did not mention continuous reelection at all), helped

---

15. Baduel was imprisoned in a military facility in April 2009 awaiting trial, while Rosales fled the country and gained asylum in Peru to avoid pretrial detention in Venezuela's notoriously dangerous prisons.

16. Venezuela still held large international reserves in early 2009 (about $45 billion), but with oil production declining and large commitments both domestically through the social missions and internationally through Venezuela's various partnerships and aid programs, these reserves were not expected to last more than a year without rising oil prices.

produce a strong "yes" vote of 54 percent. Thus, terms limits were removed for all elected positions in Venezuela, and Chávez would be eligible to run again in the 2012 presidential elections.

The Opposition Advances

Tensions with the media erupted again in 2010 when the government stopped the broadcasts of RCTV's remaining cable operations, allegedly because it broadcast only part of the president's public addresses, and arrested the president of the 24-hour news channel Globovisión for making critical comments about Chávez. Two students were killed in subsequent protests and the U.S. government, along with many NGOs, condemned these actions.

Elections for the National Assembly in September 2010 gave the opposition an opportunity to regain a presence in the body that it had boycotted five years earlier. This time, opposition parties formed a unified slate of candidates under the Democratic Unity banner and won an important victory in breaking the PSUV's supermajority, which had allowed it to approve constitutional amendments and constitutional-rank laws (66 percent of votes required), appoint public authorities, and approve enabling laws delegating legislative power to the president (60 percent required). Counting another small party that broke away from the governing coalition, opposition parties won 40 percent of the seats and 52 percent of the popular vote. Redistricting prior to the vote and the creation of additional single-member districts led to the difference between the popular vote and the seats won in the assembly.

The lame-duck assembly approved a number of laws in the month before the new assembly took office in January 2011 to further develop the goals of "twenty-first-century socialism." Among those laws were several developing the concept of popular power and creating a "communal state" organized around communal associations at the neighborhood, city, federation, and confederation level. These laws further elaborated on one that had been approved earlier in 2010 to implement the concept of the Federal Council outlined in the 1999 Constitution to manage the transfer of resources from the central to the regional and municipal governments. The 2010 law gives the president the right to transfer competencies (and presumably funds) of municipal and departmental governments to the new communal system established under the so-called popular power laws. Other laws approved in December 2010 focused on the development of social property and social accountability, based on the encouragement of "socialist ethics."

Perhaps most controversial was the enabling law delegating legislative power to the president to be able to respond to severe floods in late 2010. The length (eighteen months) and breadth (covering not only housing and reconstruction from the floods, but also infrastructure, tax policy, international cooperation, economic system, personal security, telecommunications, and armed forces) of the law led to accusations from the opposition that the outgoing assembly had essentially usurped the powers of the incoming assembly through most of the period leading up to the December 2012 presidential elections.

The Disengagement of the Third Parties

Both the Carter Center and the OAS were invited to observe the October 2004 regional elections, but the invitations came only in October, so both organizations declined. To observe an election generally requires a presence on the ground four to six weeks before an election and an invitation two months prior to that to allow time for fundraising and organization. The OAS was heavily engaged in observing other elections in the region during that time period. In addition, the Carter Center noted that the opposition continued to question the work of the international observers and, under such conditions, it would not be seen as a trusted external observer by some of the contenders. The Carter Center considers trust to be an essential condition for international observation.

The Carter Center's efforts at reconciliation between the government and the media and the private sector following the recall referendum did not bear fruit. The government managed the negotiations by consulting with each individual media organization, telling the Carter Center that it was very difficult to talk with the media as a group, stating that they were "impossible to deal with." The largest private media directors told the Carter Center that they would accept William Ury and that the government should be the one to invite Ury to bring the media and government together to talk about the law, but the government declined to do so.

Meanwhile, the Carter Center's proposed economic-social dialogue between the government and the private sector was declined by the government, which instead began individual talks with businessmen and industrial sectors. The various chambers of commerce and industry, as well as the largest family-owned businesses in Venezuela, largely took the view that, since the government had won and would be in place for some time and since the government was actively involved in the economy as a client, supplier, contractor, and licensor, they should negotiate with the government to advance their own business positions.

The lack of interest on the part of the government in external help with social or political dialogue was made clear in a phone call between President Chávez and former president Carter on November 2, 2004, in which Chávez responded to Carter's question about the timing for Ury's visit: "We were waiting for the regional elections, but now we're making an internal effort. If it turns out that we do not have the internal capacity, then we will call you for help, like a medical doctor."

Knowing that there was no opening for high-level dialogue after the recall referendum, the Carter Center remained concerned about how to sustain the societal level initiatives for dialogue and tolerance that had grown over the two-year conflict: Aquí Cabemos Todos and the Strengthening Peace in Venezuela Program. The Carter Center had been supporting both of these groups with technical assistance through the visits of Ury and Lederach, as well as with the guidance of Francisco Diez and another Argentine specialist the Carter Center had brought to Caracas for these purposes, Ana Cabria Mellace. The UNDP had supported these efforts by providing salary support to local Venezuelan coordinators and to some of the groups' activities.

After the recall referendum, the Carter Center began to help these groups establish themselves as self-sustaining entities and seek funding for themselves from the World Bank and elsewhere. The Carter Center continued to provide salary support for Cabria Mellace to provide technical assistance to them, but the World Bank funding did not come through and eventually the UNDP ended its support as well after a new resident coordinator arrived in October. The Aquí Cabemos Todos group of intellectuals initiated its own efforts to help facilitate talks on the electoral conditions, and some of the members created the national electoral observation organization known as Ojo Electoral (Electoral Eye).

The Carter Center also maintained a part-time consultant in Caracas to monitor political developments, and it remained focused on individual cases of judicial harassment and pretrial detentions throughout 2004 and 2005. Specifically, it raised its concerns with President Chávez and the attorney general about several cases, including those involving Súmate and the opposition mayor, Enrique Capriles Radonsky.

The OAS basically disengaged from Venezuela except for electoral observation missions in 2005 and 2006. Even during the RCTV episode, the reaction of the OAS secretary general (and of the government of Brazil) was to conclude that the decision not to renew RCTV's license was within the purview of government administrative authority.

After the opposition boycott of the December 2005 legislative elections, President Carter wrote to President Chávez to present some ideas for increasing the legitimacy of the electoral process and to arrange a meeting between Jennifer McCoy and the president in January 2006. During that trip, McCoy found Chávez and the government very concerned about the possibility that the opposition (particularly AD and Copei, which would not be running candidates and had little to lose in urging a boycott) would threaten to boycott the presidential election scheduled for December 2006 in an attempt to delegitimize Chávez's potential reelection. Chávez welcomed the Carter Center's ideas about how to raise public confidence in the electoral process by making it completely transparent. McCoy proposed four things: to complete an external audit of the voter list, an action the Carter Center had also recommended following the recall referendum; to review the electoral laws and make them consistent with each other, the constitution, and new technology; to return to a manual vote or to count 100 percent of the paper receipts from the electronic machines; and to choose a nonpartisan, permanent CNE through a consultative and open process that included international monitoring of the appointment process, perhaps involving Mercosur.[17]

President Chávez and the president of the National Assembly expressed interest in these ideas, and the presidents of the CNE and the National Assembly requested that the Carter Center prepare a study of Venezuela's electoral laws and inconsistencies and offer recommendations for reform based on best international practices.[18] McCoy's impression at the end of the trip was that the government was more interested in international assistance—specifically, that the Carter Center help shore up its legitimacy—than it had been in 2005 following its recall referendum victory. In fact, after asking the National Assembly president to meet with McCoy in his absence, Chávez cut short an international trip, at least in part, to see McCoy before her scheduled departure. Nevertheless, Chávez and the National

17. The Carter Center got the idea for international monitoring from the Ecuadoran 2005 case in which an international body composed of the United Nations, the OAS, and the Andean Community of Nations monitored the selection process of a new Supreme Court following a constitutional crisis in Ecuador.

18. The Carter Center commissioned four experts from four different Latin American countries to write the report, focusing on the issues that had raised the most disputes about Venezuela's elections. See The Carter Center, *Reflexiones y Aportes para la reform de la Legislacion Electoral Venezolana* (Atlanta, GA: The Carter Center, July 2006), http://cartercenter.org/resources/pdfs/peace/americas/EstudioElectoralVenezuela1%20CarterCenter.pdf .

Assembly president said they would have to think about the international monitoring idea but in the end never responded to it. Instead, they made a different strategic calculation and had the National Assembly (now 100 percent controlled by government-allied parties) appoint a new CNE that was more technically proficient but that was widely viewed as having a 4:1 partisan bias in favor of the government (including three carryovers from the previous CNE).

The Carter Center continued to work on improving electoral conditions and in a May 2006 visit to the country, McCoy encouraged the new CNE president to consult with the political parties and establish clearly the rules of the electoral game (including audit procedures) before the presidential candidate registration deadline in August, so that candidates would know the conditions under which they would be competing and thus have no reason to boycott so long as those conditions were met. This happened to a large degree, and in the end the opposition united behind Governor Rosales and participated in the December election.

The Carter Center decided to field a small observation mission to focus on the electronic machines as part of its larger effort to develop techniques and criteria for international election observation of automated voting systems, in conjunction with other large organizations—the United Nations, the OAS, the European Union, the OSCE. The Carter Center wanted to pilot the methodology it had been developing in Venezuela. It ended up presenting an extensive report on the Venezuelan system and the methods of observation in 2007.[19]

The Carter Center felt that keeping political space open in 2007 through the electoral process would be important for focusing on two key issues. First was the government's growing control of the country's resources, which was very evident during the 2006 presidential campaign, as the government had extraordinary economic resources at its disposal, and the government's growing control over and access to the media. By 2007 the tide had changed from a predominantly private and critical media market to one with a growing presence of government-owned or government-influenced media.[20] Second was the growing possibility of moving to a majoritarian

---

19. See Carter Center, *Observing the 2006 Presidential Elections in Venezuela: Final Report of the Technical Mission* (Atlanta, GA: The Carter Center, November 2007), http://cartercenter.org/resources/pdfs/news/peace_publications/democracy/venezuela_2006_eng.pdf.

20. By 2007 the government had greatly expanded its media reach after it bought out four private television stations, created cooperative relationships with other private stations, created hundreds of communal radio stations, established Telesur (South America's CNN), and then canceled the license of the oldest private station and the one with the furthest national reach (RCTV).

Students ask for NO vote on the 2007 constitutional reform program.
Courtesy of SURpress.

electoral system that favored the governing party. The Carter Center co-sponsored an electoral seminar with the Venezuelan NGO Ojo Electoral to explore these issues.

Given the continued polarization within the media itself, with private and public media continuing to present very different pictures of the country, the Carter Center began a new project in late 2008 that was focused on bringing together journalists from across the political spectrum to exchange views about the practice of journalism in Venezuela and encourage professional reporting over partisan reporting. The project offered training in specific areas of professional journalism as well as colloquia and forums for discussion and debate.

The International Front

After the defeat of the recall referendum in 2004, Chávez shifted his focus to external adversaries, primarily the United States and Colombia. This competition with the United States made it more difficult for Venezuela's regional neighbors to react to the consolidation of presidential power inside Venezuela. The United States' attempts to enlist other countries into isolating Venezuela were resisted by most of Latin America. Indeed, Latin American countries resented being put in the position of choosing between the two countries. At the same time, Venezuela's volatile relationship with neighboring Colombia—which was the main ally of the United States in South America during this time period—demonstrated the capacity of Chávez for both brinksmanship and pragmatism when national interests were at stake.

United States

Venezuela and the United States entered into a rivalry for regional allies reminiscent of the Cold War competition for influence between the United States and the Soviet Union. Although the Bush administration was fairly quiet during the fall 2004 U.S. presidential campaign, after Bush's second inauguration in January 2005, U.S. secretary of state Condoleezza Rice stepped up the verbal volley. In a January hearing at the Senate Foreign Relations Committee, Rice succinctly depicted the U.S. argument against Chávez, stating that Chávez's government was "unconstructive" and that Chávez was a "democratically elected leader who governs in an illiberal way."[21] The United States claimed that Chávez was threatening democracy in Venezuela and supporting radical elements in South America.

Venezuela publicly responded, saying that the United States was planning to assassinate the president, destabilize the government, and invade the country through Colombia. Chávez privately told McCoy in February 2005 that he wanted help to improve relations, and that Presidents Lula da Silva and Álvaro Uribe were both talking with Bush along these lines as well. Meanwhile, the Venezuelan government was forming armed militias and beefing up the army reserves, ostensibly to be prepared to repel a U.S. invasion.

The "diplomacy by microphone" damaged both sides. In Venezuela, Chávez's talk about a U.S. threat instilled fear in some sectors of the population, creating a rally-around-the-flag effect of political support, and justified his forming armed militias under his control, apart from the regular armed forces. Chávez terminated counternarcotic operations with the U.S. Drug Enforcement Agency in August 2005 and repeatedly threatened to cut oil exports to the United States were the United States to invade Venezuela. On the other side, the United States' verbal provocations provided political ammunition to Chávez, while its heavy-handed attempts to push other Latin

---

21. Remarks by Secretary of State Condoleezza Rice to the U.S. Senate Foreign Relations Committee, January 18, 2005.

American governments to oppose Chávez in a new "containment" strategy created a backlash within the region. A Venezuelan human rights lawyer told McCoy in February 2005 that he feared the U.S. was falling into a trap: by responding to Chávez's provocations with its own threatening messages, the United States would eventually allow Chávez to declare a state of emergency.

The competition between Venezuela and the United States was played out vividly in the contest to choose a new OAS secretary general in April 2005. After U.S. attempts to rally support for its initial candidate (from El Salvador) failed, the next U.S. candidate (from Mexico) went head-to-head with a Venezuela-backed candidate (from Chile) in five rounds of voting at OAS headquarters. Finally, the Venezuelan-supported candidate, Chilean José Miguel Insulza, won. In a contest at the United Nations in November 2006 for a rotating seat on the Security Council, the United States aggressively opposed Venezuela's bid, fearing that Venezuela would be disruptive on a multitude of foreign policy issues. After forty-seven rounds of voting without a resulting winner, Venezuela and Guatemala agreed to step down from the race in favor of consensus candidate Panama.

In May 2005, another incident occurred involving the Venezuelan request to the United States to extradite Luis Posada Carriles, a Venezuelan-Cuban accused of being the mastermind of violent attacks against Cuba, including hotel bombings and the 1976 bombing of a Cuban jetliner in which seventy-three people were killed. Posada Carriles had recently entered the United States from Panama, where he had been hiding. Chávez argued that the U.S. government would be hypocritical if it refused to extradite a known terrorist such as Posada Carriles while carrying out its own war on terror and indefinitely detaining prisoners in Guatanamo, Cuba. The Bush administration, meanwhile, under pressure from Cuban-Americans who regarded Posada Carriles as a hero, resisted the extradition request, arguing that he would not gain a fair trial in Venezuela's partisan judicial system. In the end, Posada Carriles was detained for two years on immigration charges and then released in Miami.

Yet another incident with the United States involved the resurgence of the Súmate case—the Venezuelan NGO that had supported the opposition during the Venezuelan recall referendum and been accused by the government of conspiracy for accepting a grant from the U.S.-based National Endowment for Democracy. Súmate's director Maria Corina Machado became a cause célèbre when she was invited to the White House to meet with President Bush in May 2005 as Venezuela was investigating her ties to the Carmona government during the April 2002 coup. The National Endowment for Democracy announced it would increase financial support to Venezuelan NGOs, and shortly after Machado's White House visit, she and three other Súmate leaders were scheduled to go on trial for conspiracy. The trial was continually postponed over the following three years but served as a warning to other NGOs to take care in their financial and political relationships with the U.S. government.[22]

Chávez opened another front in the rivalry with the United States when he opened a new regional twenty-four-hour news station meant to compete with CNN and the "imperialist news media" and to provide the news from the South's perspective. Inside the United States, Chávez responded to the catastrophic flooding of New Orleans after Hurricane Katrina by offering fuel oil and aid, reaching out to the American people while criticizing the Bush administration's failure to provide for its own citizens.

Although the microphone diplomacy calmed down in 2007 and 2008 under Assistant Secretary of State Tom Shannon's leadership in the U.S. State Department, the relationship deteriorated further in September 2008 when Venezuela expelled the U.S. ambassador in solidarity with Bolivia's complaint that the United States was supporting secessionist movements there. Nevertheless, with the inauguration of the Obama administration, Venezuela signaled that it was willing to try a more cooperative relationship with the United States and the two countries reinstated their ambassadors in mid-2009. Shortly thereafter, however, a scene from the past was replayed as Venezuela protested the signing of a U.S.-Colombia defense cooperation agreement that gave the United States access to Colombian military bases, an act that Venezuela viewed as threatening to its own sovereignty. U.S. waffling on Honduras further infuriated Venezuela, leading Chávez to increase his criticism of U.S. policy. At the Copenhagen Summit on Climate Change in December 2009, Chávez made a personal attack on Barack Obama, saying that there remained the smell of sulfur from the devil in the room—a direct reference to a line in his 2006 speech at the United Nations General Assembly that followed George W. Bush.

The most recent irritant between the two countries in 2010 was the naming of a new U.S. ambassador to Venezuela. After private testimony critical of Venezuela by the nominee, Larry Palmer, was leaked in August, Venezuela declared that he was no longer suitable to be ambassador. The Obama

---

22. Machada was eventually elected to the National Assembly as an independent (nonpartisan) deputy in September 2010, winning the highest number of votes of any opposition deputy and positioning herself as a leader of the opposition.

administration maintained its support of Palmer and revoked the visa of the Venezuelan ambassador at the end of 2010. As of this writing, the issue remains at an impasse.

Colombia

On December 15, 2004, Colombian bounty hunters captured Fuerzas Armadas Revolucionarias de Colombia (FARC) "foreign minister" Rodrigo Granda in Caracas and brought him to a Colombian border town where he was arrested by Colombian police. This set off a diplomatic crisis between Venezuela and Colombia that involved other regional neighbors and was repeated four years later when Colombia bombed a FARC guerrilla camp in Ecuador.

The volatile relationship between Venezuela under Hugo Chávez and Colombia under Álvaro Uribe simply deepened an historic national rivalry kept in bounds by mutual trade dependence. Uribe and Chávez appeared as polar opposites: Uribe was elected on a security platform of getting tough with the Colombian guerrillas, maintaining a close alliance with the United States, and promoting strong free trade. Chávez was anti-United States and antineoliberalism, and seemed to befriend the Colombian guerrillas. Yet in reality the two men shared common traits: both were charismatic and populist, with autocratic streaks. Both centralized control and changed their respective countries' constitutions to stay in power long enough to try to solve the primary problems they defined for their respective countries (security for Colombia and social justice for Venezuela).

In the case of Granda, news emerged that this high-level FARC leader had lived unrestricted in Venezuela for some time and was rumored to even have received a voter identification card. The Venezuelan government argued that no request for extradition and no Interpol report had been presented to it, and therefore it had no basis to restrict his stay in the country. Further, he had a valid Colombian passport when he entered and, with 1.2 million Colombians in Venezuela, it asked how immigration officials could be expected to stop him.[23] When Colombian authorities reportedly entered Venezuelan territory without prior warning or authorization, Chávez suspended all agreements with Colombia and recalled Venezuela's ambassador, demanding an apology from Colombia. Brazilian president Lula da Silva mediated, while the United States demanded that Venezuela stop harboring guerrillas. Six weeks after the incident, Colombia issued

---

23. Maripili Hernandez, Venezuelan vice minister for North America, in conversation with McCoy, February 9, 2005.

an apology for the "inconvenience" and promised the incident would not be repeated.

Venezuela's on-and-off relationship with Colombia continued, illustrated by Venezuela's attempted cooperation to secure the release of hostages held by the FARC in 2007. Uribe approved Chávez's role as negotiator with the FARC in September but cancelled that authorization in November. Chávez continued his efforts and secured the release of two hostages in January 2008, but was unable to resolve the high-profile hostage cases that he had been working on. Colombia subsequently managed to secure the release of the high-profile hostages in a daring rescue mission conducted by the Colombian military.

A Colombian raid into Ecuadoran territory on March 1, 2008, in pursuit of the FARC first produced an aggressive reaction not from the Ecuadoran president but from Chávez, who amassed troops at the border, closed border trade, and broke diplomatic relations with Colombia. Colombia embarrassed Venezuela by subsequently leaking to the press that the computers captured in the Ecuadoran raid showed that Venezuela had provided material support to the FARC (a claim that Venezuela denied and for which proof was not made public).

Nevertheless, the trade relationship between Colombia and Venezuela was so important to both countries that their leaders repeatedly acted pragmatically in patching up differences and restoring diplomatic relations to protect their commercial relationship. Chávez renewed relations with Colombia again within months of this incident, only to freeze trade in 2009 in reaction to Colombia's defense cooperation agreement with the United States. He broke relations completely when, just days before leaving office, Uribe formally accused Venezuela in the OAS of aiding the FARC. It took a new president—Juan Manuel Santos—to reach out to Chávez and overcome the diplomatic crisis, beginning a new honeymoon period between the two countries.

Analysis and Lessons

Lessons Learned by the Third Parties in the Recall Referendum

The first lesson learned by the third parties following the recall referendum is that the reactions by each side to a recall outcome may restrict the possibility for national reconciliation. At a September 2004 presentation to the Inter-American Dialogue, McCoy laid out three potential scenarios for postreferendum Venezuela. As a means of setting up these scenarios, she reviewed the two contrasting explanations of the results of the recall referendum that emerged in Venezuela after the referendum: according to the first explanation, the government believed that the election would be tight and wanted to ensure a victory by "fixing" the machines to pad the results; according to the second explanation, the government managed to leverage natural incumbency advantages to win, and thus opposition cries of fraud were an attempt to shift attention away from its own political errors and loss.

The future of Venezuela depended on which of these two interpretations gained most strength in the country. The three possible scenarios that she envisioned at the time were as follows:

- *The government conspiracy theory is proven correct.* Although it would not be possible to prove the government actually lost the referendum, as opposed to simply added to its numbers, the mere fact of any proven manipulation would delegitimize the government and the CNE. Therefore, the door would be open for genuine negotiations to change the country's institutions and rules, and the OAS would be pressured to act.

- *No government conspiracy is proven, but the opposition continues to refuse to accept the results.* In this case, the electoral process would be discredited in the eyes of 40 percent of the population, leading to abstention in the October 2004 regional elections and no electoral gains for the opposition. The opposition would fail to win significant concessions from the CNE and no real political dialogue would occur, though economic dialogue would be possible. International actors will have been discredited by the opposition for accepting Chávez's victory and would therefore not be able to help oversee regional elections. Hemispheric governments would not be motivated to intervene.

- *No government conspiracy is proven, and the opposition accepts the results.* In this case, the opposition would negotiate some greater transparency and controls from the CNE. Internal and external actors would encourage more genuine dialogue, and international observers would help ensure transparency of regional elections. The opposition could then begin the hard work of organizing in the *barrios* (poor neighborhoods) rather than continue to play media games. The opposition could then also shift its time-horizon to the long term (e.g., 2006 elections) to match the government's long-term perspective and strategy.

The second scenario is the one that emerged, as the social opposition (the labor unions, private media, and private sector) essentially returned to its traditional role of defending its own sectoral interests, and the political opposition undermined its own electoral viability with the fraud allegations (although the new committee of governors and mayors was able to win some concessions from the CNE). In fact, during all of the Carter Center's scenario planning prior to the referendum, the one scenario it never predicted was that the opposition would commit political suicide. It had a significant 40 percent of the population behind it but failed to mobilize its supporters either for future electoral victories or for confrontational politics. Instead, it remained divided, looking for someone to blame for the loss, and effectively removed one of the "poles" from the polarized political context for the next three years.

The Carter Center's earlier prediction about the prospects for reducing conflict after the recall referendum was only partially correct. As described in chapter 7, the Carter Center thought that if there was no opening for dialogue and reconciliation before the recall, there would be none after, and confrontation would escalate because neither side would be completely eliminated. While some in the opposition believed that Chávez would be forced to negotiate and seek more consensus in order to govern and deliver services to the people, Chávez was willing to negotiate only with those willing to come into his revolution on his terms. Indeed, the principal dynamic after the referendum was one of the government expanding its control in the wake of a virtually shattered opposition. Thus, although there was no real effort at national reconciliation, direct confrontation did not reemerge.

The second lesson learned by third parties following the recall referendum is that the parties to the conflict will end their invitation for third-party involvement when it no longer serves their interests. Both sides wished to have the OAS and the Carter Center present in the country because they believed that these external actors could assist them in their goals. The government wanted the international legitimacy that the moral authority of Jimmy Carter's interventions could provide and came to accept the OAS role as facilitator and observer—though reluctantly—for the same reasons. Once the recall referendum was over, the government no longer needed this international legitimating factor and was happy to see all international parties go. Meanwhile, the opposition expected the international actors, especially the OAS, to mediate a real agreement between the opposition and the government and help enforce the government's compliance with the agreement. Although the opposition had a closer personal relationship with Gaviria, it also came to see the value of Carter's personal relationship with Chávez and hoped Carter would be able to persuade Chávez to agree to and follow fair rules in the contest. After the recall referendum, the Coordinadora Democrática leaders found it difficult to explain their loss given their high poll numbers the previous year and their conviction that no rational citizen could support the president. Rather than analyze the shortcomings of their campaign or the contextual changes in the bases of the president's support, they looked for other actors to blame. In addition to the CNE and the automated voting machines, and later the voter list, various opposition leaders and groups blamed a weak international observation for failing to enforce stricter rules and ensure an opposition victory. They focused their blame primarily on the Carter Center, even though the OAS and the Carter Center had jointly carried out the observation, made joint statements, and organized joint press conferences, and came to the same conclusion that the recall reflected the will of the people with no evidence of electronic fraud.

Conspiracies abounded and outlandish rumors resurfaced, including the report from 2002 that the government had paid the Carter Center more than $1 million. The accusations ranged from simple charges of naïveté and incompetence on the part of the observers to allegations of nefarious conspiracies between Bush, Carter, and Chávez to ensure oil supplies to the United States, or between Carter, Cisneros, and Chávez to endorse a fraudulent recall in exchange for profits by Cisneros (it is not clear what Carter was to gain in this last theory). These conspiracy theories were so outlandish that the Carter Center did not even respond to them. Individual citizens wrote e-mails to McCoy and Carter holding them personally accountable for all the "evil" deeds of the president and for the government's continued existence. Op-eds and newspaper editorials in Caracas and the United States joined in the chorus. In this sense, Venezuelan citizens were expressing their own feelings of impotence to control their own lives and attributing an exaggerated power to the international actors.

Lessons Learned by the Opposition in the Electoral Contests

The opposition boycott of the 2005 National Assembly elections had a devastating effect on the opposition's capacity to stem the Bolivarian Revolution or build its own electoral alternative. With no justification in terms of electoral malfeasance or poor electoral conditions, the boycott could not delegitimize the new National Assembly. Furthermore, with an assembly completely under the control of government allies, the government was free to legalize its deepening of the revolution. Within the opposition, those who consistently led the abstentionist strategy lost power and credibility (primarily the traditional parties of AD and Copei), while the newer parties emerged as the new leaders. The quick acceptance of defeat of the opposition candidate in the 2006 presidential elections, Manuel Rosales, illustrated a changing attitude of the new opposition. It also showed signs that these new leaders recognized the need to build their parties from below and offer constructive messages beyond simple calls for Chávez's ouster.

The opposition had learned following the 2007 constitutional reform referendum not to overread the victory. The votes against the constitutional reform reflected an uneasiness about its content, not necessarily a vote *for* the opposition. The mixed results of the 2008 regional elections demonstrated that voters could be counted on to vote on the actual performance of local governments. For example, voters rejected several prominent Chavista candidates in areas where Chavista incumbents had performed particularly poorly. A second lesson for the opposition from the same election, however, was that it tended to lose in those races in which it was divided and presented more than one candidate. The opposition learned that lesson well going into the 2010 National Assembly elections and met their goal of impeding a government supermajority in the new assembly.

Lessons Learned by the Government in the Electoral Contests

Just as the opposition learned lessons from the electoral contests, so too did the government. First, divisions within Chavismo that emerged over the 2007 constitutional reforms showed the limits of arbitrary change. For the government, the specific lesson was that the people would not automatically support the government's political project, just as it did not automatically support the Punto Fijo regime. The people would only support it if it was clearly a democratizing project, and the 2007 constitutional reforms seemed to go backward, reversing the gains from the 1999 Constitution.[24] Combined with a breach between promises, expectations, and actual government performance, these perceptions resulted in the defeat of the reforms through an active "no" vote and a passive abstention, and highlighted the tensions within the Chavista base.

Second, following the defeat, it became clear that although the old state had been destroyed, a new, capable state had not yet replaced it. The "punishment" aspect of the vote was a clear signal from the population that it wanted basic issues of governance and public service addressed and that the constitutional reforms were not going to be able to address these issues. An historic problem of Venezuela is a weak and ineffective state. As Ana Maria San Juan points out, Chavismo should not try to transfer state func-

---

24. For an analysis of this point, see San Juan, "Referendum del 2D en Venezuela."

tions to popular sectors (such as through the communal councils). Rather, it should learn lessons from elsewhere in Latin America and strengthen the state to carry out public services and strengthen the capacity of the people to hold the state accountable.[25] Specific lessons from other countries include those related to participatory budget oversight, effective direct democracy, access to public information, and popular accountability mechanisms over public officials.

By the time of the 2010 National Assembly vote, the virtual division of the electorate into two equal voting blocs produced two different readings for Chavismo: the radical view that the government needed to move faster to implement and demonstrate the benefits of socialism and regain popular support; and the pragmatist view that it needed to slow down, correct the problems of corruption and mismanagement, and pursue change at the pace of the population's capacity to absorb it. One thing was clear, however: both the government and the opposition were reading the results in light of the all-important upcoming 2012 presidential election.

Conclusions

Once the invitation for outside intervention was ended, it became very difficult for international actors to influence the internal conflict or political developments inside Venezuela, particularly given two factors: the strong electoral legitimacy of the government and the absence of leverage over an oil-rich state in terms of aid and loan packages. Most Latin American neighbors declined to react to the country's internal political dynamics, even when the concentration of political power was evident, citing the electoral legitimacy of the government. Other actors such as the OAS and European Union restricted themselves primarily to the traditional role of election observation. The United States tried an isolationist strategy, but without leverage from aid or loan packages, and with the mutual constraint of the commercial oil relationship, it could do little more than make public criticisms.

However, the mutual trade dependence between the United States and Venezuela, and between Colombia and Venezuela, restrained the United States and Colombia from initiating permanent breaks with Venezuela, and vice versa, despite severe ideological differences. The behavior of the Venezuelan voters in the 2007 constitutional referendum and the 2008 regional elections also demonstrated the limits of the people's tolerance for

---

25. Ibid.

change and poor government performance. It may also be indicative of the constraints that the people will place on aspiring revolutionary leaders who come to power, and maintain power, through electoral democracy.

In many ways, the Chávez administration represented a continuation of Venezuelan political life that defined the forty-year Punto Fijo democracy, though with intensified characteristics. Dependence on oil revenues continued, though government control and use of the revenues increased. Centralized control during Punto Fijo was centered in two political parties, while under Chávez it came to be centered in a single party and a single leader. Control of foreign currency has always been used by political leaders to assert their control over economic activity in Venezuela, and this continued under Chavismo. Corruption and a more assertive foreign policy have typically increased during petroleum booms, and this has been the case with Chavismo as well.

In contrast with Punto Fijo, however, the Bolivarian Revolution does not seek stability through consensus building. Rather, it seeks change through confrontation. After the presidential elections in 2006, the government showed no interest in dialogue with the 40 percent of the country who opposed it. After the losing candidate recognized the president's victory and the opposition's minority status for the first time, the president declined to reciprocate by engaging that opposition leader (or any other opposition leader) in political dialogue. Ministers with whom the Carter Center met said they could not or would not meet with anyone the government considered opposition, including academic experts. Generally speaking, the government brooked no criticism and continued with the view that the opposition should be eliminated rather than be seen as a counterpart with which to negotiate or reach compromises.

The vulnerabilities of the current administration were clear: the extreme concentration of power in the president's hands with no clear successor or institutional legacy meant that the country was not only subject to his own changing ideas but also vulnerable to any accident or illness befalling him. The incapacity of the government bureaucracy to keep up with the speed with which the president aspired to transform the country risked increasing popular dissatisfaction and deterioration of services. The president's announcements of nationalizations and changes in economic policy discouraged foreign and private investment. Currency controls and government policies contributed to a shortage of imported inputs for manufacturing and shortage of locally produced foods with controlled prices. Perhaps as a reaction to these vulnerabilities, the government became even more hostile to dissidence, arresting high-profile critics and curbing the powers of opposition-elected leaders in 2009–10.

Finally, the abrupt decline of oil prices in the wake of the 2008 worldwide financial crisis highlighted the vulnerabilities of a petrostate to external shocks, whether governed by the Left, the Right, or the Center. Although the Chávez government included as a major part of its strategy the revitalization of OPEC, thus helping to engineer the cuts in production and rise in prices of the 2000s, the inability of OPEC to control the price free fall in late 2008 put in stark relief the vulnerabilities of governments dependent on oil rents.

Despite these vulnerabilities, Chávez until 2010 consistently maintained approval ratings well above 50 percent and won every vote at the polls except one referendum. The willingness of so many citizens to accept the growing concentration of power in exchange for the empowerment they felt from the president's recognition of them, as well as for the material benefits they were receiving, illustrates the level of the country's grievances and deep desire for political and social change over the last decade. The Chávez administration's extension of control over the remaining independent institutions after the recall referendum became a self-fulfilling fear of the opposition, while the opposition's lack of understanding of the Chavista base impeded its ability to compete effectively with Chávez.

In fact, in each of the conflict cycles analyzed in this book, the opposition gave up a part of its power base, as it withdrew from each contest and contributed to Chávez's victories. In the authors' analysis, Chávez did not begin with a clear plan of how to consolidate power but rather took advantage of each challenge presented by the opposition and bested it. A potential shift in this balance began to emerge in 2010 as the opposition more effectively united and began to develop alternative messages credible to the population, and as the internal vulnerabilities of the Chávez movement began to be reflected in electoral outcomes. The challenge for the opposition remained convincing the population that the social changes enacted under Chavismo and enshrined in the 1999 Constitution would be protected in a post-Chávez world, while the challenge for Chavismo remained institutionalizing the social changes while also protecting the political rights enshrined in the 1999 Constitution.

10

Conclusions

T he Carter Center began its work in Venezuela in July 2002 at the invitation of the Venezuelan government to help facilitate a national dialogue following a failed coup. It found a society deeply divided and a potentially violent social and political crisis threatening governability of the country. The roots of the crisis lay in the long-term social and political exclusion of large sectors of the population, the struggle for political control and redistribution of national resources and the concomitant clash of development strategies, and the confrontational style and strategy of the Chavista movement led by President Chávez. The consequences of these factors (and symptoms of the crisis) were weakened political institutions and eroded checks and balances, extreme polarization, personal insecurity, and two opposing camps, each with some sectors willing to negotiate and some "spoilers" who wanted simply to eliminate the enemy.

The Carter Center's initial aim was to foster a legitimate, inclusive, and multisectoral dialogue seeking reconciliation and the restoration of functioning, trusted political institutions in Venezuela. Its ultimate aim was to prevent escalation of the conflict into violence, as it saw warning signs and increasingly feared this possibility over the course of the next months. McCoy and Diez initially believed they could reach an agreement with Venezuelan actors on the design for a longer-term national dialogue with national and international verification mechanisms, and a short-term truce between government and media. For the longer-term dialogue, they hoped to build an international coalition to provide technical and financial assistance to the dialogue, and incentives and disincentives to encourage compliance by the actors with any agreements reached.

As discussed in this book, the authors' initial ideas did not go as planned, and the intervention, which they initially thought might last two months, stretched into two and a half years. The intervention came to involve an unprecedented coalition of two intergovernmental organizations and an international NGO. The secretary general of the OAS personally spent seven months, several days a week, facilitating a dialogue table. An international Group of Friends involving six nations was formed.

Through this intensive involvement, the international community strove to prevent a deep political conflict from turning violent. The intervention was thus unusual not only in its organization and depth, but also in that it was occurring before any violence had actually erupted. Indeed, throughout the intervention, Venezuelans managed to avoid the widespread bloodshed that many thought likely in July 2002 and largely resolved the question of the legitimacy of President Chávez's mandate through their rejection of a recall initiative to shorten his term in office. Even so, Venezuelan society remained polarized—a large number of citizens questioned the validity of the recall vote and the underlying elements of the dispute remained unresolved. Conflicts persisted over whether and how to guarantee a separation of powers and independent political institutions; what the role of the state should be in the economy; whether and how resources should be redistributed to address social exclusion and inequality; and what constitutes legitimate and effective political participation and representation. The ultimate goal of preventing violence was achieved by the intervention, but the underlying issues producing polarization and new forms of political exclusion were not resolved.

What explains the mixed results of such an unusual international intervention? The explanation is found at several levels. First, although new opportunities for international influence arose from post–Cold War democracy norms, there are structural constraints on how much influence international actors can have on a resource-rich state. This helps explains both the ability of international third-party actors to prevent violence and promote electoral democratic practices in Venezuela and the limits of the same actors to sustain an international intervention capable of addressing the underlying disputes and influence the course of domestic events once the express invitation for their involvement had been withdrawn.

Second, the competing perceptions and values of the opposing sides in Venezuela made it necessary for the mediators to attempt to sufficiently change those perceptions to alter the calculus of each side and open spaces for negotiation. The mediators were able to take advantage of only some of the opportunities for changing perceptions, however, due to the personalities of the mediators themselves, the personal relationships among the actors and the mediators, the nature of the mediators' respective organizations, and the mediators' own real-time analyses, which lead them to miss certain opportunities.

Third, a sustained peacebuilding initiative at the societal level was fundamental to transforming the Venezuelan conflict, but organizational and resource constraints on the part of the Carter Center and the UNDP prevented this from occurring.

This chapter elaborates on this explanation for the mixed results of the international intervention and identifies lessons for international relations theory and democracy promotion and for conflict resolution theory and practice.

Lessons for International Relations Theory and International Democracy Promotion

As described in chapter 2, the international actors faced three dilemmas in their attempts to prevent conflict in Venezuela. These related to issues of sovereignty and constraints on international intervention; the actors' potentially competing roles as mediators/facilitators and as observers/monitors; and the potentially competing goals of peace and democracy. These dilemmas are explored again in this section to extract lessons for future interventions in similar contexts and to help explain the eventual outcomes in Venezuela.

Applying International Norms and Leverage and Respecting Sovereignty

The nature of the conflict within Venezuela was deeply affected by the international context of the early twenty-first century, which in turn created certain dilemmas for international third-party actors in Venezuela related to international democratic norms and state sovereignty. The international community had a good deal of experience globally in applying universal human rights, intervening in humanitarian crises, and postconflict peacebuilding. Venezuela, along with the rest of the hemisphere, approved the Inter-American Democratic Charter in 2001, committing itself to a particular form of democratic practice and to international sanctions if those forms were violated. These norms both inspired and constrained the Venezuelan actors as they sought international allies and legitimacy in their struggle for power. The government sought recognition and legitimation of its authority as the elected government; the opposition sought help to remove a government it considered to be violating democratic norms. The ideas and norms of the early twenty-first century further inspired the Venezuelan actors in their search for domestic legitimacy in terms of identity politics, empowerment of marginalized groups, and individual rights and freedoms.

The post–Cold War international context also empowered the international community to intervene in Venezuela to protect democracy as the Inter-American Democratic Charter was invoked to protest the coup against Chávez and then the OAS, the United Nations, and the Carter Center received and accepted invitations to facilitate dialogue in an attempt to prevent violent conflict, promote the resolution of conflict within democratic procedures, and consequently help protect human rights. The established practice of international election monitoring had previously been applied in the 1998 and 2000 elections in Venezuela and provided the context for the invitations to the OAS and the Carter Center to observe the unprecedented signature collection and recall referendum.

International democracy norms also constrained both the Venezuelan actors and the international community in important ways. The international condemnation of the military coup against President Chávez in April 2002 helped to fracture the coup coalition and overturn its outcome within forty-eight hours. Further unconstitutional acts were contemplated by radical anti-Chavistas but never carried out due to a lack of international and domestic support. The government also felt the constraints of the new international context as it highlighted its electoral legitimacy, accepted international election observation, avoided excessive use of force and curtailment of civil liberties in its struggle against its opponents, and sought legal backing through legislation and judicial rulings for each of its actions. As demonstrated in chapters 6 and 7, the joint international election mission played a crucial role in ensuring that Venezuelan rights to petition for a recall referendum were respected, though it was a slow and tortuous process.

However, international democracy norms have their limitations, as they have focused on elections as the fundamental component of democracy. International monitoring capacity has evolved much more extensively in the realm of electoral processes than in other components of democracy, including participation, rule of law, and civil liberties.[1] The Inter-American Democratic Charter itself provides for international intervention only when the

---

1. Extensive reporting and monitoring mechanisms for human rights protection have also been developed through the UN system and the Inter-American system, but in the Venezuelan case, human rights violations have been less flagrant; the Inter-American Commission on Human Rights has been impeded in its monitoring role in situ by the requirement to have government invitations, and the UN system did not detect sufficient violations to send special rapporteurs there until 2010.

constitutional order is altered or interrupted, but it does not define such an alteration. Thus, the charter's application has been limited thus far to the traditional military coup. It is ill-equipped to deal with more modern democratic threats involving constitutional crises among competing branches of power or threats from armed and even unarmed nonstate actors.[2] The charter does provide for international assistance when requested by governments, but that assistance has also tended to focus on the electoral arena, in both technical assistance and election monitoring.

While the international community was heavily involved in the Venezuelan conflict between the 2002 coup and the 2004 recall referendum, it scaled back its involvement dramatically following the recall referendum, in spite of continued political polarization and a growing concentration of power in the hands of the executive and ruling party, leading to complaints from the opposition of growing violations of democratic norms and civil rights. Several factors discussed in this book explain this withdrawal from the Venezuelan context. First, the OAS and the Carter Center could no longer play a facilitating or mediating role when one party to the conflict—the opposition—lost its confidence in and withdrew its invitation to them, attributing the outcome of the recall referendum at least in part to the international actors' incompetence and even alleging their collusion in electoral fraud.

Second, the gradual nature of the concentration of executive power and the ambiguity of its democratic character impeded international reaction. A growing political science literature on "gray zone" democracies—neither full liberal democracies nor outright dictatorships—attempts to analyze the characteristics of these alternative political regimes and the movement from one type of regime to another.[3] In Venezuela, the transition from the Punto Fijo (or Fourth Republic) political regime of 1958–98 to the Bolivarian Revolution (or Fifth Republic) represents a transition from a low-quality liberal democracy to a more limited electoral democracy, with tendencies toward electoral authoritarianism.[4]

2. Jennifer McCoy, "Transnational Response to Democratic Crisis in the Americas, 1990–2005," in *Promoting Democracy in the Americas,* ed. Sharon Lean, Tom Legler, and Dexter Boniface (Baltimore, MD: Johns Hopkins University Press, 2007).

3. Thomas Carothers, "The End of the Transition Paradigm," *Journal of Democracy* 13, no. 1 (2002); the 2004 issue of *Democratization* (11, no. 5) edited by Croissant and Merkel; Larry Diamond, "Thinking about Hybrid Regimes," *Journal of Democracy* 13, no. 2 (2002); Levitsky and Way, *Competitive Authoritarianism;* and Schedler, *Electoral Authoritarianism.*

4. McCoy and Myers, eds., *The Unraveling of Representative Democracy in Venezuela;* Javier Corrales and Michael Penfold, "Venezuela: Crowding Out the Opposition," *Journal of Democracy* 18, no. 2 (2007): 99–113; and Michael Shifter, "In Search of Hugo Chavez," *Foreign Affairs* 85, no. 3 (2006): 45–59.

This conceptual ambiguity was reflected in international politics as different foreign governments emphasized different aspects of Venezuelan democracy: the Bush administration in the United States tended to downplay the electoral legitimacy of the Chávez administration while highlighting deficits in its governance, claiming that it was an "illiberal democracy" that failed to govern according to democratic rules. Brazil and other neighboring governments highlighted the repeated electoral mandates won by the Chávez administration and the legal basis of the government's actions, while refraining from criticizing such actions as the Chávez administration's refusal to renew RCTV's television license or its politicization of the judiciary. Another view of Venezuela emerged as well, highlighting the progressive nature of Venezuelan democracy in terms of its participatory mechanisms and empowerment of popular sectors.

These competing views of Venezuelan democracy remained largely at the rhetorical level as a result of the third factor limiting more decisive international action in Venezuela: the limits of international influence and leverage in a resource-rich state. As indicated in chapter 2, Venezuela's significant petroleum revenues and the related commercial interests of foreign governments both reduced the leverage of those international actors who might otherwise have made international loans and aid conditional upon domestic political reform, and influenced the actions of foreign governments benefitting from commercial relationships with Venezuela and discounted Venezuelan oil. The mutual energy and trade dependence between the United States and Venezuela, and between Venezuela and Colombia, in particular, constrained all three governments from breaking relations or otherwise damaging their relationship for extended periods of time.

The limits and opportunities provided by petroleum resources became especially evident during the 2002–03 petroleum strike. At that time, the United States was preparing to invade Iraq and was especially concerned that the Venezuelan oil strike end so that world petroleum supplies would not be further interrupted in the wake of the invasion. As a result, the United States pushed for an end to the strike even if it meant keeping Chávez in power.

Finally, the traditional notions of sovereignty and nonintervention, historically strong in the Western Hemisphere, came to play a role in the international community's withdrawal from Venezuela in two ways. First, neighboring Latin governments remained reticent to comment on, much less intervene in, the internal affairs of a fellow government for several reasons. In addition to the conceptual ambiguities regarding democracy and the economic interests noted earlier, the fear of setting precedents for international monitoring and sanctions on internal domestic affairs restrained many Latin governments, lest they be next to receive unwanted international attention. Second, the Chávez government played up the sovereignty card in its calls for South-South alliances and in its constant warnings against U.S. imperialism and alleged invasion and assassination plots, particularly in the wake of U.S. approval of the 2002 coup and after 2004. Other governments in the OAS resisted U.S. pressure to isolate Venezuela or to be caught in the competition between the United States and Venezuela in the international arena.

Dealing with Shifting Mandates and the Competing Roles of Mediation and Monitoring

A second dilemma, as noted in chapter 2, arose from the shifting mandates given to the international actors by the Venezuelan parties to the conflict and the potential contradictions and conflicts among these roles. From the beginning of the international involvement, Venezuelans were divided over whether the Tripartite Working Group's role should simply be as facilitator (the government's view) or as a guarantor of a negotiation process that would lead to binding agreements (the opposition's position). As the international participation evolved and the May 2003 agreement eventually reached to respect the constitutional rights of citizens to petition for a recall of the president, the role of the same international actors (particularly the OAS and the Carter Center) shifted to an electoral focus. This role included both facilitation of the negotiations over the continually evolving rules for the unprecedented referendum process and monitoring of the ten-month referendum process.

The dilemma was whether the same actors who had mediated a conflict could and should objectively monitor and "judge" its outcome (i.e., serve as international observers at the recall referendum). At the time, the Carter Center and OAS secretariat considered the recall process to be a continuation of the political conflict and its attempted resolution. The two organizations viewed their mandate to include facilitating the implementation of, and monitoring compliance with, the agreement they had facilitated, in this case the constitutional right to petition for a recall of the president. At the practical level, they also recognized that no other international actor would be able to serve as international monitors—the United Nations did not observe elections without a Security Council mandate, usually in civil war contexts, and the European Union did not have sufficient time or guarantees to mount a mission.

Several decision points involving this dilemma arose for the Carter Center during its two-plus-year intervention in Venezuela, such as whether it should

- leave at the conclusion of the May 2003 agreement, as the OAS temporarily did;
- help negotiate the conditions for the recall process, but decline the invitation to observe the signature-collection process beginning November 2003;
- leave in protest of the *planas* (similar handwriting) decision in March 2004;
- leave after the repair process was concluded in May 2004, which resulted in the recall referendum being announced;
- leave July 1, 2004, when the CNE declined to guarantee the Carter Center conditions for observation during McCoy's visit;
- leave after the August 15, 2004, vote without conducting the second audit.

The Carter Center could have decided at any of these points to withdraw, but as discussed in chapters 3–8, after careful consideration of each point, it believed the benefits of remaining in Venezuela outweighed the potential risks and costs.

With hindsight, however, McCoy and Diez now believe that the proper time to have ended the Carter Center's involvement as observers was June 2004. The decision to hold the recall referendum, announced on June 3, 2004, at the conclusion of the repair period, completed the terms of the May 2003 accord that indicated that the political crisis could be resolved through application of the constitutional provision for citizens to petition for recall of their elected officials. As noted, the May 2003 accord in reality did not represent any negotiated concessions; instead, it simply ratified both sides' acceptance of the existing constitutional right to petition for the recall of the president and recognized that this right had an associated procedure to determine whether the recall referendum would be held. The recall referendum itself would produce an *outcome* that both sides hoped would "resolve" the conflict—in short, the defeat of the other side. Of course, the Carter Center was never under any illusion that a referendum would resolve or transform the underlying conflict. Indeed, the international community at large generally favored the referendum as a democratic and constitutional "solution" to a political crisis, preferable to a coup or violent conflict.

The Carter Center continued to mediate the terms of the petition procedure through early June 2004. Its help in facilitating and monitoring the creation of the procedural aspects of the signature-collection and -verification process were simply part of the implementation of the accord and did not have an outcome per se. The procedure simply provided the opportunity for citizens to call for a voting process (referendum) that would itself produce an outcome, with a winner and a loser. When that petition procedure concluded by triggering the recall referendum, the Carter Center could have decided to let another organization assume the responsibility of monitoring the recall referendum itself. This was a fundamentally different type of process, requiring observers who would evaluate and judge the process (and by implication legitimize or not its result).

By declining to shift to the role of election observer, the Carter Center would have been more likely to preserve its own role as potential mediator for the inevitable conflicts that would arise in the aftermath of the recall referendum. That decision would have had costs as well, however: Gaviria and the OAS would have had to make the decision to observe alone and would have been held responsible for the outcome. Given the eventual reaction of the losers, the OAS's ability to play any further role in Venezuela could have been damaged, with longer-term costs to that organization.

If the OAS had also declined to observe, it is unlikely that any other organization would have stepped in to fulfill the monitoring role necessary to continue to provide confidence in the process, for the reasons previously discussed.

Navigating Peace and Democracy

A third dilemma specifically faced by the Carter Center involved the potential competition or conflict between the Carter Center's own goals in Venezuela. As noted in chapter 2, the Carter Center's overall goal was to provide facilitation that could help resolve the conflict in a peaceful way—avoiding violence and enabling the country to collectively address its significant social transformation and accompanying tensions within a democratic framework.

The very concept of democracy was being debated inside and outside of Venezuela, contributing to the conflict. The competing conceptions were never understood by the other side. Chavistas (and the Left in the United States and Europe) focused on democratic deepening from a participatory point of view, such as by creating a strong electoral legitimacy, increasing avenues for citizen participation through referenda and community councils, and promoting the social inclusion and empowerment of the previously marginalized popular sectors. Venezuelan opposition figures (and many in the U.S. scholarly community and U.S. administration), on the other hand, focused on formal procedures of democracy, protection of property and other rights, and legal formalities in identifying democratic deficits in Venezuela: the erosion of the rule of law, curtailment of civil liberties and property rights, and the recentralization of power in the national government and the presidency.

While they recognized some legitimacy emanating from Chávez's electoral victories, opposition leaders failed to recognize (and never understood) the main source of Chávez's political legitimacy: the visibility, human dignity, and hope that he gave to those who felt invisible.[5] This lack of understanding of Chávez's base prevented the opposition from presenting a convincing alternative message and offer to the electorate. Combined with the message of fraud, this failure to provide a convincing alternative contributed to the opposition's repeated losses at the ballot box between 2004 and 2006, and to Chavismo's domination of elected positions at all levels in the country. The Chávez administration subsequently used that electoral dominance to extend its control over other institutions in the country between 2006 and 2010.

An important question for conflict resolution and democracy theorists and practitioners is whether the goals of peace and democracy are always mutually reinforcing, or whether they can be potentially conflicting at different stages of the conflict. The latter may be the case especially with elections, an inherently divisive process that becomes even more so under conditions of conflict.[6] In the Venezuelan conflict, the Carter Center was consciously

---

5. The competing views of political legitimacy are illustrated in two contrasting anecdotes: (1) during the collection of signatures to demand a recall referendum against the president, an old dark-skinned man began to yell at the well-dressed people standing in line: "We will not return to being invisible" (*"No nos vamos a volver a ser invisibles"*); (2) in a meeting at the foundation of one of Venezuela's richest families, a former minister of the interior during the Punto Fijo political period, Asdrubal Aguiar, told the story of how he handled the problem of security within the poor and violent slums ringing the capital city in the mid-1990s. He first sent police inside the slums to collect arms, but soon learned that this led the amount of violence to actually increase. He concluded that the slums had their own system of justice in the form of gangs and their bosses who imposed order, and that the intervention of the state would disrupt that order. So he decided instead to simply cordon off the slums from the rest of the city, thus protecting the "real citizens." This strategy of physically separating, and ignoring, the poor met with approval from the others in the room, and admiration for its creativity. This same segregation and lack of attention also applied to other public policy areas, with an absence of schools, hospitals, and doctors in the *barrios*, and explains the popularity of the Chávez government "missions," which brought public services for the first time to the *barrios*.

6. For a discussion of postconflict elections and the conditions under which they may contribute to peace or encourage a return to war, see Andrew Reynolds and Timothy D. Sisk, eds., *Elections and Conflict Management in Africa* (Washington, DC: United States Institute of Peace Press, 1998); Pauline H. Baker, "Conflict Resolution versus Democratic Governance: Divergent Paths to Peace?" in *Turbulent Peace: The Challenges of Managing International Conflict*, ed. Chester A. Crocker, Fen Osler Hampson, and Pamela Aall (Washington, DC: United States Institute of Peace Press, 2001), 753–64; Timothy D. Sisk, "Democratization and Peacebuilding: Perils and Promises," in *Turbulent Peace: The Challenges of Managing International Conflict*, ed. Chester A. Crocker, Fen Osler Hampson, and Pamela Aall (Washington, DC: United States Institute of Peace Press, 2001), 785–800; Terence Lyons, "The Role

striving to promote inclusiveness and preserve political space for dissent. The authors, representing the Carter Center, recognized the possibility that pursuing negotiations could simply be buying time for both sides to build their capacity for undemocratic actions. As long as the two sides resisted the concept of coexistence and the possibility of negotiating issues of democracy, such as those related to the preservation of separation of powers or the guarantee of political space for the marginalized poor, the ability to protect and expand democratic spaces in the country was restricted.

An important lesson for democracy promotion theorists relates to the use of elections as a conflict management tool. Although the international community espoused the recall referendum as the best solution to the crisis, and the only democratic alternative for the opposition to remove Chávez, the Carter Center knew a vote could not resolve the conflict and carried the risk of actually deepening it. Therefore, all along, the Carter Center strove to focus on the two sides' actual grievances and policy differences and on de-politicizing institutions so that both sides would have guarantees if they lost power. It also focused on social reconciliation and finding a shared vision of the country that would move the parties away from zero-sum calculations toward stable coexistence.

The Carter Center tried to get the actors to talk *before* the recall about the rules for the recall and a governability accord so that whoever won would not be facing destabilization after the recall for the next two years. However, since the Carter Center knew this would be very difficult to achieve, it also planned a strategy for immediately *after* the recall to sit the two sides down and talk about what safety guarantees each side needed.

In the Venezuelan case, the counterintuitive logic of electoral contests identified by Laurence Whitehead was not witnessed: generally speaking, electoral campaigns produce intense periods of partisan confrontation and politicization, which are abruptly replaced once the vote counting begins by an equally intense collective discipline for the winners and losers to accept a legitimate outcome.[7] This requires strong institutions and multiple sources of reinforcement or compensating factors that can be domestic or external, local or national, legal or societal.

---

of Postsettlement Elections," in *Ending Civil Wars: The Implementation of Peace Agreements*, ed. Stephen John Stedman, Donald Rothchild, and Elizabeth M. Cousens (Boulder, CO: Lynne Rienner Publishers, 2002), 215–35; and Paris Roland, *At War's End: Building Peace after Civil Conflict* (Cambridge: Cambridge University Press, 2004).

7. See Whitehead, "Closely Fought Elections and the Institutionalization of Democracy," and Jennifer McCoy, "The 2004 Venezuelan Recall Referendum," *Taiwan Journal of Democracy* 2, no. 1 (July 2006): 61–79.

In the Venezuelan recall referendum, both sides told their supporters in the campaign that the vote would determine the very future of their society, raising the stakes in a context of high distrust. McCoy examines the potential compensating factors to determine why this case did not follow the positive outcome posited by Whitehead that a "hotly contested election that inflames partisan passions may actually precipitate intensified efforts at institutionalization strong enough to reinforce the inclinations of all parties to work within agreed rules from then onwards."[8] In this case, the potential compensating factors included institutions, such as the CNE and Supreme Court; societal actors, such as the media and moderating population sectors; and foreign actors, such as governments and international election observers. The potential domestic moderating factors, however, were weak: the CNE and Supreme Court were perceived as partisan, no clear rules existed for the signature-collection process for the referendum; the media moderated its coverage during the campaign but for the most part returned to its partisan stance immediately after; and no independent domestic observer group formed. International actors thus became the primary compensating mechanism, and in the end they were insufficient to compensate for the absence of domestic mechanisms and generate full acceptance of the results.[9]

Although it is not the intent of this volume to characterize and explain the Venezuelan political regime as it evolved, the authors have considered how national and international perceptions of the integrity of the referendum process may have impacted the national and international actors' perceptions of the legitimacy of the political regime. These perceptions in turn influenced the strategic calculations of national and international actors during and after the referendum process, as these actors sought to influence or react to the power struggle and nature of democracy in Venezuela.

Lessons for Conflict Resolution Theory

Two central elements in the field of conflict resolution theory are the notion of timing of the intervention (ripeness) and the use of track $1^1/_2$ diplomacy within a conflict transformation approach. Although it is not possible to predict a moment of ripeness for intervention in a conflict, it is very useful to revisit both created and missed opportunities to intervene and influence the course of a conflict. The Carter Center identifies its approach as track $1^1/_2$ which, as will be explained, is more consistent with the concepts of conflict transformation and

8. McCoy, "The 2004 Venezuelan Recall Referendum," 6.
9. Ibid.

peacebuilding than with the more traditional concepts of conflict or dispute resolution. As this section argues, when designing interventions as third parties in conflicts similar to the one discussed in this book, it is essential to lengthen the horizon of the planned intervention to more than three years.

The Question of Timing

Conflict resolution literature offers various analyses concerning the "ripe moments" of conflicts.[10] Christopher Mitchell's questions regarding ripeness are particularly salient: "ripe for what? to solve it? to start negotiations? to introduce a third party? to present solution options? to end it or change its level?"[11]

In the Venezuelan case, the Carter Center asked itself, from the very beginning of its intervention, whether the conflict was ripe enough for an international facilitator to usefully intervene. Indeed, Carter's initial facilitation offer was rejected, while Gaviria's was accepted, even though the objective circumstances of their initial involvement was mostly the same and separated only by three months. The actors were the same, the level of "hurting stalemate" between both sides was the same, the costs and fears were essentially the same, and the external conditions of the conflict were the same and did not seem to present extraordinary opportunities. Why, then, was Carter's initial offer rejected, while Gaviria's was accepted?

As discussed in Chapter 3, the difference between the two offers has to do with two factors. The first factor is that the Tripartite Group (OAS, UNDP, and Carter Center) performed detailed and precise preparation work and focused on prenegotiations for two months before Gaviria's first visit, which was not possible to do in the short time (one week) between the Carter Center's initial assessment mission and Carter's initial visit. The second factor relates to the perceptions of the decision makers from both sides. For the opposition to have the OAS secretary general as facilitator was especially meaningful, both because the government had been reluctant to accept an OAS role (what is bad for my opponent must be good for me, and vice versa) and because the OAS attributed to him supranational authority and an ability to exert great pressure on the government. For its part, the government perceived something different, attributing a different meaning to the same thing (as usually happens in all conflicts). The government saw the participation of the OAS secretary general as a guarantee that

---

10. For a useful analysis of the four models, see Christopher R. Mitchell, "Cutting Losses: Reflections On Appropriate Timing" (working paper 9, Institute for Conflict Analysis and Resolution, George Mason University, 1995).

11. Ibid.

the "coup-monger" sectors of the opposition (especially the military sectors condemned by Gaviria) would be controlled and a reassurance of the government's international legitimacy.

These two cases demonstrate that the willingness of parties to accept third-party intervention—specifically, its ripeness for intervention—is not constant: their willingness may be affected by work done at preparatory stages and may change as the perceptions of decision makers change. In the end, it was the Carter Center's initiative to create the Tripartite Working Group—that is, combining the Carter Center (insisted upon by the government) and the OAS (insisted upon by the opposition)—that influenced the comfort level of the actors regarding international intervention and allowed them to accept third-party facilitation.

In the authors' experience, "ripe moments" are not predictable. The concept could be useful for an ex-postconflict analysis about what important elements were taken into account at a given moment in a given situation. But as an analytical tool for diagnosis and prescribing future action, the danger is that it could be used to justify inaction or failure, as in the Aesop's fable about the wolf not being able to gather grapes and concluding they are not yet ripe.

As Jeffrey Rubin says, the "ripe" moment can undoubtedly be created by the third party.[12] Expanding this reasoning, it is obvious that when one works in a conflict situation, entering as a third party, one becomes part of a dynamic system and has some influence on it, as an element of the system. The art is in understanding when and what kind of influence can be exerted on this system from within, as well as what move the third party needs to make to generate a change of the system in a given direction.[13] In that sense, the right question is not whether the conflict is "ripe or not ripe" for a given intervention, but rather what kind of influence third parties can have at a given time over the system they are involved in. It is relevant because the burden of the question, and the responsibility for the answer, is placed on the third party. In other words, the conflict situation, from the third party's perspective, cannot be seen as an external situation that can be analyzed and dissected in pieces. At the very moment the third party begins to interact with the actors in the conflict, his or her mere presence influences the whole

---

12. Rubin, "The Timing of Ripeness."

13. Paul Watzlawick, John Weakland, and Robert Fisch, *Change: Principles of Problems Formation* (Barcelona: Herder, 2003).

system and begins to generate new realities.[14] And that generation of new realities is a process that unfolds over time. It is a process that responds not only to structural variables and the wide set of decisions taken by the actors in the conflict but also to a number of influences impossible to predict and control, making uncertainty a distinctive feature of every conflict.

As a third party in a broad sociopolitical conflict, one sails into a sea of uncertainties, where one's own values are the only constant, where pursuing the prevention of violence and creating conditions for coexistence is the general direction, and where the navigation route is built upon a balanced set of interpersonal relationships, structural analysis, experience, and intuition.

A Series of Missed and Created Opportunities

To learn from the Venezuelan case about the relative usefulness of the concept of "ripeness" and the Carter Center and OAS's ability to create those conditions, it is first necessary to review their work as third parties in Venezuela, identifying both the opportunities that they missed to influence the course of the conflict and the opportunities that they created. There are several key moments at which they could have influenced the situation and perhaps spawned a more positive course for the conflict situation, including the following:

- *November 2002.* As recalled in chapter 4, Gaviria had the opportunity to stop the strike (or to prevent it from turning into an oil strike), but he missed it. He did get the opposition to offer to stop the strike in exchange for the government's ending of the intervention with the metropolitan police. But when he received the phone call from the government representative asking the opposition to cease the street protests, he understood it as a frivolous demand since it was obvious (for him) that the protestors were far out of the reach of the opposition leaders. He rejected the request, telling the minister of labor on the phone, "Call me again if you are seriously ready to negotiate," thus closing the moment of opportunity.

  Although he was right about the objective situation, and perhaps about the government not being serious about making a deal, it is now possible to posit alternatives and ask what would have happened if, for example, he had offered to go personally to the presidential palace to

---

14. As Chavista leader Elías Jaua told Diez privately in an informal conversation in Uruguay two years after the Carter Center and OAS left the country, "It is a relief to know you are no longer there, watching everything we are doing, because when you were present all the time, we in the government needed to consider at every moment what the internationals would say about this or that decision."

discuss the government's needs for an agreement, instead of staying at the hotel with the opposition leaders waiting for the government representatives to call back. Here the personality of the facilitator becomes important: Gaviria's understanding of how third-party impartiality should be enacted (at a distance from both parties) most likely prevented him from "offering his assistance" to one of the parties or from going to the government's headquarters to try to help the government come up with a proposal that could be accepted by both sides.

- *December 2002.* Chapter 4 describes a November 26, 2002, phone conversation between Carter and Chávez, in which Chávez expressed his willingness to personally participate in negotiations facilitated by Carter and Gaviria, and Carter expressed his willingness to travel to Caracas after the Nobel Peace Prize ceremony on December 10, if Gaviria agreed. Gaviria declined the offer and the Carter Center decided not to push for the negotiations. It is impossible to say what the opposition's reaction at that point (mid-December) would have been to negotiations with Chávez, with the petroleum strike still in full steam and the government beginning to respond with oil and food imports. Looking back, however, it was clearly one of the few opportunities in which Chávez himself was open to becoming personally involved in negotiations with the opposition.

- *February 2003.* After Carter presented his electoral proposals on January 29, 2003, the Carter Center failed to provide sufficient follow-up. Carter would not stay in Caracas and Gaviria was not committed to the proposals, but the Carter Center staff could have pushed both parties to give better and more comprehensive answers to the proposals. Part of the problem lay in the bargaining system established by the negotiation table, where the proposals were presented. The table became a black hole, leaving Carter's initiative and the electoral proposals in a kind of "limbo," just as it became with all of the other products generated by the members of the table that awaited the outcome of the power struggle taking place somewhere else.

- *July 2004.* Throughout 2003 and leading up to the recall referendum in August 2004, the Carter Center conducted a series of scenario-planning exercises. It planned for various contingencies, such as the recall never happening (e.g., if no CNE were named, if sufficient signatures were not collected, or if the government was able to avoid it in other legal or illegal ways). It also planned for all possible referendum results including how to provide guarantees to the losers and assure governability for the postrecall period. It even planned for a challenged result if the vote was very close. But it never planned for one side to reject the results in the face of a clear margin of victory and to then blame the international observers for the outcome. Of course, that is what happened, and the Carter Center was unprepared to react.

- *August 17, 2004.* After the recall vote, when the OAS and Carter Center were trying to forge an agreement between the CNE and opposition leaders for the second audit (as presented in chapter 8), Jorge Rodriguez had, at a certain point, refused to continue talking directly with the opposition delegates. The OAS and Carter Center could have tried harder to push Rodríguez to reach out to the opposition negotiators to try to involve them in the second audit. But the Carter Center team accepted that he was angry with them and tired. Furthermore, it thought that the prospects of convincing the opposition to participate were low, so it also stopped trying to convince it.

  Likewise, the OAS and Carter Center could have pushed harder to convince the CNE to accept the statistical program proposed by the opposition to select the sample for the second audit of the votes. Although the programs were equally acceptable in a technical sense, and a change would not have changed the opposition's position on participating—the opposition had already rejected the audit publicly and refused to come to the planning meeting—using the opposition-proposed statistical program would have affected perceptions of the audit and could have alleviated the primary complaint posed by the opposition afterward in rejecting those audit results as fraudulent. The change also might have had an effect on the ensuing debates and thus minimized confusion about the validity of the electronic vote results.

The OAS and Carter Center not only missed opportunities but also created some opportunities for decision makers to try to change the course of the conflict in a more positive way and to avoid further confrontation. These include the following:

- *January 2003.* As discussed in chapter 4, Carter's fishing trip posed a particular dilemma for the Carter Center team. The team decided to turn a potential public relations disaster into an opportunity to break the table-negotiation impasse. Carter's proposals gave the table a new breath and electoral options were formally introduced into the draft agreement that the table members were working on at that time.

- *February 2003.* The second Ury visit and the breakfast with the media owners were planned to create an opportunity to open negotiations between the government and the private media. The Carter Center had not been able to set up this negotiation scenario during Carter's first trip in July 2002 and it knew that these negotiations were a key element for de-escalating the conflict. The Ury visit did succeed in opening negotiations.
- *May 2003.* In closing the May agreement, as presented in chapter 5, McCoy and Diez leveraged Chávez's interest in getting Gaviria and the Carter Center out of the country and in presenting a closed deal at the upcoming Rio Group meeting of presidents in Cuzco, Peru. This interest was not related with the content of the agreement that was being worked on, but the authors knew that going to the meeting with an agreement in hand was a powerful incentive for Chávez, and they were proved right.
- *May 2004.* As noted in chapter 6, the Carter Center and OAS pressed hard between March and May to get a good process for the repair phase and to ensure that the signatures confirmed by the citizens would be accepted by the CNE. Looking back, it seems that the CNE members may have been more afraid of going into the recall referendum than Chávez himself and that they were trying to figure out what to do with the confirmed signatures that they knew would open the door to the recall referendum process. The Carter-Gaviria late night visit to the CNE headquarters after the repair process is another good example of creating the conditions to prevent additional conflict.
- *June 2004.* As mentioned in chapter 7, as the campaign for the recall referendum was approaching, the Carter Center knew that the CNE had decided to impose new rules for media ads, so it facilitated negotiations between the media and the CNE. It created an opportunity for the media to receive rules that they would be able to comply with and for the CNE to maintain its authority, setting up rules accepted by all.

The Advantages and Disadvantages of Track 1½ Diplomacy

Track I diplomacy is defined as the official activity of states and governments in the area of conflict resolution. Track II diplomacy, meanwhile, encompasses all nonstate and unofficial conflict resolution activities, such as those mediated by NGOs, the media, civil society, etc.[15] This distinction has its origins in the early 1980s as a result of the proliferation of nonstate

---

15. Diamond and McDonald, *Multi-Track Diplomacy.*

actors in international conflicts and in their increasing participation in conflict management and resolution, whether as third parties that participate
indirectly as mediators to a conflict or as members of one or both parties to
the conflict who start influencing the way a conflict is addressed.

With the general shift of conflicts away from the international sphere to
the intranational one, the distinction between track I and track II diplomacy
that had been applied at the international level is now being applied to political and social conflicts within states. In addition, the theoretical developments in the field of conflict resolution have become increasingly concerned
with a systematic approach to understanding and managing conflicts. This
approach allows for the inclusion of different sets of actors working with
one another at different levels and in interconnected and interdependent
ways, which in turn allows for a broader understanding of the possible roles
that can exist in conflict resolution and conflict management. In the 1990s,
Louise Diamond and John McDonald coined the term "multitrack" diplomacy as a comprehensive approach that can encompass the different actors
in international conflicts, thereby multiplying (at first by four and then by
eight) the relevant nonstate actors and underscoring the need to work systematically using this multicentered approach.[16]

In Venezuela, the Carter Center used an approach it calls track $1^1/_2$ diplomacy. This means that it performed its activities in a particular realm located somewhere in between what is known as track I and track II.[17] (The
Carter Center's approach is not a multitrack approach because it possesses
its own distinct characteristics.) For instance, as explained in chapter 3, the
Carter Center designs its programs only after receiving the explicit invitation of governments (and the leaders of the opposition when acting as a
third-party mediator or monitor), and generally after having direct contacts
with the president and/or some of the ministers of the country in question. As founder of the Carter Center, Jimmy Carter establishes direct communication with the country's political leaders and members of the Carter
Center staff always discuss the proposed activities and initiatives with the
highest authorities in the government and other national leaders. These
communication channels remain open throughout the time the Carter
Center's program is carried out in a given country.

The Carter Center's work thus comes close to track I not only because
governments, political leaders, and states are involved in its activities but

---

16. Ibid.

17. According to Diamond and McDonald, "Because of his prominence as a former President, Carter
is able to serve as a bridge between Track One and Track Two diplomacy." Ibid., 43.

also because of the close relationship between the Carter Center and the political actors, and because of the Carter Center staff's sense of the political dynamics, interests, and restrictions imposed by the exercise of politics and governance upon official actors. Led by a politician and former president, the Carter Center shares these political and governmental experiences and understands how important it is to build trust and create personal relationships with the actors. When created effectively, such trust, coupled with the Carter Center's moral weight as a principled organization, gives the Carter Center a special ability to influence social and political issues.

The Carter Center, as a nongovernmental entity, does not have the restrictions, bureaucracy, and restraints of other international organizations, such as the OAS and the United Nations, which are accountable to governments. On the other hand, of course, the Carter Center lacks the power, financing, and personnel of these important international actors, as well as the legitimacy that emerges from formal international legal agreements. These comparative advantages of each type of organization were good reasons for the Carter Center, the OAS, and the UNDP to form the Tripartite Working Group.

Despite its high-level access, the Carter Center is still an international NGO, and in that sense it is very close to the social and civic issues typical of other national and international organizations working at a track II level. It depends on external funds for its programs, focuses on specific issues, and has all the institutional dynamics of an NGO. But it also has considerable convening power to bring governments and civil society together, and to direct the attention of the public and the media to its issues. The Carter Center works with a wide range of mid-level social and political actors, community groups, civic associations, and NGOs. In fact, one of the operating principles of the Carter Center is to establish partnerships with domestic unofficial actors, organizations, and groups that work locally on the issues promoted by the Carter Center.

As an NGO, the Carter Center works on an equal footing with these community and civil society sectors, understands their language, and shares many of their expectations and disappointments regarding politics. It seeks out networks already present and strives to enhance the capacity of those actors to participate and influence local public policies, hoping to create a sustainable strategy to propel collective action toward peacebuilding. The large Strengthening Peace in Venezuela Program presented in chapter 5 was based upon this approach. The Carter Center designed comprehensive interventions and proposals, taking into account the need to integrate those who are part of the problem so that they may become part of the solution.[18]

From the track 1½ perspective, the Carter Center was able to put together initiatives involving governmental and nongovernmental actors, thereby empowering the spaces of cooperation and the capacity of both sides to act. In situations where the government actors could not participate due to political or legal restrictions, the Carter Center was able to create an unofficial space that was both trustworthy and safe to discuss critical situations or sensitive topics. This is how it operated with the private media and the CNE in Venezuela to set the rules for the recall referendum ads, as explained in chapter 7.

In situations where nongovernmental actors in a country are unable to provide visibility to their initiatives or have a hard time influencing official policies, the Carter Center can help them secure the participation of public officials, create provocative channels and contexts of dialogue, draft agreements between governments, communities, and civil society, in addition to providing them with needed media attention.[19] The statements by the group Aquí Cabemos Todos or the activities of the network of social organizations known as Paz en Movimiento gained a greater public scale with the help of the Carter Center.

The Processes of Conflict Transformation and Peacebuilding

The theoretical field of conflict resolution has seen the evolution and increased conceptual clarity of the terminology used to identify the types of activities required in all conflicts, as well as those specifically designed for political and social conflicts. When dealing with social and political conflicts, it is more realistic to talk about processes of "conflict transformation"—a concept that is broader and deeper than simply focusing on the specific conflict situation.

The concept of conflict transformation recognizes that conflict is natural and often an engine for social change, but that the resulting tensions need to be channeled in a constructive manner to reach a peaceful resolution of those confrontations.[20] It is no longer only about solving disputes but also

18. John Davies and Edward Kaufman, *Second Track/Citizen Diplomacy: Concepts and Techniques for Conflict Transformation* (Lanham, MD: Rowman & Littlefield Publishers, 2002).

19. As Jeffrey Mapendere says, "In most of its interventions, The Carter Center not only communicates what it is doing at the grassroots level to government officials and the president, but also operates as a communication link for other smaller Track Two actors with limited access to the political elite. If well coordinated within a strategic framework for peace, these levels of diplomacy can have a quick and direct impact on conflict." Jeffrey Mapendere, "Track One and a Half Diplomacy and the Complementarity of Tracks," *Culture of Peace Online Journal* 2, no. 1 (2006): 66–81.

20. John Paul Lederach argues, "Conflict transformation is accurate because the core of my work is indeed about engaging myself in constructive change initiatives that include and go beyond the resolution of particular problems. It is scientifically sound because the writing and research about

about trying to help the actors transform their manner of relating to each other, and thus about peacefully and constructively managing the natural tensions of social and political conflict and favoring sustainable processes of democratic change.

The Carter Center's participation in the Venezuelan domestic political conflict forced it to face its particular activity from a more global perspective, using a multifocal perspective and a multilevel approach.[21] As briefly explained in chapter 5, these complex processes did not require one intervention but a set of interventions with multiple areas or action focuses—each with its own intensity and projection—to be deployed at different levels in the social ladder and at different points in the decision-making process.[22] The Carter Center developed three basic activities that fit the theoretical framework of peacebuilding:[23] (1) directly negotiating, facilitating, and mediating at mid- and high levels of the decision-making system, using different formats, and including a variety of procedures as described in this book; (2) providing training and assistance to a multiplicity of NGOs and groups of political and social leaders including women and youth, in themes of conflict transformation and management, as an effective way to participate in the construction of networks of social actors that would sustain peace-creation processes;[24] and (3) creating spaces of dialogue among key actors with the ability to influence the conflict situation and providing a safe environment where participants can carefully listen and try to understand each other and perhaps develop empathy and acceptance of "the other's" experiences and perspectives and create constructive working relationships. This constitutes one of the foundations of

---

conflict converge in two common ideas: conflict is normal in human relationships and conflict is a motor of change. And transformation is clear in vision because it brings into focus the horizon toward which we journey, namely the building of healthy relationships and communities, both locally and globally. This process requires significant changes in our current ways of relating." Lederach, *The Little Book of Conflict Transformation* (Intercourse: Good Books, 2003).

21. Lederach, *Building Peace.*

22. Ibid.

23. As described by Boutros Boutros-Ghali, "Peace building is a process that facilitates the establishment of durable peace and tries to prevent the recurrence of violence by addressing root causes and effects of conflict through reconciliation, institution building, and political as well as economic transformation." Boutros-Ghali, "An Agenda for Peace: Preventive Diplomacy, Peacemaking and Peace-Keeping," UN doc. S/24111, June 17, 1992.

24. In an article published by *El Nacional* newspaper on December 4, 2003, Marianela Palacios wrote: "The group Peace in Motion, comprising 110 public and private organizations that respond to various political positions, carried out a series of sporting, cultural, recreational and educational initiatives in Caracas, Maracaibo, Barquisimeto, Merida, Ciudad Bolivar, for the purpose of creating spaces to depolarize the Venezuelan society, to facilitate national reunification and strengthen tolerance, democratic pluralism and respect for differences."

conflict transformation and was the key element in the formation of the Aqui Cabemos Todos, which in turn became the single nonpartisan national organization able to observe elections, Ojo Electoral.

The Venezuelan case demonstrates the long time frame required to develop societal capacity for conflict transformation. Based on Lederach's theory, Diez foresaw the need to develop such societal capacity and promoted long-term initiatives (such as extensive training programs and the creation of institutional platforms), while being conscious of the Carter Center's short-term plan of intervention. Nevertheless, the Carter Center failed to provide a sustainable strategy for its efforts in Venezuela. It designed its Strengthening Peace in Venezuela Program counting on the support of UNDP-Venezuela, which would remain in the country and, it assumed, would be independent enough of the domestic polarized actors to continue supporting the initiative, which was strongly anchored by a myriad of individual peace activists and domestic NGOs. But UNDP personnel and priorities changed after the recall referendum and, in the new political context, the new authorities were anxious to not appear political in their work. The funds needed to support the work of the small team sustaining the efforts were not continued. Although a group of Strengthening Peace in Venezuela Program staff members and volunteers decided to create a domestic NGO and the Carter Center sought to help them organize and write grant proposals,[25] they had difficulty raising funds, thus dramatically diminishing the scope of their work.

A lesson from this experience is that, in this kind of context, the Carter Center (or any other institution interested in working with conflict situations) needs to design its interventions with a medium-term time frame of three to five years. It must explicitly work to build alliances with local and international partners with roots in the country and a desire to stay in the location, and with a commitment to continue working after the Carter Center (or any other international third party) leaves, so that its contributions as a catalyst for these processes to be truly effective.

Lessons for Conflict Resolution Practice

For conflict resolution practitioners operating as a third party in political conflicts, the Venezuelan case yields three lessons. The first explores the chain of hypotheses that the authors used to look at the perceptions and

---

25. It was called Fortalecer la Paz en Venezuela, Asociación Civil (Strengthening Peace in Venezuela, Civic Association).

interactions between the parties; the second underlines the importance of personal relationships among the parties and between the parties and the third party; and the third concerns the level of expectations created by the third party.

Understanding the Relevance of Perceptions and Interactions

As illustrated throughout the book, a third party should be attentive to the ways in which the parties in conflict perceive the situation and how this set of perceptions affects the interactions of the parties.[26] The following premises further develop this idea.

- *Conflict exists only within the kinds of interactions the parties build and maintain. Thus, to change the course of conflict, it is necessary to change, even if slightly, the nature of the interactions between the parties.* In the Venezuelan case, the conflictive interaction would have changed radically if the opposition had explicitly recognized Chávez as the legitimate president, entitled to fulfill his entire mandate, and had declared its willingness to support some policies for social change (even while opposing all of the other policies and the government itself, as any political opposition does in a democracy); or if Chávez had assumed a more conciliatory position toward traditional elites, powerful businessmen (including the owners of mass media), and the interests of the United States and had negotiated with them spaces of power instead of trying to evict them altogether. This conciliation actually happened only in the case of the Cisneros-Chávez relationship during the meeting facilitated by Carter.
- *The interactions among the parties to the conflict are based on the set of perceptions each party has of itself, its counterparts, and the conflictive situation.* Therefore, in order to change the nature of the interaction, it is necessary to change (at least to a degree) the perceptions the parties have of themselves, the other, and the conflictive situation. In the Venezuelan case, the Chavistas clearly perceived that if they were ousted, they would not only lose their position but also their freedom, their property, and perhaps even their lives; at the same time, many opponents clearly perceived that Chavistas were installing a repressive regime that would deprive them of their property, freedom, and way of life. Had it been possible to change those perceptions so that both sides

---

26   Francisco Diez, "How Perceptions Are Shaped?" (thesis presented as a working paper for the International Mediation Research Program at the London School of Economics International/Conflict Resolution Department, March 1995, London).

felt more confident that they could coexist, the outcomes would have been very different. During the table negotiations, this line of thinking could have been explored since the parties many times opened a door for the mediators, but such exploration was not encouraged.

- *Each party's perceptions are created, maintained, and changed when new elements are introduced, such as through changes in the environment, the introduction of a third party, or the passing of time.* In the Venezuelan case, several decision makers belonging to the opposition became enthusiastic about the military rebellion of Plaza Altamira and thought that it could lead to a great movement of civil disobedience; however, Gaviria's immediate reaction against it became a powerful dissuasion. Carter exercised similar influences on Chávez and Cisneros at different points.

- *Decision makers have their own internal systems to interpret situations and interactions differently, giving different meanings and values to the same event. Thus, in order to be able to influence decision makers and their perceptions, it is necessary to understand how they attribute value and meaning to events and to work within their system.* In the Venezuelan case, the Chavistas saw the petroleum strike as an opportunity to "make a real revolution and return to the people their wealth,"[27] by gaining control over PDVSA and its resources. The opposition, meanwhile, considered the strike a patriotic feat for the defense of freedom, with which it would be able to force Chávez to resign. Neither side actually tried to understand how the opponent attributed meaning and value to the strike, because their starting points were very different. As mediator, the Carter Center was able to see that difference and it could have worked more to help the opposition understand the Chavistas' perception of the strike as very risky for the opposition's own position, just as William Ury did with the media owners.

- *In interactions with decision makers, the mediator appears as another element in each party's internal system of awarding value and meaning and calculating probabilities of success, and cannot avoid influencing them to some degree. Therefore, if the mediator understands each party's internal system and interests, he or she can consciously choose the manner and timing of his or her interactions to help generate a positive change in perceptions on the evolution of the conflict.* In the Venezuelan case, Carter's personal interaction with Chávez and his clear messages that he would publicly

---

27. These words were spoken by one of Chávez's ministers shortly after the beginning of the petroleum strike.

support the populace's right to petition for a recall exercised decisive influence on Chávez's decision to accept the challenge of a recall referendum. Likewise, Gaviria's interaction with the opposition leaders had decisive influence on their decision to sign the May 2003 agreement. In both cases, the third parties exercised their influence from within the parties' own perceptions and calculations, appealing to their interests in international legitimacy that could be derived from exercising democratic rights.

In conclusion, a focus on the sets of perceptions each party has and the kind of interactions going on among them and between them and the third party is key to understanding how mediators can help the parties address a conflict.

Promoting Personal Relationships

Personal relations matter, always. In many sociopolitical conflict situations, analysis focuses on the structural features of the situation (economic and social cleavages, historic developments, bases of political power, legal issues, etc.). But equally relevant in sustaining or fueling a conflict situation is the personal relationships among the main actors. These relationships and the personal relationships between the third party and the protagonists of the conflict are key elements to be considered when working within a political conflict.

Relations among the parties. Throughout the Carter Center's experience in Venezuela, the need for understanding the role played by personal relationships among the parties was clear. Personal relationships can advance or impede negotiations between the conflicting parties. For example, as mentioned in the lessons in chapter 5, even though an agreement was reached between the media and government, it was impossible to hold direct meetings between Minister of Information Diosdado Cabello and RCTV director Marcel Granier because of their poor personal relationship. Something similar happened with the relationship between Nicolas Maduro (on the government side) and Asdrubal Aguiar (on the opposition side), who were both members of the liaison mechanism following the May 2003 accord that in the end did not function. Similarly, within the opposition, the coleadership of Henrique Salas Römer and Enrique Mendoza did not work in large part due to their respective personalities, as mentioned in chapter 7.

In all of these cases, the Carter Center could have more systematically tried to generate a few options to overcome the obstacle of personalities. For example, Cabello could have met with other television directors who could also have represented the interests of RCTV (as actually happened later) or the Carter Center could have requested another representative from RCTV (like the son of Marcel Granier, who had a very different style). The Carter Center also noted that Maduro had much better dialogue with the other member of the opposition in the liaison mechanism, Timoteo Zambrano, and it could have promoted individual meetings between them. Finally, in its work with the Group of Five leaders of the Coordinadora Democrática, the Carter Center avoided dealing with Mendoza and Salas Römer at the same time and basically worked with the others.

Negotiations between the CNE and the private media were more successful at least in part because the personalities of Jorge Rodríguez and Alberto Federico Ravel (from Globovisión) were quite compatible. In the same way, some communications at the table worked better if Timoteo Zambrano and José Vicente Rangel were able to talk directly, while the climate deteriorated if Minister of Labor María Cristina Iglesias and the representative of the private entrepreneurs, Rafael Alfonzo, were presenting their views.

For the third party, identifying the positive and negative relationships between the individual actors can help the facilitation, allowing the third party to put together the more compatible personalities to negotiate agreements, or to strive to improve the relationship between the clashing personalities. When the context does not allow for that kind of work, the third party should limit the interactions between the clashing personalities and either create distinct spaces where other individuals can interact in representation of the principals or use the mechanism of the third party as a go-between.

Relations with the third party. As described throughout the book, Gaviria had a difficult personal relationship with Chávez and much better relations with the opposition leaders and the media owners, while Carter had a good personal relationship with Chávez and much less patience with opposition representatives. Carter is very good at creating personal relationships with individual parties at conflict, and he is very comfortable working on a one-to-one basis because he relies on his own personality as a source of influence over the decision makers. On the other hand, Gaviria relied more on his institutional position as the OAS secretary general and placed less emphasis on personal relationships.

Gaviria was able to spend many hours listening to all the members of the Coordinadora Democrática at very large meetings; Carter never liked to do the same. Gaviria was able to sit at the negotiation table for months, just listening to the members giving speeches, something that Carter would never do. On the other hand, Carter liked to be proactive and make proposals he considered fair and feasible to solve the conflict; Gaviria refrained from taking such a proactive stance. Carter took the risk of failure in his attempts to foster agreements as something natural; Gaviria avoided that risk as much as possible. All of these personal characteristics were important to the kinds of relationships they created and, in turn, shaped the kind of interventions they were able to perform.

As Carter Center staff working closely with the secretary general of the OAS in the field, the authors placed special emphasis on the task of building personal relationships of trust with key actors within the opposition and the government. They succeeded in most cases and were able to count on the collaboration of leaders of both sectors to support the Carter Center's peace-building initiatives and to be receptive to proposed negotiation initiatives. The political and social opposition was always more open to international collaboration and it was natural for the international representatives of both the Carter Center and the OAS living in Caracas to establish personal relationships with them, since they lived in similar neighborhoods, sent their children to the same schools, and went to similar public places. They developed good relations with some leaders and also with some social and civic peace activists, many of them very close to the opposition. This was not the case with government officials or community leaders supporting Chávez, since they usually felt very different from the international representatives.[28] For precisely this reason, building personal relations based on trust was particularly important when dealing with the Chavista movement, because due to its very nature, it operates as a set of rather fragmented sectors and is based on a network of personal contacts that is not necessarily reflected in party institutions or the position of its officials. The relationships that the Carter Center forged with some low-level pro-government activists during the many activities of the Strengthening Peace in Venezuela Program, in addition to the good personal relationship that Carter had with Chávez, helped the Carter Center build more confidence among the mid-level leaders of Chavismo. In the same way, the personal relationships it developed with the CNE directors and the media owners provided a door for various Carter Center's initiatives.

---

28. During the recall referendum campaign, Nicolás Maduro asked the Carter Center team for an urgent meeting on a Sunday afternoon, which was held at Diez's private home in the neighborhood called Valle Arriba. Looking through the window down at the view of the city, he said, "The city looks very different from this side. I would like all the houses in Caracas to be able to enjoy this privileged view." Of course, most of the people living in the building (except for the guards) were sympathetic to the opposition.

Managing Expectations

A great lesson of the authors' time working in Venezuela has to do with the Carter Center's inattention to managing the expectations of the parties about what the Carter Center could and could not deliver as a third party. Many citizens on the opposition side believed that the Carter Center would "save" them from Chavismo and help them to preserve the "American way of life" that they so valued. For example, individuals would come up to Carter Center staff in the airport to say, "Please come back, you are our only hope against Chávez." In addition, due to the personal relationships that the Carter Center team created with many of the opposition leaders and the team's ability to understand them and their concerns, the opposition leaders felt safe with the Carter Center team and expected from it results beyond its role and power.

The Carter Center staff knew intuitively, even if not consciously, that expectations about its ability to work as a third party were being confused with expectations about its power "to put Chávez under control," or even worse, "to get rid of Chávez once and for all." Still, the Carter Center did not consciously attempt to manage these expectations beyond reminding in all of its public statements that it was simply an invited third-party facilitator without any decision-making power in Venezuela. The Carter Center did not consistently include the problem of expectations in its scenario-planning or conflict-analysis exercises, and it did not design an adequate communication strategy to lower expectations. This became especially clear after the recall referendum, when President Carter accepted the results of the recall referendum and asked the opponents of Chávez to do the same, while their political leaders—unable to take responsibility for their own electoral defeat—claimed a massive fraud. The level of frustration and anger against the Carter Center increased exponentially.

Concluding Remarks

The Venezuelan case illustrates a pressing question about the capacity of democracy to manage conflict over the redistribution of resources. In any social context, the struggle by one group to gain a greater share of political and economic resources naturally produces a reaction from those who control and benefit from those resources. Conflictive processes are normally the result. In some contexts, the institutional framework is capable of managing the conflict through a gradual, though usually limited, redistribution of resources (reformist governments). In other cases, the demand for such redistribution can produce more radical change and violent backlashes.[29] This was the case in Venezuela, as the Chávez administration responded to demands for change with a confrontational strategy, and elites resisted their loss of power. The resulting political polarization trapped all sectors of society, as even those who sought to promote tolerance or find a third way were labelled as supporting one side or another and their attempts were thus delegitimized.[30] The society suffered a coup and countercoup, a devastating national petroleum strike, massive protest marches with some violence, and months of uncertainty and ungovernability.

In this context, international third parties were invited to Venezuela to bridge the divide between two apparently irreconcilable camps, with the overarching goal of preventing a serious political conflict from turning violent. This larger goal was attained: violence was contained, despite conditions being present that predicted bloodshed. While it is impossible to prove a counterfactual—in this case, the absence of violence—the direct role of the third parties in preventing an escalation could be seen on several occasions, such as in the negotiations for safe conditions for the July 2002 opposition march during the first visit of Jimmy Carter; the negotiations at the table for safety measures during additional protests and the petroleum strike; the mediator's resistance to the military "sit-in," which helped to deter more overt military action; the turn from potentially dangerous street strategies and tests of physical power to the electoral strategy emerging from the table negotiations; the negotiation of the procedures for the recall referendum, resulting in a peaceful outcome of the petition process in June 2004; and the widespread international acceptance of the recall referendum, which helped to deter a violent reaction to the outcome of the recall referendum after August 15.

Even so, polarization within the country was not eliminated and one side was largely able to impose its views and strategy of change on the other. The recall referendum itself would not have occurred without the active participation of the third parties in the negotiation of the May 2003 accord, the procedures for the recall process, and the acceptance of the government to hold the recall. Nevertheless, an electoral strategy could not resolve the underlying disputes, as explained in this volume, and the limitations of the

---

29. Jennifer McCoy, "Democratic Transformation in Latin America," *Whitehead Journal of Diplomacy and International Relations* (Winter/Spring 2008): 19–29.

30. For an analysis of how the student movement in 2008–09 fell victim to the logic of the political polarization, see the paper by Maria Pilar Garcia and Ana Mallen presented at the Congress of the Latin American Studies Association, Rio de Janeiro, June 2009.

international actors in changing the perceptions and attitudes of the Venezuelan actors were clear.

This volume has sought to identify and analyze both the limitations and contributions of the international role in the Venezuelan conflict through a critical self-reflection by two third-party actors in Venezuela and through the lens of conflict resolution and political theory and practice. It is the authors' hope that the information and the lessons provided herein will contribute to comparative studies and even better prospects for international third-party attempts to prevent conflict in future situations.

Appendix A

May 2003 Agreement of the Table of Negotiation and Agreements

Agreement between the Representatives of the Government of the Bolivarian Republic of Venezuela and the Political and Social Groups Supporting It, and the Coordinadora Democrática and the Political and Civil Society Organizations Supporting It

We, the undersigned members of the Forum for Negotiation and Agreement, representing the national government and the political and social groups supporting it as well as the political and civil society organizations comprising the Coordinadora Democrática hereby sign this agreement in a spirit of tolerance, in order to contribute to strengthening the climate of peace in the country. It is in this spirit that we reaffirm the principles and mechanisms that brought us to this table, as set forth in the Executive Summary agreed to by the parties from the time it was established, as well as our conviction with regard to finding a constitutional, peaceful, democratic, and electoral solution.

We express our full adherence to and respect for the Constitution of the Bolivarian Republic of Venezuela. The rule of law is based on respect for this Constitution and for the legal system that underpins it. The Constitution envisions a system of values and norms to govern fundamental principles of social and political coexistence and establishes mechanisms for reconciling differences. Any change in response to recent experiences with the political process should be based on these norms and should preferably be made through consensus.

We are aware that at this historic moment, we must agree upon fundamentals for ensuring a participatory, pluralist, robust, and genuinely representative democracy, where we shall continue to have room for all and where social justice, tolerance, equal opportunity, the rule of law, and democratic coexistence are the essential values. We are aware that these values must be held above any political or partisan strife and that they must guide policy, especially in areas where there is a preponderant social interest.

We wish to state our conviction that Venezuela and the Venezuelan people will continue along the path of democracy with a sense of fraternity, respect for the beliefs of each and every Venezuelan, and the desire for reconciliation.

We are aware that our society must consolidate pluralism, as embodied in the Constitution, where policy exercised by all actors in national life is consistent with the values of the Constitution. Venezuela needs the cooperation of all to continue along the path of peace and democracy, so that each and everyone may express his or her ideas, adopt his or her respective position, and choose from among the various political options that exist.

We express our adherence to the principles enshrined in the Inter-American Democratic Charter, which proclaims the right of peoples to live in democracy and the obligation of governments and all citizens to promote and defend it. In light of the provisions of Article 6 of the Constitution of the Bolivarian Republic of Venezuela concerning participatory democracy, all sectors share the values set forth therein, such as those that advocate that power may only be exercised according to the rule of law; the holding of free, fair, and transparent elections; the separation and independence of branches of government; representative democracy reinforced and enriched by ongoing, ethical, and responsible citizen participation within a legal framework; strict respect for human rights, the rights of workers, and freedom of expression, information, and the press; and the elimination of all forms of discrimination and intolerance. Both parties also recognize the close links between democracy and the war on poverty, between democracy and development, and between democracy and the effective exercise of human rights.

We invoke the principles of the Charter of the Organization of American States (OAS), the American Convention on Human Rights, international law as the standard of conduct among states in their reciprocal relations, respect for sovereignty and the principle of nonintervention, the principle of self-determination, the juridical equality of all states, and the peaceful settlement of disputes.

We ratify the validity of and our full adherence and commitment to the Declaration Against Violence and for Peace and Democracy, signed on Feb. 18, 2003, which should be considered an integral part of this agreement.

We fully agree that monopoly on the use of force by the state through the national armed forces and the metropolitan, state, and municipal police is a basic and inalienable prerogative in combating violence and guaranteeing the essence of a democratic state. Civilian authorities exercising the powers conferred on them by the Constitution and the law shall determine the role of the police. This requires full compliance with the legal provisions and judicial decisions governing citizen safety coordination. In any event, the possession of weapons by the police or any other security force having national, state, or municipal jurisdiction must be regulated in strict accordance with the law. None of these forces should be used as an instrument for arbitrary or excessive repression or to engage in actions that connote political intolerance.

We agree to undertake a vigorous campaign to effectively disarm the civilian population on the basis of the law passed by the National Assembly, making sovereign use of all mechanisms and resources provided for therein and with the technical support of the international institutions. We, the parties, shall abide by the conclusions of the Forum for Dialogue conducted by the National Assembly in its quest for a consensus plan for disarmament of the civilian population.

We urge the parliamentary groups of opinion represented in the National Assembly to finalize the law on the formation of the Truth Commission, to enable it to help shed light on the events of April 2002 and cooperate with the judicial bodies in identifying and punishing those responsible.

In pursuance of the objective established in the Executive Summary of seeking agreement as a means of contributing to resolution of the crisis in the country through the electoral process, we, the parties, agree that this resolution of the crisis should be achieved through application of Article 72 of the Constitution of the Bolivarian Republic of Venezuela, which provides for the possible holding of recall referenda on the mandates of all those holding positions and serving as magistrates as a result of popular election, where they have served one-half of the term for which they were elected (governors, mayors, regional legislators, and representatives in the National Assembly) or will have served one-half of their term in the course of this year, as is the case of the president of the republic, in accordance with the judgment of the Supreme Court of Justice of Feb. 13, 2003. Such referenda, including those already called for and those that may be called for in future, will be possible if they are formally requested by the requisite number of voters and approved by the new National Electoral Council, once it has been established that the constitutional and legal requirements have been met.

We agree that it is essential to have as soon as possible a trustworthy, transparent, and impartial electoral arbiter, to be designated in the manner prescribed in the Constitution. In that connection, the work under way in the National Assembly is considered to be of the utmost importance. We, the two parties, state our willingness to assist in facilitating understanding in all matters relating to the formation and workings of the electoral arbiter, without interfering with the standard procedure being conducted by the national legislature.

We are committed to freedom of expression, as enshrined in our constitutional and legal provisions; to the American Convention on Human Rights; and the Inter-American Democratic Charter. We, the two parties, intend to work with the public and private media to promote their espousal of the aims set forth in this document and in the Declaration Against Violence and for Peace and Democracy. In particular, we intend to work with the public and private media with a view to quelling violence and with respect to their role in making citizens aware, in an equitable and impartial manner, of their political options, which would contribute significantly to creating the most conducive climate to the successful conduct of electoral processes and referenda provided for in Article 72 of the Constitution.

We assume that the Constitution and laws of the republic provide for the appropriate and necessary requirements and mechanisms in order for the competent public authority to proceed with the timely financing of recall referenda and any other mechanism for popular consultation, which must be conducted once the admissibility has been confirmed by the competent public body. With regard to the Republic Plan, this plan will be activated in response to a request from the electoral authorities, under the same terms and conditions that have applied in previous electoral processes.

The OAS, The Carter Center, and the United Nations have expressed their willingness to provide such technical assistance as the competent authorities of the Bolivarian Republic of Venezuela might request of them for holding any type of electoral consultation; any such request shall be in accordance with the principle of law contained in the Constitution of the republic. This technical assistance could range from preparatory or pre-election activities to actual electoral observation. With regard to direct support that may be given to the CNE, emphasis should be placed on the willingness of these three organizations to collaborate with both human and material resources that they have offered.

Once the pertinent legal and constitutional requirements have been met, the CNE shall determine the date for the recall referenda already requested, as well as any that may be requested later, in an expeditious and timely manner in accordance with the Law on Suffrage and Political

Participation, and we, the parties, agree neither to propose nor to promote amendments to that law.

We, the parties, recognize the support and facilitation provided to this forum by the representatives of the OAS, particularly its secretary-general, by The Carter Center, and by the UNDP, which, upon the signature of this agreement, constructively concludes its task. We recognize the importance of the follow-up work these institutions may conduct in the future for the execution of this agreement, and we intend to continue to avail ourselves of international assistance.

Lastly, we, the parties, agree to establish the joint follow-up body provided for in Article 7 of the Declaration Against Violence and for Peace and Democracy, each appointing two representatives to open channels of communication and take measures for the effective fulfillment of the provisions of that declaration and of this agreement, maintaining contact with the international facilitation when the parties consider it necessary.

—Caracas, May 23, 2003

Members of the Forum

José Vicente Rangel
Timoteo Zambrano
Roy Chaderton Matos
Alejandro Armas
María Cristina Iglesias
Manuel Cova
Ronald Blanco La Cruz
Américo Martín
Nicolás Maduro
Eduardo Lapi

Advisers

Omar Meza Ramírez
Juan Manuel Raffalli

Facilitators

César Gaviria (OAS)
Francisco Diez (Carter Center)
Antonio Molpeceres (UNDP)

Appendix B

Jennifer McCoy and Ben Hoffman, Briefing Memo, July 2002

Ben Hoffman, Jennifer McCoy, Laura Neuman, Council member and former president of the Dominican Republic Leonel Fernandez, and mediation consultant Francisco Diez traveled to Caracas June 24–29, 2002, to explore the invitation to President Carter from the President and Vice President of Venezuela to facilitate a national dialogue to help resolve the current crisis of governability in the country. This memo is based on that trip in preparation for a trip by President Carter to Venezuela July 6–10, 2002.

I. Summary

Despite the deep polarization, high level of anxiety and insecurity, and directly competing interests of the players, we see the possibility for a targeted effort to reduce tensions in the short-term and open the political space for concrete negotiations on an accorded agenda. The next moments of uncertainty occur in July—with the annual promotions of the military by July 5 and the opposition march and possible strike scheduled for July 11; followed by a deepening of the economic crisis in the fall as public employee contracts come due, inflation rises, and major public debt obligations come due. We plan a two-step negotiation process immediately in July–August to help reduce tensions now and to put in place a longer-term dialogue process to get them through the next year, described in more detail below.

II. Context

The essential polarization in Venezuela arose from the following long-term and short-term factors:

- **Long-term exclusion of large sectors** of the population from decision-making and social-economic benefits. The forty year democracy known as the Fourth Republic or the Punto Fijo democracy achieved a stable democratic system buoyed by oil revenues, but with a political elite increasingly out of touch with the population, growing corruption, administrative incompetence, and eroding public infrastructure, institutions, and living standards. The political system was unable to cope with declining revenues from the early 1980s, poverty grew to 70%, and public services deteriorated. Large sectors of previously unmobilized citizens responded to Chavez' message blaming a corrupt elite for the ills of the majority of the population and the need for radical change when they elected him in 1998.
- **Venezuelan myth that the country is rich** and that the growing poverty is due to corruption. In fact, petroleum revenues are unable to sustain the growing population. The revenues generated by petroleum have fallen from $10/day/capita in 1980 to $1/day/capita in 2002.
- **Heightened class consciousness, racial consciousness, and hatred** and resentment sowed by Chavez' harsh rhetoric against the prior "ruling class" of political parties, church, entrepreneurs, and media.
- **Exacerbation of traditional Venezuelan poor public management** due to the Chavez administration extreme inexperience and incompetence in public administration, and prioritizing loyalty over merit and expertise. This has led to a lack of confidence by investors, economic and social paralysis, and extreme concern by workers and businesses.
- **Personal insecurity** exacerbated by the Bolivarian Circles organized by the governing party ostensibly for social programs in poor urban areas, but also alleged to be armed to "defend the revolution." In response, a growing hysteria among middle and upper classes, particularly in Caracas, appears to be leading to a new arms race as families and individuals across the board arm themselves for protection and defense.
- **Extreme concentration of power in the person of the president.** All policy decisions are made by this president. The new constitution further provides greater institutional powers to the president, for example, removing the legislative oversight over the military and providing for direct consultation of the people on legislation and officials through plebiscites and recall referenda.
- **Personal style of the president.** Chavez is a nineteenth-century leader—charismatic, populist, with autocratic tendencies. He appears

incapable of controlling his passion during public speeches, leading to strong rhetoric that scares and alienates many sectors. His discourse is moralistic, classifying any critics as enemies of the revolution to be defeated at all costs. It incites violence, and gives the impression he is incapable or unwilling to follow through on any commitments.

- **Weakening and politicization of institutions and checks and balances.** The naming of the former vice president and close confidant of the president as the attorney general has generated a widespread perception that there is no possibility of objective investigation of the president. The president's own words saying he would not abide by the Supreme Court rulings if they moved toward impeachment cause a complete lack of confidence in his respect of constitutional and democratic institutions. The majority control of the National Assembly and the strong influence of the president over the electoral branch, the judicial branch, and the citizen's branch of government (attorney general, comptroller general and ombudsman) through their appointment under temporary conditions rather than the new constitutional procedures leads to the perception of a complete lack of checks and balances. (This has begun to change recently with apparently more independent rulings of the Court and some defections in the National Assembly.)

- **Dissolution of political parties and rise of civil society.** The collapse of the political party system during the 1990s led to a vacuum of representation in which civil society organizations, including labor, business and media organizations, stepped in. During the last three years, the latter groups have formed the core of the opposition to the Chavez administration, mobilizing street protests, stepping in during the coup attempt, and becoming political actors themselves. IN response, the government has attempted to argue that civil society does not represent the citizenship, and there is a new court ruling that may impede civil society organization. There is a strong need to revitalize political parties as the legitimate representative institutions, allowing the other organizations to pursue sectoral interests and monitor government actions.

- **Military fragmentation.** From a professional military under civilian control, though with some institutional autonomy, during the Fourth Republic, the military has seen an expanded internal mission and growing politicization during the Fifth Republic. Growing resentment at interference in promotions (based on loyalty to the president rather than merit), corruption among civilians and military officers, government ties to leftist causes such as Cuba and the Colombian guerrillas, and violence against citizens have led to a serious fractionalization within the military. The extreme opposition also believe the government is consciously weakening the military, as it loses control over it, and organizing its own armed militia with dependence on Cuba. Chavez concession—he did stop wearing his uniform after April 11, which had been an irritant, and he told us he was planning to follow the high command's recommendations with regards to promotions July 5, according to merit.

- **Church and media** transformed from neutral, autonomous players to perceived opposition players. The church and media came under attack by the president as the last two autonomous, respected institutions in Venezuela. Hostility and personalized attack by the president has risen over the past two years as both institutions took an increasingly critical position towards the government. The president appears to be willing to broach reconciliation with these two institutions now.

- **Spoilers.** The dissatisfaction with the status quo has grown so intense that there is a group of spoilers on both sides who want to force an end to the conflict with a clear victory by one side. The radical opposition wants Chavez out by any means and opposes any negotiations that will give him breathing room to consolidate his power. The radicals on Chavez' side want to eliminate the opposition and consolidate the revolution, with some of his supporters ready to defend him with force rather than risk losing the only representative they have ever identified with.

- **Presidential Dialogue Commission.** Chavez made several concessions after his return to power in April: changed Cabinet members; reinstated the professional PDVSA (oil company) board members, whose ouster had prompted the strike before the April events; stopped wearing his uniform; ended preemptive TV appearances ("chains"); and initiated a national dialogue under Vice President Rangel's leadership. The latter step erased all confidence of the president's commitment to change generated by the first steps, because the dialogue was seen as a farce. It was convened by the presidency in the presidential palace rather than a neutral place, its membership was chosen by the president rather than the actors, members were invited to participate in their personal capacity rather than institutional representation, and it has not produced anything.

In short, the main actors are not participating—the CTV because it's president has not been formally recognized; therefore the business group Fedecámaras withdrew. The political parties have not joined. The media walked out after a particularly heated exchange between media reps and the president in one of the dialogue sessions. Of 30 members, five are seen as non-government supporters. The commisson continues to meet periodically and some of the five subtables are working on reports (economic, international, territorial, labor; political does not meet). But there is very little confidence in the process.

III. Issues to be Resolved

- **Disarmament**. General disarmament of the population (very difficult). Ending government resources provided to organize Bolivarian Circles.
- **Separation of Powers**. Agree to a timetable to appoint the public powers (attorney general, controller general, ombudsman); judges; and electoral authorities according to the constitutional provisions. Of these, the easiest to reach an agreement on appears to be the electoral authorities (government is interested) and ombudsman (no real power). The attorney general, controller general, and courts are perceived as actors who can be used politically to attack the president.
- **Term of the president's mandate.** Opposition parties are working toward one of four strategies to shorten the president's mandate through constitutional terms: recall (revocatory) referendum (Aug 2003) which, if he is defeated would lead to elections within 30 days in which the president might be able to run again (preferred option by Chavez); constitutional amendment to shorten the term and add a second round to elections (preferred by some of the opposition); resignation in light of massive street mobilizations and strikes, leading to new elections; or impeachment through the courts.
- **49 decree laws.** The National Assembly delegated decree power to the president in 2001 under the Enabling Law. Consequently, the president decreed 49 laws in December 2001 without consultation with the sectors affected. Particularly controversial are the hydrocarbons law, fisheries law, and land laws. These laws created a general concern about the government's disrespect of property rights. The private sector demanded suspension of the laws. After the April 11 coup, the

government agreed that 17 of these laws should be reviewed under the National Assembly, with consultation of the private sector, a process which is now under way.

- **Labor sector.** National election of new labor leaders last October resulted in accusations of fraud by the government and refusal to recognize the (opposition) labor leader who apparently won a clear majority of the vote. The matter is still unresolved by the electoral authorities, leading the government to initially exclude the CTV (labor confederation) from the national dialogue initiated after the April 11 coup, and to delay negotiation of collective contracts.

- **Freedom of Expression.** The media continues to perceive a tightening of their freedoms. Recent reports by the Inter-American Commission of Human Rights emphasize the dangers of the aggressive public remarks of the president naming media owners and journalists as opponents of the revolution (and implicitly inviting attacks on them), and cite journalists who have been beaten up in the streets. Television and radio owners are concerned about a new telecommunications law which may allow the government to suspend access to the airwaves to those who oppose the government, and all are concerned about a draft law on Contents of Media.

  Nevertheless, the press continues to freely criticize the government (Human Rights Watch notes that the press is clearly biased against the government), anti-government talk shows abound, and the government perceives the media as its primary political opponent. Chavez also made one concession after April 14—he stopped the TV "chains" in which private stations were obligated to carry his remarks live, preempting regular programming, and which had been used to an extreme by Chavez.

- **Church.** The church has traditionally been respected in Venezuela, though it is not a highly religious country. The church is now perceived by the government as part of the opposition, and a war of words has occurred. Need reconciliation to allow the church to return to a potential role of facilitator/arbiter/reconciler.

- **Establishment of Truth Commission.** Following the events of April 11–14, the establishment of an independent and investigative truth commission was promised to determine responsibility for deaths and arrests on both sides during the chaotic days. This has not yet developed in such a manner as to appease the opposition and continues to be called for as a critical agenda item.

IV. Conflict Analysis

This is a multi-party, multi-issue, deep-rooted, volatile and potentially lethal conflict. It is marked by extreme hardliners, personalized and vitriolic hostility between certain key actors, especially the President and media and labour. There is little apparent middle ground and only a tenuous balance of power (hurting stalemate) inclining the parties to negotiate rather than prevail by force (whether by non-violent pressure or violent). While focused on the person of the President Chavez, suggesting that accommodation on his part may lead to a workable truce, the deeper problems of institutional erosion, structural economic shortcomings, and heightened expectations of the newly mobilized urban poor call for more.

This is more problematic as there is little evidence that the President is capable of honoring commitments in the absence of pressure, resulting in a deep lack of confidence in the possibility of holding meaningful, durable negotiations. In this atmosphere there would naturally be concerns by each of the parties about the nature of any third party intervention: some will want an authority that can arbitrate and impose commitments and enforce them; others will look to "friendly" third parties who will play into their agenda; some will boycott any effort that might lead to a negotiated settlement as they simply wish the other side removed; others will participate, but do so for the express (hidden) purpose of undermining the negotiations.

Our approach must therefore, be a disciplined, step-wise intervention directed, ultimately, at the long-term root causes of the conflict and the elements required to restore Venezuela. We need to take the requisite time and efforts to build confidence in our presence (which was explicitly rejected by the opposition at first, but is softening) and our approach. We need to continually assure ourselves that we believe a negotiated process is viable (that there is growing commitment to goodwill efforts by the key parties). Finally, we need to unblock in the immediate short-term the bilateral stumbling blocks to a full multi-party accord; to set in place sufficient demonstrated success to build a working trust between the parties and momentum for peaceful resolution; and to ensure that the critical components of verifiability and enforcement are in place.

From the beginning to the end, we must remember that it is Venezuelans themselves who must own the process and the outcomes for there to be a sustainable resolution. The estimated time of our active involvement is one year.

V. Negotiation Strategy

Our *goal* is to develop a process to negotiate a political accord leading to a legitimate, inclusive, multi-sectoral dialogue seeking reconciliation and the restoration of functioning, trusted political institutions. This is expected to take place over the next year.

Our short-term *strategy* is to initiate a two-round elite-centered effort in July to achieve the political accord, resolving some immediate issues and providing the foundations for a longer-term negotiated solution to various dimensions of the governability crisis in Venezuela. More specifically, the strategy seeks to:

- Lower tensions immediately by achieving a truce in the war between the media and the president of the Republic and help to diffuse tensions before the scheduled July 11 march.
- Build confidence among the players by encouraging unilateral signals from the key players, particularly the president.
- Give hope to Venezuelans that there is an orderly and peaceful way forward by designing and securing agreement among the key players on a dialogue process, including identification of the actors, an agenda agreed to by the actors, sequencing and timetable to address specific issues, and verification mechanisms by both national and international actors.
- Provide sustainability of the effort through an international coalition and support group that can provide technical and financial assistance to the Venezuelan dialogue process, and a series of incentives and disincentives to encourage compliance by the parties to the accords.
- Have the dialogue process in place within two months in order to help the country navigate the difficult economic and social terrain expected in September–December.

The methodology to accomplish the above goals and strategy is:

1. Visit by PC to Venezuela July 6–10 to:

- Meet individually with each actor toward developing a single-text agreement on agenda items, players, facilitators, and timetable for the negotiations toward a political accord.
- Agreement by all actors to participate in a second round of negotiations within one month, sitting at the table together in a location to be determined outside of Venezuela with the facilitation of PC and an agreed set of international facilitators.

- Negotiate a truce between the media and the president, which might include a commitment from the president to name a presidential spokesperson and change his weekly radio programs to monthly programs in order to reduce his public contact "facetime"; a commitment by the president to end the personal attacks on individual media owners and journalists; a commitment from the media to provide balanced coverage and develop a voluntary code of ethics; agreement on a process of negotiation to resolve the business/policy interests of the media concerning unrenewed licenses, government time on TV/radio, etc.
- Potentially obtain additional bilateral agreements between the government and individual actors, such as recognition of the labor confederation CTV; agreement with the private sector organization Fedecámaras on deadlines for the modification of decree laws of concern to them; agreement with the church to end the mutual recriminations between them; or agreement with the political parties on the immediate reform of the electoral authorities and law.

2. Second round of elite negotiations with PC in neutral location in July/August.

Bring the key actors to the table in a neutral location, preferably The Carter Center, to negotiate substantive accords on the previously agreed upon agenda, including the design of the long-term dialogue process and international and national verification mechanisms. This should take place within the next month, with PC and a small group of international actors facilitating. This round of negotiations would include the participation of the international support group, potentially UNPD, OAS, Council of Presidents and Prime Ministers, other eminent person.

3. Longer-term, inclusive, multi-sectoral Dialogue Process for national issues.

We would provide assistance in designing a dialogue process to address the longer-term issues confronting Venezuela, such as poverty, property rights, unemployment, corruption, personal security, foreign policy, oil policy, decentralization. Such a dialogue process would need the assistance of the UNDP, the OAS, or other such organizations. The agenda would be agreed upon in the elite negotiation table, but the participants of the dialogue might be a second ring of intermediate-level actors and experts. There may be several different dialogue tables, or different arenas and mechanisms to deal with each issue. The international community would provide technical and financial assistance, and the Carter Center would continue monitoring and facilitating this process through a field office in Caracas.

Appendix C

Francisco Diez, Private Memo,
September 30, 2003

To: Jennifer McCoy and Matthew Hodes
From: Francisco Diez
Reg.: Political Analysis
Date: September 30, 2003

Dear colleagues,

The conflict in Venezuela is far beyond Chavez himself. We all know that. We said many times the Recall Referendum will not solve the conflict, because there are many deep divisions in this country fuelling the internal conflict. Those divisions were "masked" many years by the "democratic" system established by the dominance of the AD-Copei politicians. Thousands of people were increasingly "invisible" during those years and the poverty of the barrios was avoided by the public policy of the oil-driven, rich democratic state. We have now a country with more than 50% of its work force out of any records, in the "informal" sector, and everyone knows there is no way to implement public policy within the Barrios. There is no health, education, security, no social policy at all there, and most of them have their own self regulated mechanisms of coexistence based upon violence. The frontier dividing the Barrios and the city are clearly marked only for them, because the City is geographically united, but there are many frontiers all along Caracas. The situation is similar (but less dramatic) in other parts of the country.

During the 4th Republic, as a consequence of the oil revenues, most of the people lived under the "illusion of harmony" Venezuela used to be, until el Caracazo in 1989 when the people of the Barrios expressed themselves for the first (and only) time. There were up to 5,000 deaths. After that, everything changed because the illusion of harmony started to coexist with the anger and the fear of what happened and the social injustice that became evident. The "traditional" political system collapsed and the process drove the country to the Chavez regime. His rhetoric promised a deep change of the system, and he did so using symbols and language with the new Constitution and he created a new dynamic on the political scenario. The—for too many years—"invisible" people felt (and many of them still feel) represented by Chavez. But, at the same time, he did not "deliver" the kind of change most of the people were waiting for. In trying to change the system, Chavez entered into a self designed trap. He decided not to negotiate with the traditional factors of internal and external power and he progressively isolated himself and undermined his capacity for governing. So, he started to blame "the others" and the fight against the unfair and unjust system became the fight between Chavez and the others. He lost allies and friends constantly. The remaining people with him are people who have no other place to go because most of them will be "invisible" again if Chavez, personally, is not there. Because also it is true Chavez prevented (and aborted) any possibility of creating something beyond himself within the borders of his political force.

Now, the many true divisions this country really has, again, are "masked" by the fight between Chavez and the others. This fight is a "power struggle" including the most powerful position in this country, which is the presidency, and involving very basic human needs like the life, property and freedom of many of the actors involved.

My feeling (and all the polls say that) is 30% to 50% of the country are involved in that fight, representing the extremists of both sides (giving a higher % in favor of opposition, it does not matter) BUT the remaining 50% to 70% of the people are not involved and are against that fight. They, basically, want to coexist and be able to focus on solving their daily difficulties, improving their own personal situation, with or without Chavez.

The issue is that most of the people within the upper circle of power in this country are fighting for or against Chavez, and that is the dominant polarization (although not the only, nor the most important one).

On the other hand, the prospect for violence is omnipresent. In fact, there actually is a lot of crime-related violence, intra-family and community and organizational violence and the trend is increasing dramatically. All the elements for social violence are in place and **the way the political crisis is addressed (I am not saying resolved) will have a lot of influence on the "channeling" of that violence.** *This rationale* was the main reason for our (the Tripartite) involvement and, in fact, it was the focus of all our efforts.

What should we do? How should we intervene to help on that situation? What kind of intervention will help to create a different political dynamics?

To think we are facing the risk of having a government undermining the "democratic system" is a very naïve and unproductive approach. Mainly because this country has, in fact, "produced" the deeply unfair social situation using the democratic system!! Based upon the democratic system the country went down into the tubes!! So, **democracy by itself** is not something we should focus on. Consensus is, agreement, coexistence, ways to share a common future, civilized disagreement, the rule of law and many of the elements characterizing democracy are incredible important, and we should understand them as useful "instruments" to address the present conflicts.

I still think the main purpose of our presence here is to help them avoid violence, not to strengthen a truly democratic system, but to find a way to coexist and address their social and economic problems cohesively. And we cannot be in the position to judge. If we let the parties push us into making judgments we should condemn, first, the mass media. Openly and frankly, the private media is putting democracy at risk down here. They try to extort the public institutions, the same way they blocked the negotiations around the CNE, they pressure the National Assembly, they buy judges and lie and create news whenever they want. They also finance violent groups. We have the same vague proof of all of this as we have about the Government undemocratic behavior: "just stories," told by some adversary. How can we judge? How can we make a condemnation of the Government or the media or the political opposition. Both parties felt, with a lot of legitimacy, they are being attacked by the other side in a very unfair way. Both parties are afraid. They are in a "psychological war situation."

In terms of the conflict situation, in the months to come we will face a lot of challenges. The main problem regarding the recall referendum is how the parties are prepared to read the results, whatever the results are. **Because the "reading code" of the electoral solution is the elimination of the other.** As it was since the actual fight begun, last April, as the coup and the strike clearly showed. *The "electoral solution" is not a democratic solution at all.* The opposition is looking for the recall as the way to get the power and be able to "eliminate" chavismo. They openly say that, everybody understands that. On the other hand, Chavez is looking at the failure of the recall as the way to eliminate opposition for his "revolutionary" project and consolidate power. None of them are thinking about coexistence after elections. That is the major challenge.

On the other hand, the recall (as any other electoral process) poses a great opportunity as long as both parties think they could win or lose because the results are uncertain. The opportunity is to help both to think on both scenarios and try to change their common "reading code" of the results *before* the results are out there. We were talking about reconciliation and coexistence because *try to reshape the meaning* of the process is highly needed. If there is not a clear "opening" before the electoral struggle, I do not see how it will be possible after. The winner will impose its retaliation and, because neither side will be actually killed, the confrontation can escalate dramatically.

I am not sure what feeling the Government side has regarding the recall now. If they are sure they will lose, we are facing a very different situation. Let us work on both hypotheses.

1. Government thinks they have the chance to win the recall process (because the opposition is not able to collect the signatures or, in a second step, the votes needed). They will try to prevent the recall to take place, but finally they will face it.

2. Government thinks the opposition will win the recall. In this case they will not accept the process to take place, pushing a state of siege or violence or autogolpe or through resignation or looking for general elections or any other move to avoid the recall.

The main reason to act that way is because they know the "reading code" of the results the other side has. They themselves have the same idea, if they win the battle and the recall is defeated, opposition should shut their mouth and they can proceed to deepening their revolution.

In any case, the tendency is towards more and more isolation and a deep defensive positioning. At the same time, they are trying to strengthen ties with their own supporters, the people represented only by Chavez, and the movements "excluded" from the international community. In all of the cases, the prophecy of prosecution and revenge against the chavistas is strengthened by the increasingly aggressive way they are talking and functioning while they read this behavior as just defending themselves. They see plots against them everywhere.

On the opposition side, those who think they can win the recall whatever the conditions are, will go for it and will take the burden (as they are doing) of fighting against the power of the President because they think they will finally win and, after that, they will "get rid of the problem." Which means eliminate chavismo whatever it takes. Those who think the government is yet too strong and they will not be able to impose the recall (or some other electoral solution to put Chavez out of office) will be constantly looking for a violent outcome. The media people were talking to me about using "other means" because they feel Chavez will not allow the opposition to win the electoral battle.

But, due to the internal fight and competition among them, I think it will be difficult for the opposition to be united and strong enough to push the recall cohesively and to present a viable option. This fact, clearly read by many within the same opposition, pushes them to underline the argument Chavez is "the only" reason of the possible failure, so, violence is needed because that is the only language he understands. So, the circle of open violence is there, increasing its dominance.

Meanwhile, we can see more and more people tired of the confrontation and hopeless.

We were working hard during these months trying to position TCC as a place for common sense and, against, any kind of violence. At the level of the social images we have moved from the pro-government NGO (paid) or the naïve "gringo-like" organization to a place of discreet respect from everyone, and, again, a place for strengthening common sense, peace and coexistence. Until now, we are the single international institution able to put together pro-government and anti-government actors in a private or public forum.

We are now being able to build bridges over the many invisible frontiers dividing groups, asking them to work together for peace. We are slowly but consistently building a peacemakers` network at different levels. Not only for a 2 days event. Now we are setting the basis for a more consistent and prolonged strategy for building peace and reconciliation. We are facilitating alliances between the biggest local NGOs, some Governmental institutions and other networks working at social level (including the Church), some media allies (Cadena Capriles) to give scale to the initiative and a cohesive group of distinguish academic people from both sides working together and ready to go public.

We are not the actors, but we are the conveners, we create the safe room they need to express themselves.

We are operating under the premise the leaders cannot decide to make peace if most of the supporters are asking for war and open confrontation and NOBODY is talking or asking for coexistence, tolerance and understanding of the other. If those who actually think tolerance, coexistence and understanding are needed cannot express themselves, polarization will drive everyone to a violent outcome. So, *because* we saw there are many people anxious to work for peace we are trying to help them and we are facilitating only "articulations and linkages" between lower and upper levels and across the ideological borders dividing them. And I think a network could emerge. It all depends on the will and determination of the people involved, not on us. I do not know if they will succeed and a strong network will result, I do not know if the political confrontation will destroy everything. But I can assure you only TCC can push this kind of activity within this environment.

I think the place TCC has is a result of our coherence. We have been acting as facilitators, channeling communication among the parties, with a lot of respect for everyone and without making judgments about them. The only thing PC told me is he needs the confidence of the President. And that "capital" was the main basis to build our activity here, because that confidence is unique. I think we should continue trying to work on the same direction. As soon as we lose the confidence of the President we will need to change our strategy and evaluate the continuity of our work down here. We can continue doing things and saying things, we can observe and judge, and make statements, but we will not be able to build a thing. At the end, we will collaborate with the dynamics of confrontation as most of the local international actors are doing now. Any meeting with foreign ambassadors will show an anti-government discourse being built. That one is another polarization going on (nationalism vs. pro-US/foreigners) and we can easily fall in the dynamic of that struggle.

Well, I'm sorry I was so long and poorly organized in my thinking.

General guidelines about what I think we should do:

1. Check where the government is going and try very hard to pull them out from the isolation trend. PC should check his relationship with HCF, try to reinforce reliability and confidence in order to push him to his democratic commitments.

2. Openly start talking about "coexistence" far beyond any electoral contest. And start pushing the debate about the conditions for that coexistence, stressing the idea this is something the "political elite" should address now. It is their responsibility.

3. Continue building bridges between the leaders on both sides, pushing the Enlace and trying to create other spaces for joint negotiation at the high political level (NA, Parties, leaders).

4. At the same time try to strengthen the arbiter, asking for respect of the decisions taken at the CNE and the TSJ, and offering them our help to push negotiations or to build consensus on delicate issues for the parties.

5. Not focus ONLY on electoral matters but continue building the peace-makers' network and making efforts to give them more visibility. "Integrate" our work on the electoral process to the larger activity of helping them to build a peaceful coexistence.

6. NOT make judgments or evaluations about the process UNLESS we are asked by both parties or by the CNE to do so. NOT condemn only one side, especially without solid proofs. It is always better to PROMOTE good behavior, values and actions designed to sustain values. If we make condemnations, condemn behaviors linked not to people but to values (lie, put unfair pressure, egotistic behavior, corruption, intolerance, etc).

7. Look for domestic and international allies out of the polarization dynamics or with some support on both sides, at the same time we distinguish within each side the collaborative and democratic from the authoritarian and violent.

8. Have a media strategy to reinforce the above trends.

Cheers,
Francisco

Index

About the Authors

Jennifer McCoy is director of the Carter Center's Americas Program and professor of political science at Georgia State University in Atlanta. She has led the Carter Center's election-monitoring missions in Venezuela since 1998 and its mediation of Venezuela's political conflict in 2002–04. She is coeditor of *The Unraveling of Venezuelan Representative Democracy* (Johns Hopkins University Press, 2006).

Francisco Diez is an Argentine mediator and has worked as a private consultant, maintaining a working relationship with the Carter Center since 1991. He served as the Carter Center's field representative in Caracas from 2002 to 2004 and the Carter Center's representative in Latin America from 2007 to 2009. He has also been a member of several international electoral observation missions and is coauthor of *Tools for Working in Mediation* (Editorial Paidós, 1999).

United States Institute of Peace Press

Since its inception, the United States Institute of Peace Press has published over 150 books on the prevention, management, and peaceful resolution of international conflicts—among them such venerable titles as Raymond Cohen's *Negotiating Across Cultures*; John Paul Lederach's *Building Peace*; *Leashing the Dogs of War* by Chester A. Crocker, Fen Osler Hampson, and Pamela Aall; and *American Negotiating Behavior* by Richard H. Solomon and Nigel Quinney. All our books arise from research and fieldwork sponsored by the Institute's many programs. In keeping with the best traditions of scholarly publishing, each volume undergoes both thorough internal review and blind peer review by external subject experts to ensure that the research, scholarship, and conclusions are balanced, relevant, and sound. With the Institute's move to its new headquarters on the National Mall in Washington, D.C., the Press is committed to extending the reach of the Institute's work by continuing to publish significant and sustainable works for practitioners, scholars, diplomats, and students.

—Valerie Norville
Director

About the
United States Institute of Peace